KARL MARX

SECRET DIPLOMATIC HISTORY OF
THE EIGHTEENTH CENTURY
STORY OF THE LIFE OF
LORD PALMERSTON

SECRET DIPLOMATIC HISTORY OF THE EIGHTEENTH CENTURY

and

THE STORY OF THE LIFE OF LORD PALMERSTON

KARL MARX

edited and with introductions and notes by
LESTER HUTCHINSON

1969
INTERNATIONAL PUBLISHERS
NEW YORK

Introductions and Notes © *1969 Lester Hutchinson*

Library of Congress Catalog Card No. 69–20356

Printed in Great Britain
by The Camelot Press Ltd., London and Southampton

PUBLISHER'S NOTE

In this volume are reprinted two works by Karl Marx, originally written in English, which have for long been unavailable. Their last publication in English was in two pamphlets, edited by Marx's daughter Eleanor, published by Swan Sonnenschein in London in 1899—some years after Marx's death and shortly following the tragic death of Eleanor Marx.

The two pamphlets are devoted to exposing the long-term collaboration of English with Tsarist Russian diplomacy for the aid and comfort of reaction in Europe. Marx's attention was particularly drawn to the subject by the contemporary anti-Russian agitation conducted by David Urquhart in the English press and in various political pamphlets.

Secret Diplomatic History of the Eighteenth Century was originally published in part, under the title "Revelations of the Diplomatic History of the Eighteenth Century", in *The Sheffield Free Press* in June, July and August 1856. Shortly afterwards the complete work was published, in successive issues from August 1856 to April 1857, in Urquhart's journal, the London *Free Press*.

As reprinted by Swan Sonnenschein in 1899, several paragraphs were cut out at the conclusion of Chapter 5. In the present edition this passage has been restored, so as to accord with the full text printed originally in *The Free Press*. Apart from this cut, one or two minor stylistic improvements were made in the text as edited by Eleanor Marx, and in the spelling of Russian names the "w" used in *The Free Press* version was changed to "v" (for example, "Iwan" to "Ivan"). We have incorporated these editorial corrections by Eleanor Marx in the present edition.

The Story of the Life of Lord Palmerston was originally published in 1853 in the *New York Tribune* and in England in the *People's Paper*. At the close of 1853 the third chapter was published under the title "Palmerston and Russia" in the *Glasgow Sentinel* and as a political flysheet by E. Tucker in London. This flysheet was republished by Tucker in 1854 under the title "Palmerston and Poland". Tucker also published Chapters 4 and 5 in 1853 under the title "Palmerston, what has he done? or Palmerston and the Treaty of Unkiar Skelessi". The whole work was republished in successive numbers of the London *Free Press* from November 1855 to February 1856.

In this edition the text of *The Story of the Life of Lord Palmerston* reproduces the text as edited by Eleanor Marx in 1899. As with the other pamphlet, she introduced some minor stylistic improvements. She also corrected some errors in the text as published in the *Free Press* (for example, some obvious misprints, such as "Turkish" for "Grecian" on page 17 of the pamphlet, and an incorrect date in one of the Parliamentary quotations).

In Chapter 7 of his polemical work *Herr Vogt* (*Werke*, Vol. 14, page 474, Dietzverlag, Berlin) Marx himself explained in a lengthy footnote how these two works came to be written:

"Vogt naturally ascribes the attacks made by the Marx clique against Lord Palmerston to my opposition to his own bumptious person and to his friends. It would therefore seem to be useful if I were to outline briefly my relations with D. Urquhart and his party.

"I was excited but not convinced by Urquhart's writings on Russia and against Palmerston. In order to arrive at a definite standpoint I made a very close and careful study of Hansard's *Parliamentary Debates* and the diplomatic *Blue Books* as of 1847–50. The first fruit of these studies was a series of leading articles in the *New York Tribune* at the end of 1853 in which I outlined Palmerston's connections with the Cabinet in Petersburg in relation to his dealings with Poland, Turkey, Circassia, etc. Shortly after this I agreed to the republication of these articles in the *People's Paper*, the organ of the Chartists, edited by Ernest Jones, which included new material about Palmerston's activities. In the meantime, the *Glasgow Sentinel* also printed one of these articles, which was drawn to the attention of Mr. Urquhart. Following a meeting between us, Mr. Urquhart asked Mr. Tucker of London to print parts of this article in pamphlet form. This

Palmerston pamphlet was later issued in various editions and sold between 15,000 and 20,000 copies.

"As a result of my analysis of the Blue Book which dealt with 'The Fall of Kars' (this appeared in the London Chartist paper in April 1856), the Foreign Affairs Committee in Sheffield* sent me a letter of appreciation. In digging at the British Museum into diplomatic manuscripts, I came upon a series of English documents going back from the end of the eighteenth century to the time of Peter the Great, which revealed the secret and permanent collaboration of the Cabinets at London and St. Petersburg, and that this collaboration dated from the time of Peter the Great. I want to devote to this subject a detailed study to which I have so far published only the introduction under the title 'Revelations of the Diplomatic History of the Eighteenth Century'. It first appeared in the *Free Press* of Sheffield, then in the *Free Press* of London, both Urquhartist journals. To the latter journal I have contributed various articles ever since its foundation.

"As can be seen, my preoccupation with Palmerston and with Anglo-Russian diplomacy in general proceeded without the slightest intimation that behind Lord Palmerston there stands—Herr Vogt."

The footnotes in the text are those of Marx. Supplementary notes by the present editor are indicated by superior figures.

---

* This was one of a number of committees established in English cities by Urquhart and his followers for the purpose of fighting against Palmerston's policies.

CONTENTS

SECRET DIPLOMATIC HISTORY OF THE EIGHTEENTH CENTURY

INTRODUCTION

I

In 1897, fourteen years after his death, Karl Marx's *Eastern Question*, edited by his daughter Eleanor Marx and Edward Aveling, was published by Swan Sonnenschein & Co. The Eastern Question was the term used to describe the dangerous condition of south-eastern Europe, resulting from the decay of the Ottoman Empire and the attempts of the rival supra-national empires to expand at the expense of Turkey. The Balkans were regarded as the "cockpit of Europe"; the new States, Greece, Serbia and Bulgaria, fought and conspired against each other as proxies for the Great Powers; Britain bolstered up Turkey to prevent Russian expansion into the Aegean which, she thought, might endanger her life-line to India; plots and assassinations culminated in the murder in 1895 at Czarist instigation of Stambulov, the pro-Austrian regent of Bulgaria; and in 1898 the German Kaiser entered the cockpit by visiting Constantinople, where he exchanged German military instructors for valuable commercial and railway concessions.

The publication of Marx's *Eastern Question* was therefore timely and it aroused considerable interest. The *Daily Chronicle* declared it to be "a very masterly analysis of the condition, political economic and social, of the Turkish Empire, which is as true to-day as when it was written"; the more conservative *Westminster Review* could not but admire the man's strength of mind, the courage of his opinions, and his "scorn and contempt for everything small, petty and mean", although it deplored "his extravagant abuse of high political personages"; the *Liverpool Post*, however, relished "the biographical interest of the volume . . . for prominent men of that period are dissected and analysed with a vigour and freedom which are as refreshing to readers as they would be disconcerting to their subjects were they alive"; *Justice* praised "the indefatigable energy, the wonderful grasp of detail, and the keen and marvellous foresight of a master mind".

All the papers agreed that the book was necessary, in the words of the *Liverpool Post*, "for a clearer perception of the later Eastern issues, which are now engaging the attention and testing the diplomatic talents of the ambassadors at Constantinople". These diplomatic talents led to the Balkan War of 1912 and the Great War of 1914.

In the Preface to the *Eastern Question*, the editors referred to two earlier works by Marx, touching on the same subject, which they promised to publish at an early date. These were the *Secret Diplomatic History of the Eighteenth Century*, and *The Story of the Life of Lord Palmerston*, one of the "high political personages" so thoroughly "dissected and analysed" in the *Eastern Question*. Eleanor Marx undertook the work, but died tragically before she could see the papers through the press, but the interest in them was so great that the same publishers decided to issue them in 1899, without the editor's final revision, as two separate two-shilling pamphlets.

2

European radical opinion in the first half of the nineteenth century equated the Czarist autocracy in Russia with reaction. The Holy Alliance of 1815 of the Czar, the Austrian Emperor and the King of Prussia to revert to the *status quo* before the French Revolution and to crush Jacobinism wherever it might emerge; the perpetuation of serfdom; the ruthless repression of liberal thought in Russia and Poland; Czarist expansion at the expense of the Turkish empire: all served to reinforce and justify this opinion. Above all the progressive movement in Europe closely identified itself with the struggle for the liberation of Poland, finally partitioned among the three Holy Allies in 1795. In Marx's phrase, Poland was "the external thermometer" of the revolutionary movement.

The equivocal attitude of the British government, the devious and mystifying policies of Palmerston, and the loud anti-Russian noises made by Liberal politicians, encouraged European radicalism in the belief that Britain to serve its own interests was an ally against Czarist imperialism and repression. Marx, however, was not deceived. In the *Life of Lord Palmerston* he denounced the British government as "the tool and accomplice" of the Russian autocracy, and in the *Secret History* he produced

contemporary evidence to prove that this connivance dated back
to the beginning of the eighteenth century.

The *Secret History* is the product of Marx's researches in the
Library of the British Museum. It consists with Marx's com-
mentary of documents ignored by "Whig writers, because none
has dared to publish them". The argument is introduced by a
series of secret despatches from English envoys at the Russian
court from the reign of the Empress Anne to the beginning of the
reign of the Emperor Paul, "thus encompassing the greater part
of the 18th century", which tend to show that Britain was prepared to betray her allies to serve the interests of Imperial
Russia. An extract from a manuscript written by the Rev. L. K.
Pitt, chaplain to the Factory of St. Petersburg and a near relative
of William Pitt, contains a blunt statement of the delusion
common to the Whig oligarchy of the time: ". . . the ties which
bind her (Great Britain) to the Russian Empire are formed by
nature and inviolable." But Marx's main purpose in this work is
to show that the pro-Russian character of Whig foreign policy
dated back to the Great Northern War (1700–21) and the emergence of Russia as a great European power. To this end he
reprints English pamphlets of the time of Peter the Great, which
clearly show that "the plans of Russia were understood, and that
the connivance of British statesmen in these plans was denounced
by English writers". The first of these pamphlets *The Northern
Crisis*, published in 1716, at the time of the alliance of Russia,
Denmark, Poland, Prussia and Hanover for the partition of the
Swedish empire, probes Russian policy and reveals the dangers to
England of the Russian domination of Sweden; the second, *The
Defensive Treaty*, records the violations by Britain of her treaty
with Sweden of 1700; and the third, *Truth is but Truth, however
it is Timed*, shows that British acquiescence in Russia becoming
the dominant power of the Baltic was in opposition to traditional
English policy. The three pamphlets reveal that from 1700, the
date of the Anglo-Swedish Treaty, to 1719, England was continually "assisting Russia and waging war against Sweden, either
by secret intrigue or open force, although the treaty was never
rescinded nor war ever declared". Marx found it strange that
"modern historians" should ignore these unpleasant facts
by a conspiracy of silence.

Apart from the reference to the British surrender of Kars

there is no mention of the Crimean War. It is evident that Marx did not consider that the outbreak of this war invalidated in any way his argument that the Whig oligarchy was Czarist Russia's accomplice. On the contrary many events in connection with this futile war tend to support the argument. The Whig government of Russell and Palmerston had resigned in 1851, and a coalition government of Peelite Tories and dissident Whigs first under Lord Derby and then under Lord Aberdeen had taken its place. At the same time there was strong anti-Russian feeling in Britain as a result of the dreadful repressive policy of Czar Nicholas I which created political and intellectual suffocation at home and bolstered up reaction abroad. It was Nicholas who broke the Hungarian rebellion against Austria; who threatened to destroy any republic created by the 1848 revolution in Prussia; who also in 1848 issued a manifesto warning the peoples of Europe to submit themselves to their rulers, "for God is with us". It was Nicholas who frightened the British Indian government by fomenting trouble on the northern frontiers of India.

The Crimean War was primarily a conflict between Russian and French imperialism. France had long had greedy eyes on the decaying Turkish empire, had been behind the rebellion of the Turkish governor of Egypt, Mehemet Ali, in 1831–33. The conflict became more acute after the *coup d'état* of Louis Napoleon in 1851. Nicholas saw clearly that Louis Napoleon would be obliged to distract attention from the instability of his government at home by rash adventures abroad, and was not therefore surprised when France countered Russia's claim to be the protector of orthodox Christians in the Turkish Empire by proclaiming herself to be the protector of all Catholic subjects of the Sultan. Nicholas had already on his visit to England in 1844 told Palmerston that on the question of Turkey, "the dying man", he was afraid of no one except France. As the conflict between France and Russia became dangerous, Nicholas, confident in the traditional pro-Russian policy of the Whigs, expected Britain's neutrality if not her active support. At the beginning of 1853, he cynically suggested the partition of Turkey between Russia and Britain, "if the sick man (Turkey) died". Britain was to have Egypt, as well as Crete, "if the island suits you". The Aberdeen government rejected the proposals. To have accepted them would have meant not only immediate war with France but an outcry from an outraged world. Yet at the insistence of Britain the Powers meeting in Vienna in August of that year sent a note to the Sultan advising him to accede to the Russian demands. Turkey refused and war became inevitable. The Aberdeen government, one of the most incompetent in a long history of incompetent administrations, blundered into the war ostensibly on the side of its traditional enemy, France, for a variety of reasons: to satisfy British public opinion, to warn Russia to keep out of the Mediterranean, and most important of all to keep a close eye on France, which was not to be trusted alone with an army in Turkish territory. France was considered to be a far greater threat to British imperial interests than Russia, and it is not entirely without significance that Lord Raglan, the British commander in the Crimea, should at allied councils of war by a curious *lapsus linguae* frequently refer to the enemy as the French.

Marx's motive in writing the *Secret History* was political. He wished to refute "the prejudice common to Continental and English writers, that the designs of Russia were not understood or suspected in England until at a later, and too late, epoch", and to correct the Anglophils in the European revolutionary movement. He was providing an historical background to political issues which were then live. Now, over a hundred years after it was written, it has acquired historical value of an uncommon kind; Marx's insight and pungency provide a necessary corrective to the more orthodox academic histories. But as the issues involved are not contemporaneous, the modern reader may find a general historical introduction acceptable.

3

If history is regarded as a record of human society in motion, each century must be studied in relation to those that preceded it. The sixteenth century in Europe was one of profound social, economic and ideological changes. It was a time when man emerged from the blanket of the middle ages and began to challenge the old values; it was an age of discovery, of political and economic development, of social progress, in which the economic conflict between rising capitalism and the old privileged orders of feudal Europe took an ideological form which resulted in fierce religious wars, collectively referred to as the Reformation and the Counter-Reformation.

The basic conflict thus begun in the sixteenth century was continued and extended in the seventeenth century, which was a period of war and rebellion, during which there were only seven years of peace: 1610, 1669–71, 1680–82. Now capitalists in alliance with the country gentry attacked not only the monopolies of the Roman church but also the absolute monarchies which they themselves had created in the struggle against the feudal nobility. Absolute monarchies were costly and extravagant; they created bureaucracies each member of which was expected to make casual profits at the expense of the country. The monarchies were obliged to reward their favourites and office-holders not merely in ready money but by the grant of crown lands, monopolies and the right to levy taxes and duties on certain classes of goods. The recipients of the royal bounty rewarded their servants in similar ways, the whole burden being borne by the merchants, the smaller gentry and the peasants, who staggered under the burden of increasing and irrational taxation. Capitalism could not flourish under such a system and had to fight to change it. That is not to say that the merchants and their apprentices, the gentlemen of the Home Counties, and the canting religious fanatics, who under Cromwell overthrew Charles I, were conscious revolutionaries putting into action a particular theory. Far from it; for on gaining power they did not know what to do with it and had to restore the monarchy, but this time on special terms, establishing Parliament as the real sovereign power to protect their interests. It was only in England and Portugal that this type of rebellion was completely successful. Revolts in Catalonia, Andalusia and Naples against the Spanish monarchy failed; that in the Palatinate and Bohemia led to the Thirty Years War; and the Fronde failed in Paris so that it was another hundred and fifty years before the French bourgeoisie caught up with their counterpart in England. The striking result of this is that by the end of the seventeenth century, England, a third-rate nation under the Stuarts, when it had been a satellite first of Spain and then of France, had become a major maritime and commercial power, whereas Spain, the greatest power at the beginning of the century, was already far in decline.

In the sixteenth and seventeenth centuries the balance of power in Europe had been maintained by the antagonism between France and the Habsburg Empire, which included

Germany, Austria, Spain, the Netherlands and most of Italy. The main object of French diplomatic and military action during this period had been to break the Habsburg encirclement of France; Richelieu and Mazarin succeeded in doing this by skilful diplomacy and by indirect and direct intervention in the Thirty Years War, which had paralysed the Empire. But in doing so they upset the balance, and France in the second half of the seventeenth century under Louis XIV became undeniably the dominant country of Europe, an aggressive and expansionist colossus, rich, populous, with a great army and navy led by capable generals and admirals, a constant threat to England, Holland, Germany and Spain. The threat became intolerable when Louis accepted for his grandson the throne of Spain, left vacant by the death of the mad and childless Charles II, remarking tactlessly that "the Pyrenees had ceased to exist". In 1701 the Grand Alliance was formed against France by England, Holland and Austria, and the War of the Spanish Succession was launched. In the smoke and dust of battle few noticed that a new power had entered the Western arena, without whom nothing could henceforth be decided. It was Russia.

4

Until the beginning of the eighteenth century, Russia was scarcely more than a name to the West, where it was thought to be an amorphous geographical area occupied by barbarous schismatics owing a vague allegiance to a priest-king. It was thought of little importance to Europe save as a source of raw material and a pasture for impoverished German Baltic barons. Most of the Russian produce was marketed by Sweden, but as far back as the sixteenth century enterprising Western merchants had tried to establish a direct trade, and in the short ice-free season, French, Dutch and English ships had visited the northern ports. In particular the English merchant adventurers were anxious to obtain free transit trade down the Volga to Persia, and to explore the riches of Siberia, already being exploited by the great Russian merchant family of Stroganov.

An accident brought England into closer relationship with Russia. In 1553, Richard Chancellor, seeking the North-East Passage, came ashore in an unknown bay and discovered to his surprise that he was in Russia. He was well received by Ivan IV, surnamed the Terrible, the first Grand Prince of Moscow to assume the title of Caesar (Czar), and two years later returned to negotiate a very favourable trade agreement. Chancellor was very perceptive. He wrote: "If they (the Russians) knewe their strengthe no man were able to make match of them. For I may compare them to a young horse that knowest not his strengthe, whom a little child ruleth and guideth with a bridle, for all his great strengthe; for if he did neither child nor man could rule him."

The Czar was willing to pay a great price to obtain from England the materials and the military and technical experts he needed for the struggle against the Teutonic Order, Poland and Sweden. He agreed that the English might trade in Russia and establish a factory there without paying dues and with extra-territorial privileges. On this basis in 1555 the Russia Company was formed in London to monopolise the trade between England and Archangel.

In 1569 Ivan offered Elizabeth of England a full defensive and offensive alliance, by which each sovereign should have the right of asylum in the other's country, and by which England should cease trading with Poland and supply Russia with masters of gunnery and shipbuilding. The King of Poland begged Elizabeth to reject the alliance lest Russia with a navy, and a reformed army trained in up-to-date military technique, should become too strong for the northern powers. "We have defeated him up to now," he said, "because of his ignorance." Elizabeth and her advisers while wanting all the trade they could get could see no value in the alliance. Even Ivan's generous proposal to divorce his fifth wife and marry a lady of the English court succeeded only in terrifying the lady concerned.

Russia was isolated and technically backward because it was landlocked, being cut off from the Black Sea by the Ottoman Empire, from the Baltic by Sweden, Denmark and Poland, and from the White Sea by ice. All trade and communication depended on the great inland waterways, the Volga, the Don and the Dnieper, the last river bringing Russia in contact with Byzantine civilisation and Orthodox Christianity. The fall of Constantinople to the Turks had closed even this limited outlet.

Surrounded as they were by enemies, the Russian people were almost constantly at war. The prolonged resistance to Tartar domination combined with the disunity of the ruling factions of

Kiev and Novgorod gave the leadership to Moscow, whose princes by a mixture of guile and courage not only broke the Tartar power but created the nation of Great Russia. There were no established frontiers as these constantly moved forward in the wake of victory. Temporary movable defences and settlements of peasant-warriors, the Cossacks, were all that were required, and these were advanced as the empty lands filled with peasants escaping from tax-gatherers and equally rapacious masters. Land was plentiful but labour was scarce; landowners, therefore, tried to force peasants to stay and work the land, and this led to the state institution of serfdom, legally confirmed in 1649, by which peasants lost all rights and became the property of their masters. This led to further migrations, creating an explosive element which burst periodically into rebellion.

Russian expansion inland was thus determined first by the needs of defence and then by the domestic pressures on the population. It was first directed towards the south-east in the struggle against the Tartars, and then north-east into Siberia towards the Pacific. In 1581 a rebel Cossack with a handful of men captured the territory round the two great Siberian rivers, the Irtysh and the Obi, and handed it over to the Czar in exchange for a free pardon. Thenceforward it was a matter of occupation rather than conquest; with no help from the government, the pioneers escaping from tyranny defied the climate and, making use of the great rivers, reached the Pacific in 1643. The colonisers and merchants followed.

But the ambitions of the Moscow government lay elsewhere. It wanted access to the ice-free waters of the Baltic and the Black Sea. It considered direct contact with Europe essential for technical development, for the modernisation of the army and the creation of a navy, and for a free outlet for Russian products. But all attempts, notably by Ivan III and Ivan IV, to break through to the sea had hitherto failed. It was left to Peter the Great to realise these ambitions.

5

The Thirty Years War, in contrast to the misery it caused the people, proved very profitable to the big landowners. The open country suffered most; villages were burnt, farms and crops and livestock destroyed, and peasants killed or driven to hide in the forests. The depopulation of the countryside accelerated the process of enclosures of common land, which the German and Baltic *junkers* had started even before the war. The magnates alone were immune from attack in their fortified estates, and they did not fail to appreciate that with rising food prices and the increasing demands of the urban populations throughout western Europe, in addition to the demands of the warring armies, immense profits could be made out of large-scale farming, stock-breeding and bulk selling of cereals, timber, cattle and horses. No less was the demand for Swedish iron and copper, and especially for the timber, hemp, canvas, pitch and tallow, without which the great navies of England, Holland, France and Spain could not put out to sea.

To market these goods and realise the profits required the services of entrepreneurs. International finance was now largely in the hands of Lutheran or Calvinist bankers, who showed a remarkable elasticity of conscience in the nature of their loans. Louis de Geer, a Walloon Calvinist at Amsterdam, controlled the whole of Swedish economic life and supplied the armies and navies not only of Sweden but of all the European powers, irrespective of which side they were on. The royal French finances were controlled by Huguenots, notably d'Herwarth, until Louis XIV foolishly expelled them in 1685, and even that drastic action did not prevent him borrowing from exiled Huguenots in Switzerland nor them from lending. The Calvinist de Witte excelled them all, for he financed the Catholic powers in their attempts to destroy the Protestants, and was the supplier, paymaster and economic organiser of Wallenstein's victorious armies. *Pecunia non olet.*

Only the Russians did not get their fair share of the profits. The essential naval supplies came mainly from Russia, which since the treaty of Stolbova with Sweden in 1617 had been cut off completely from the Baltic. She was still further excluded by the eclipse of the old Hanseatic League, which by the end of the Thirty Years War had lost its privileged position in England, Russia, Sweden and the Netherlands. The Baltic was being invaded by English and Dutch merchants, who began to absorb the Hanseatic trade. The Hanseatic port of Hamburg was taken over by Dutch Calvinists, who founded the Bank of Hamburg in 1619.

This was the period of Swedish expansion. In 1621, the

Swedes began to conquer Livonia and Lithuania, and followed this up by defeating Poland and its vassal Brandenburg-Prussia, annexing the Prussian ports of Memel, Pillau and Elbing, absorbing Dantzig and occupying Pomerania. In 1645, they defeated Denmark, which by the Treaty of Brömsebro was obliged to reduce the Sound duties and to cede to Sweden the strategic islands in the Baltic which secured access to the North Sea. Denmark was reduced to a second-class power in northern waters. The end of the Thirty Years War by the Treaty of Westphalia in 1648 left Sweden the dominant power in the Baltic, controlling extensive territory apart from Sweden itself and possessing the important ports of Reval, Riga, Stettin, Bremen and Verden.

Yet the Swedish Empire was a ramshackle structure, possessing neither unity, nor great wealth, nor a large population for its support. Its political constitution was unstable, the crown being in theory elective and subject to a greedy and selfish oligarchy of nobles, always prone to obstruction and rebellion. The rise of the Swedish empire was partly due to the division of Germany, the military ability of Gustavus Adolphus, the skilful opportunism of his minister Oxenstierna, the head of the council of five which decided policy, but mainly it was due to the political, financial and military backing of France.

Ringed by envious and resentful enemies, Sweden's only friend was France. England and Holland, fearful because of their need for naval supplies, were suspicious of the French alliance; the Elector of Hanover coveted Bremen and Verden; the elector of Brandenburg-Prussia longed to get his hands on Western Pomerania; Poland wished to recover Livonia; the King of Denmark wanted to recover his lost territories and status; and the Czar Peter of Russia had his eye on the provinces stretching from the Gulf of Finland to the Dvina.

In 1672, Sweden, under a regency, joined France in the Franco-Dutch War, while Denmark and Brandenburg supported the anti-French coalition. The Swedes overcame the Danes, but when they advanced on Berlin they suffered an unexpected defeat at the hands of the Elector of Brandenburg at Fehrbellin. The Elector followed up his victory by over-running the Swedish possessions in Germany, taking Stettin and Stralsund. Sweden was saved only by the intervention of France,

which invaded the Elector's territories and forced him to restore
Western Pomerania to Sweden by the Treaty of St. Germain.
But for Sweden it was only a reprieve; when the final test came,
France was fully engaged fighting Britain and the German
Empire in the War of the Spanish Succession and was unable to
come to the rescue.

An important result of the Swedish defeat was to discredit the
Swedish pro-French oligarchy and to strengthen the monarchy,
which had not been involved in the disaster. With the support of
the lower estates, Charles XI made himself an absolute ruler and
tried to re-establish the royal finances by claiming the return of
Crown lands that had been alienated by his weaker predecessors.
This process, called the *reduktion*, not unnaturally caused fierce
indignation among the nobles who held those lands. The German
barons in Livonia were particularly outraged, and one of them
named Patkul headed a protest. He was condemned to death, but
succeeded in escaping to be welcomed by the open arms of the
Czar Peter, who employed him to organise a coalition of all the
states that wished to dismember the Swedish Empire.

Patkul's proposals were enthusiastically received by Frederick
IV of Denmark, who, among other things, coveted the Duchy of
Holstein, then under Swedish protection, and by Augustus II,
the Elector of Saxony, who had recently been made, with Russian
backing, King of Poland. Prussia and Hanover, looking hungrily
at Swedish Pomerania, sympathised but prudently held back to
see how the war would go. The Czar also delayed, but promised
to attack Sweden as soon as he had finished with the Turks
against whom, as a member with Austria of the Holy League,
he was at war.

Against this coalition Sweden signed a comprehensive defen-
sive treaty with England and Holland, ratified by King William
III on behalf of both England and Holland on February 5th,
1700. The remarkable way in which the Whig government of
George I ignored without repudiating this treaty is the subject of
Chapter 4 of the *Secret History*.

Like all wars, the war against Sweden had a highly moral purpose. Its sole object, it was declared, was to liberate the oppressed
barons in Livonia. With this no doubt in view, Denmark
launched an immediate attack on the Duchy of Holstein.
English and Dutch naval squadrons were at once sent to occupy

the Sound, the narrow strait between the Danish island of Zealand, on which Copenhagen stands, and the Swedish province of Scania, which Sweden had acquired from Denmark by the treaty of Oliva in 1660. The young King of Sweden, Charles XII, invaded Denmark and advanced triumphantly as far as the gates of Copenhagen. Denmark was obliged to sue for peace, and accepted the humiliating treaty of Travendal, by which she promised to leave Holstein alone and to abandon her alliance with Saxony and Russia.

The day after Denmark's capitulation, the Czar Peter, having patched up a peace with Turkey, declared war on Sweden and invaded Livonia. Charles hastily sailed north with his army, and fell upon Peter as the latter was besieging the fort of Narva on the border between Esthonia and Ingria. The battle was fought on November 30th, 1700, in a snowstorm. The Russian troops although greatly superior to the Swedes in number were a disorganised mass, recruited on the old mediaeval system, without transport or ancillary services, and commanded by German generals in whom the soldiers, who anyway could not understand orders given in German, had no confidence. De Croy, the commanding general, at an early stage of the battle sought refuge with the enemy, and the cavalry which could have enveloped the Swedes was ordered into a panic retreat across the Narva river. The Czar was not slow to learn the lesson; far from being discouraged he turned his immense energy to military organisation.

Peter was given time. Instead of following up his victory, Charles marched against the man he wrongly thought to be his chief enemy, Augustus of Saxony and Poland, described by Marx as "that commonplace of immorality". The Poles and Saxons offered very little resistance to the Swedish advance, and Charles occupied Warsaw and established his headquarters at Cracow. Finding it easier to defeat the Poles than to occupy their country, Charles tried to impose a political solution. Because the crown was elective, Poland called itself a republic. Power rested in the Diet, from which commoners were excluded. Each noble member of the Diet had the right of *liberum veto*, by which he could not only prevent the passing of a law but could also dissolve the Diet, so that only seven Diets ran their full course in over a hundred years, 1652–1764. Bribery and malfeasance were endemic in this constitutional anarchy, and Charles had little difficulty in persuading the Diet to depose Augustus and to elect his own nominee, Stanislas Leszczinski.

To reconcile Augustus to his deposition, Charles now pursued the unfortunate elector into Saxony, violating on his way Austrian Silesia, where he proclaimed himself the protector of all Protestants under Austrian oppression. Augustus was chased to the gates of Leipzig, which was guarded by a Russian army under Menshikov. Without telling the Russians, however, Augustus accepted Charles' terms at Altranstadt in September, 1706, and acknowledged Stanislas as King of Poland, renounced the Russian alliance and undertook to deliver Patkul to the vengeance of Charles. The only article of the Treaty that Augustus observed was the easiest one to comply with: Patkul was handed over to Charles, who had him broken on the wheel. A month later Augustus was with the Russians, still ignorant of the treaty, when they defeated the Swedish general, Mardefeld, at Kalisz.

Charles' successes and defiance of the Emperor encouraged Louis XIV to hope that Sweden would now join him against the Grand Alliance. The War of the Spanish Succession was not going well for Louis. His invasion of Austria had ended in disastrous defeat at Blenheim in 1704; he had been evicted from Italy by the imperial forces under Eugene in 1706 and from the greater part of the Spanish Netherlands by Marlborough after the battle of Ramillies, and he was barely holding his own in Spain, where the English had captured Barcelona and Madrid. If Charles could be induced to drive on Vienna, Louis could concentrate the bulk of his forces against the English and Dutch in the Netherlands. This possibility occurred also to the Allies, and at the urgent request of the worried Emperor, Marlborough was sent to Charles' camp in Saxony to remind that monarch of the sacred nature of treaties with England. Marlborough saw at once that the Allies had no need for concern: the Swedish king, his tent littered with maps of Russia, was intent on vengeance on the Czar Peter. The Emperor tossed a few concessions to the Austrian Protestants, and Charles, declaring himself satisfied, marched eastwards at the head of an army of 33,000 first-class troops.

6

While Charles was engaged in Poland and Saxony, Peter had not been idle. His "New Model" army, commanded by the Russian general Sheremetev instead of the former German, defeated the Swedish garrisons in Livonia and Esthonia and overran the country, gaining battle experience on the way. Next, Peter followed the river Neva to its mouth, and there, on May 1st, 1703, he captured the Swedish fort of Nyenschantz, which he renamed St. Petersburg and impudently announced that it was to be his new capital. He at once built the fort of Kronstadt on an island in the river, and established a cannon foundry. Proceeding along the south shore of the Gulf of Finland, he took the university town of Dorpat and at last stormed the fortress of Narva. The Swedes launched a naval attack on St. Petersburg, which was beaten off with the loss of several ships, Peter himself taking part in the battle as a subordinate. In 1705, the Russians conquered Courland, Vilna and Grodno, and began to appear in large numbers in eastern Poland.

Yet in spite of these successes Peter was not ready to meet the redoubtable Swedish king. At the time of Charles' advance, the Czar was involved in the suppression of four dangerous rebellions, including one by the Don Cossacks, provoked by heavy taxation and oppression. The Cossacks of the Dnieper were also restive, and their Hetman, Mazeppa, decided to betray Peter and join Charles. The King rejecting all Peter's offers of peace determined to march to Moscow, but finding that the Russians had destroyed everything in his path and were harrying his supply lines, he turned south with the intention of joining Mazeppa. Thenceforward misfortune dogged the Swedes. Reinforcements coming from Livonia were intercepted and decimated; Mazeppa was defeated and fled to Charles with only a handful of followers; the winter of 1708–9 was one of the severest recorded, and the Swedish soldiers suffered the same terrible privations as those suffered a century later by the soldiers of Napoleon. By the spring the Swedish army had been reduced to less than 17,000 fit men, and Charles' only hope was a swift decisive victory. To entice Peter into action he attacked the small fort of Poltava on the Dnieper. Peter rose to the bait. The Russian army was now very different from that which had been defeated at Narva and was vastly superior in numbers. The Swedes were either captured or destroyed, and Charles, wounded in the foot, and Mazeppa barely escaped across the Dnieper into Turkey.

The Northern War lasted another twelve years, but the

Swedish Empire perished at Poltava. Eager to be in at the kill, the King of Denmark, followed by the Elector of Brandenburg soon to be King of Prussia, declared war on Sweden; Augustus of Saxony repudiated the Treaty of Altranstadt and was placed back on the Polish throne by the Russians; and the Russians themselves added Finland to their other conquests and laid the foundations of St. Petersburg.

In 1715, Russia, Denmark, Poland, Prussia and Hanover entered into an agreement for the partition among them of the Swedish Empire. George of Hanover was to get Bremen and Verden. Accordingly, as Elector of Hanover, George declared war on Sweden, and waged it as King of England.

7

George of Hanover became George I of England in 1714. The previous year the Treaty of Utrecht had brought the War of the Spanish Succession to an end. Although Philip of Anjou kept the Spanish throne, the European possessions of Spain were divided between Austria and Savoy, Austria getting the Netherlands. England was no doubt the chief gainer.

The accession of George I brought the Whigs back into power, which they were to keep for another forty-five years. The Tories were suspected of having Jacobite sympathies, and were therefore regarded with suspicion by the first two Hanoverian kings.

The Whigs and Tories were not popular political parties in the modern sense of the word. They were rival oligarchies. England was governed by an aristocracy of a few great families which were interrelated by blood and marriage, the King being the source of honours and patronage. As the majority of these great landowners had inherited former Church lands they were vigorously anti-Catholic, which was the main obstacle to a Stuart restoration. They were more virile than their French counterparts, taking an active interest in their estates, conducting agricultural experiments, dabbling in the arts and sciences, and taking part in trade which they affected to despise. On the other hand they lived extravagantly, building themselves country palaces, travelling in splendour, collecting *objets d'art*, gambling recklessly and supporting a regiment of servants, and were as a result often short of ready money. Politics was intended to remedy this deficiency. It became the custom for the elder son to go into politics to benefit from royal patronage and to maintain the family interest in pensions and sinecures; if he served the country while doing so, there was no objection, but it was not felt to be necessary. Younger sons went into the army and the navy, the Church and the law.

These great families controlled not only the House of Lords, in which they sat, but through their nominees the House of Commons. The electorate was unrepresentative, the franchise being confined to owners of freehold property in the counties and to corporations in the cities. Thus, for example, the city of Bath had only thirty-five voters. Many other seats were filled by the representatives of rotten boroughs, often not in physical existence, which were sold to the highest bidders, and pocket boroughs, which belonged to the landowners, who nominated the members to represent them. Thus the Duke of Newcastle had fifty pocket members who had to vote as he directed.

Members were not paid a salary; on the contrary they often had to pay to get in. In 1730 the price to sit in a single Parliament was £1,500; in 1830 it was £7,000. Yet politics were expected to be renumerative. If a member became a minister, it was easy. Robert Walpole, "the father of corruption", provided well-paid crown offices for his three sons, the youngest, Horace, the gossip-writer, being still at school. Ordinary untied members sold their influence and votes to the highest bidders. Among these bidders were the great trading monopolies, such as the East India Company and the Russia Company.

At the beginning of the eighteenth century, direct trade with Russia was only a fraction of the national commerce, and English imports from Russia were less than half of the imports from Sweden. As a large portion of Swedish exports, especially naval supplies, came originally from Russia, and these were marketed by the Dutch merchants in Amsterdam, it occurred to the Russia Company that if Russia obtained access to the Baltic it could export all its own goods to Europe through the London Company, which would treble its trade and profits. During the Northern War, therefore, the Russia Company was enthusiastically pro-Russian and anti-Swedish. It began an active agitation, which included bribery, petitions and noisy demonstrations, to induce the government actively to intervene in the war against

Sweden. English seamen, whose ships had been stopped by the Swedes while carrying contraband to Russia, were paraded as national martyrs and a source of national grievance. "The interested faction," wrote Marx, "then raised the commerce and navigation cry, which the nation stupidly re-echoed."

The Russia Company was aided and abetted by the Dutch bankers who, oblivious to the interests of the Amsterdam Swedish middlemen, were investing large amounts of capital in Russia, and supplying the Czar with ships, arms and officer-instructors. In spite of the Treaty of Commerce of 1703 between Holland and Sweden, which expressly forbade navigation to enemy ports, the Dutch raised an outcry about the Swedish interception of their ships carrying arms to Russia. Holland and England were still very closely linked, and it is doubtful whether the Dutch proclamations against Sweden could have been made without the knowledge and consent of the English government.

The final weight in the balance against Sweden was King George. Having declared war on Sweden as elector of Hanover, he expected England to do the fighting for him to further Hanoverian ambitions. The Government of Townshend, Stanhope and Walpole effected a typical Whig compromise: it decided to make war on Sweden in the Russian interests without declaring war and without repudiating the Anglo-Swedish Alliance of 1700.

8

Charles XII spent five years of exile in Turkey, trying to persuade the Sultan to declare total war on Russia. The Turks did indeed go to war, but having recovered Azov returned home satisfied and were no longer interested in Charles' belligerent exhortations. At last he made his way overland back to Sweden, where he found the situation desperate. The Coalition had launched a full-scale attack on Pomerania and cleared the country of Swedes except for the fortress of Stralsund and the port of Wismar. The Swedish council advised the King to seek peace and salvage what he could, but Charles was determined to pursue the war to the end. He threw all his energies into the defence of Stralsund, and ordered the Swedish fleet to protect it from attack by sea. The English government, however, had lent eight warships to Hanover, which in turn had lent them to

Denmark. And in case this reinforced Danish fleet was not enough, an English flotilla, under Admiral Norris, arrived off Stralsund. The odds were too great for the Swedish fleet which, thus baulked by its ally, was unable to intervene. Stralsund fell, followed by Wismar, the King himself narrowly escaping capture.

Sweden had now lost all her extra-territorial possessions. The Coalition now planned to carry the war into Sweden itself. The English, Danish and Russian fleets were to convoy allied armies from the Danish island of Zealand to Scania, the southern Swedish province acquired from Denmark in 1660 by the Treaty of Oliva. Under the protection of the confederate fleet, which included Norris' English squadron and was commanded by the Czar in person, 40,000 Russian soldiers were transported to Zealand, where they settled down at the expense of the Danish government. The descent on Scania was to be made on September 25th, 1716, when the conditions including a good harvest in Scania were favourable, but the Czar, ignoring remonstrances by the King of Denmark, the British minister and Admiral Norris, refused to move. First he postponed the expedition until the following spring, and then announced that he could only spare fifteen battalions for the landing. Denmark could not embark on such an adventure by herself, for it was doubtful if even the few Russian battalions would have materialised. The King cancelled the expedition, but the Czar lingered in Zealand, costing the Danish government 40,000 rix dollars a month for the maintenance of his army, bribing British and Danish sailors to desert to his navy, until the Danes began to fear that he was about to seize Copenhagen and Zealand. Eventually, however, having wintered his army at Danish expense, the Czar returned to Germany.

The abortive Scania expedition was entirely Danish in conception. Frederick of Denmark hoped to use Russian troops to recover all Danish territory lost to Sweden by the Treaty of Oliva and at the same time to force the Swedes to abandon their attack on the Danish dependency of Norway. The Czar, however, had not destroyed the Swedish Empire in order to create a Danish one. Henceforth Russia was to be the paramount power in the Baltic.

But Peter's general behaviour was causing his Western allies concern and alarm. In 1716 he married his niece to the Grand

Duke of Mecklenburg, a neighbour of both the Elector of Hanover and of the Elector of Brandenburg, now King of Prussia. By the marriage treaty the Grand Duke was to put his country entirely at the disposal of the Russian army and to accept Russian protection against any domestic disturbance. In return the Duke was to have Wismar and Warnemunde which should have gone to Prussia, and Prussia was to be satisfied with Bremen and Verden, which should have gone to Hanover, which was to have nothing. George I, when he heard of it, was naturally enraged, and his English ministers looked back to their obligations to Sweden by the Treaty of 1700 and began to think of restoring the balance in the Baltic, which by their aid to Russia they had destroyed.

They were too late: Russia and Sweden were negotiating an alliance. Charles on his return from exile had given wide powers to a Holstein baron named von Goertz. While the Scania fiasco was dragging out, Goertz was in touch with the Czar Peter. He proposed that Sweden should cede her Baltic provinces to Russia in exchange for a Russian undertaking to support Sweden against Denmark and against any other power which should come to Denmark's aid. Sweden should be compensated for the loss of her Baltic provinces by seizing Danish Norway. Prussia, her claims satisfied, was not likely to intervene, nor was the Empire, still engaged in fighting the Turks. Only Hanover would prove troublesome, and she could be rendered insignificant by replacing the Hanoverian dynasty in England by the Stuarts.

The Jacobite rebellion of 1715 was only the prelude to the more dangerous one of 1745. In the meantime the English government was well aware that there were many in England and Scotland who had no liking for the Hanoverian dynasty and its foreign entanglements, and who more or less openly drank toasts to "the King over the water". With the help of France and Spain, which would naturally wish to upset the Treaty of Utrecht, as Goertz argued and the Czar agreed, it was perfectly feasible to bring about the expulsion from England of the Hanoverians.

In pursuance of the scheme, Peter visited Paris in 1717, ostensibly to offer his daughter in marriage to the boy-king Louis XV, but also to persuade France to repudiate the Treaty of Utrecht. He failed in both purposes. The Regent, with only a sickly boy between him and the throne, was unwilling to take risks. Goertz had no better luck in Holland, where he was arrested at the request of the English government. In London, the Swedish ambassador, Karl Gyllenborg, who later claimed, falsely according to Marx, to be the author of the *Northern Crisis*, was arrested and his papers seized.

Goertz was released, and in 1718 plenipotentiaries of Sweden and Russia met on the island of Aland and agreed on the terms of the alliance. In accordance with it, Charles XII at once invaded Norway, where he was killed in suspicious circumstances. The Swedish oligarchy rejoiced. They placed his younger sister on the throne, and executed Goertz who supported the claims of the elder sister, married to the Duke of Holstein. Having thus regained power, the oligarchy at once repudiated the treaty with Russia, and tried to carry on with the war. But the Russian Navy, carefully fostered by Peter during the course of the war, dominated the Baltic, and landed troops near Stockholm.

Britain now decided to intervene to bolster Sweden and to prevent the Baltic becoming a Russian lake. She had already taken steps to preserve the Treaty of Utrecht by sinking the Spanish fleet at Cape Passaro, without the formality of declaring war, and she now hoped to do the same thing with the Russian fleet in the Baltic. Admiral Norris, who by this time must have been rather bewildered, was again despatched with a naval squadron to the Baltic, with instructions to help Sweden by all means in his power. But before he could afford the Swedes any effective help, the South Sea Bubble burst on England, which suddenly found herself bankrupt. Norris was recalled and Sweden left to her own devices. The end could not be long delayed. In 1721 at Nystadt in Finland peace was concluded between Sweden and Russia. The latter obtained Livonia, Estonia, Ingria, part of Karelia, and part of Finland. In 1719, as the price of British support, Sweden had already surrendered Bremen and Verden to Hanover, and in 1720, again under British pressure, Stettin and the mouth of the Oder to Prussia, while Denmark was allowed to seize Schleswig from the Duke of Holstein. Only Poland, Saxony and the Duke of Mecklenburg got nothing. All that was left of the Swedish Empire was a part of Pomerania, which she retained on the insistence of her old ally France.

c

In his new capital of St. Petersburg, hurriedly built by forced serf labour on piles driven into an Ingrian marsh, Peter celebrated his victory with riotous feasts. He had every reason to celebrate. Russia had achieved not only her ambition in reaching the sea, but had become the dominant power in the Baltic and Northern Europe.

9

The transfer of the Russian capital from Moscow to St. Petersburg was an act of defiance. It was serving notice on Europe that Russia had not only come to stay but to expand. For the new capital could not be safe until the adjacent countries and the coastline were subdued. Some intelligent observers in the West began to wonder where the process of conquest, once it began, would stop. As Marx expressed it: "Petersburg, the *eccentric centre* of the empire, pointed at once to a periphery still to be drawn."

This was a point not overlooked by the author of the *Northern Crisis*: "We shall then wonder at our blindness that we did not suspect his designs when we heard the prodigious works [i.e. fortifications] he has done at Petersburg and Revel." The Czar's immediate designs, according to this author, writing in 1716, included the swallowing up one by one of his weakened allies, Denmark in particular, the monopolising of all the northern trade, and the control of Eastern trade by linking the great rivers by canals and making them navigable from the Caspian and Black Sea to Petersburg. The Russian navy, husbanded during the war, was numerically superior to the Danish and Swedish navies joined together. Moreover the Czar was now in a position to deny the Maritime Powers, Britain and Holland, the naval supplies on which they depended. The *Northern Crisis* was intended by its author as a warning piece to be read by "every *honest* Whig and every *honest* Tory"; ". . . let us look to ourselves," he urged; "he [the Czar] will most certainly become our rival, and as dangerous to us as he is now neglected."

The author of the pamphlet *Truth is but Truth*, to shorten the long-winded title, is equally explicit but even more belligerent. Published in 1719, when relations between Russia and Hanoverian England were strained, it was written in 1715 after the author had been dismissed from his position in the British

embassy in Moscow "because the Czar desired it". The memorandum was drawn up on the personal order of George I, who
had already quarrelled with Peter, and was handed to the
Secretary of State, Viscount Townshend.

The author is chiefly concerned with the danger to Britain's
naval supplies. The life of Great Britain, he argued, depended
upon trade, trade depended upon a fleet, and a fleet depended
upon naval supplies. Sweden could never threaten these supplies,
because her ports were but thoroughfares, the goods being
produced in Russia. If the Czar were allowed to retain the
Baltic provinces he had wrested from Sweden, then with
Archangel he had in his hands "the two keys of the general
magazines of all the naval stores of Europe", for Denmark,
Sweden, Poland and Prussia only had "single and distinct
branches of those commodities in their several dominions".
In that case, asks the author, ". . . where then is our fleet? Or,
indeed, where is the security for all our trade to any part of the
earth besides?"

Now that things had gone so far, the author would allow the
Czar to have "an inlet into the Baltic" provided he kept no
warships, and if the Czar should refuse these reasonable terms
Britain should go to war to restore the provinces taken from
Sweden, the expulsion of the Muscovite from the Baltic being
the principal end. He was suspicious, however, of the Townshend
government, and doubted the purpose of Admiral Norris'
latest voyage.

After such powerful and public warnings, the Whig politicians
could no longer plead ignorance of Czarist ambitions. But they
took no action. The temporary alliance with France to maintain the Treaty of Utrecht soon dissolved into commercial and
colonial rivalry, fought out in the War of the Austrian Succession and the Seven Years War. For the rest of the eighteenth
century and well into the nineteenth century, successive British
governments could see only one enemy, France, and her satellite
Spain. Any power which resisted or weakened France was
necessarily Britain's ally. Thus, in 1743, in the War of the
Austrian Succession, Britain alone supported Austria against
France, Prussia and Bavaria; yet in 1753 she supported Prussia
against Austria, now backed by France and Russia. Although
on opposite sides, Britain and Russia never clashed; in fact

throughout the war Britain continued to pay Russia the subsidy agreed to in 1755, by which, in return, Russia undertook to protect Hanover from any Prussian aggression.

No aggression, no rebuff could quench Whig enthusiasm for a Russian alliance. The elder Pitt, Lord Chatham, was induced by Catherine II's ministers to foster the "grand conception" of a Northern Alliance of Russia, Denmark and Sweden allied to Great Britain and directed against France; but when the Northern Alliance was formed, the Armed Neutrality of 1780, it was found to be directed against instead of for Britain. The North government affected to believe that Russia had been tricked into it by the wiles of the Spanish minister, Florida Bianca, and tried to bribe Russia by offering her the island of Minorca, which would have made her a Mediterranean power.

The Armed Neutrality Pact was one of the many rebuffs from Russia which in no way reduced the conviction, chronic in British politicians of the time, that Russia was their natural ally. They watched benevolently while Russia replaced declining Austria as the arbiter of central Europe, while it threatened Polish independence, while it contemplated the partition of Sweden, and while it drove ruthlessly eastwards against the Ottoman Empire. Obsessed as they were with the French danger, they were blind to the threat which Russia constituted to British imperial interests in the Near East and India. Yet it was a real threat. India was one of the countries that Peter the Great had indicated in his will as an indispensable object of future acquisition by Russia, and plans for its conquest were a recurrent feature of long-term Russian strategy. The French adventurer, Benoît de Boigne, afterwards commander of the Maratha armies but then in the Russian service, proposed in 1776 to travel to India from St. Petersburg by way of the Caspian Sea, Tartary and Kashmir. Before he left, he had an audience with the Empress Catherine II, who ordered him to provide full details of his route, with a view to Russia invading India by an advance in that direction. De Boigne's map was one of those given to General Orlov by the Czar Paul, when in 1800, in conjunction with Bonaparte, he ordered an overland invasion of India.

It is partly against this background that the diplomatic letters published by Marx in the *Secret History* should be studied.

10

The first letter is from the British minister at St. Petersburg to Horace Walpole, the son of the all-powerful Prime Minister, Robert Walpole. It was written in 1736, in the reign of the Empress Anne, then at war with Turkey.

Anne, one of the least attractive of rulers, was the half-German niece of Peter the Great, and before being called to the throne had been the widowed Duchess of Courland. She brought with her to Russia a number of German advisers, who with one exception were distinguished only by their rapacity. The favourite Biren was without talent or political interest, his only aim being to enrich himself; Loewenwold, the gambler, was even worse; but Ostermann, who dealt with foreign affairs, was wily and able, and Münnich was not without military ability. After having plundered Russia on a hitherto unheard of scale, this junta of German barons entered on a policy of acquisition abroad. Their sights were aimed at Poland and Turkey.

Peter's protégé, Augustus II of Saxony and Poland, died in 1733. France supported the candidature of Charles XII's nominee, Stanislas Leszczinski, who had become Louis XV's father-in-law, while Russia demanded the election of Augustus' son. In alliance with Austria, whom the French were trying to throw out of Italy, Münnich with 50,000 Russian troops invaded Poland. Leszczinski fled to France, Augustus III was elected King of Poland, which thus lost more of its independence, and the favourite Biren was foisted on the unwilling Courlanders as Duke. The war became general, and Russia was obliged to send an army as far as the Rhine to succour the Austrians against the French. England remained strictly neutral, although Austria was her traditional ally against France. Austria suffered most in the war, losing Naples and Sicily to Spain, while the Bourbon alliance of France and Spain extended its influence at the expense of the Empire and Italy. Britain was left isolated.

The Russian incursion into Poland alarmed the Turks, who had an adjacent frontier with Poland. Their alarm was justified. Hardly was the War of the Polish Succession over than Russia was proposing to the Habsburg emperor that he should recoup his losses in Italy at the expense of the Ottoman Empire. Russia's object was to obtain the Crimea. The two empires, therefore declared war on Turkey in 1735.

The Ottoman Empire, in spite of a brief resurgence under the Kiuprili viziers, had been rapidly declining under the effects of economic and social stagnation and incompetent and corrupt governments since the middle of the sixteenth century. After the Turkish rout at Vienna in 1683, the Turks ceased to be a military menace to the West, and were themselves forced on the defensive. From then, under the steady pressure of the Empire and Venice, the Turks were driven back into their own territories, losing Hungary and Transylvania to the Empire, and Morea and the Dalmatian coast to Venice. The third crusader in the Holy League, Peter the Great, advanced on the Sea of Azov, and in 1697 captured the fort of Azov itself, but had to give it back again in 1711. In 1699, Turkey was forced to accept the humiliating Treaty of Carlowitz, ceding to the Holy League nearly all the the conquered territory. From that moment the Turk became the "sick man" of Eastern Europe, as was Poland in the North, with the Great Powers gathering impatiently to divide up his effects.

The war of 1735 was undisguisedly predatory. Russian armies under Münnich and Lacey invaded and devastated the Crimea, capturing Azov and Ochakov, and planned a naval expedition down the Dneiper to Constantinople. The Turks in their extremity appealed to Britain and Holland for help. The kind of help they received is revealed in the letter from Rondeau, the British minister in St. Petersburg, to Horace Walpole. Rondeau's idea of mediating and inducing Russia to make peace was to reveal to the Russian minister, Ostermann, the contents of two secret letters written by the Turkish Grand Vizier to the King of England, in which there were several "hard reflections" on the Russian Court. With astonishing *naïveté* he asked the Russians not to let Turkey know that he had betrayed their letters, for if they knew it would only "aggravate matters".

Fortunately for the Turks, the attack on Constantinople did not materialise owing to incompetence and the dishonesty of army and naval contractors, and Austria, having fared badly in the Balkans, for the Turkish peasants still made good soldiers, made peace at Belgrade, in which the Russians were forced to acquiesce. Turkey recovered the Crimea, but undertook to dismantle the fortress of Azov. But for Turkey it was only a temporary reprieve.

II

The second letter is from the British Minister in St. Petersburg, Sir George Macartney, to the disreputable Earl of Sandwich, Secretary of State in the Grenville government.

It was written early in the reign of the Empress Catherine II, at a time when Britain was negotiating a commercial treaty with Russia. But Catherine and her chief minister, Panin, had more important matters on hand, and were deliberately cavilling and delaying the commercial treaty in order to ensure British acquiescence in their aggressive plans. For Catherine and Frederick II of Prussia had just formed an alliance for the partition of Poland and Sweden and for a new Russian attack on Turkey.

Macartney's letter throws much light on events which have hitherto mystified English historians. It shows that the Tory government of Grenville was prepared to be even more subservient to Russian interests than the Whigs.

Poland was the first victim. Augustus III died in 1763. Catherine and Frederick, who had foreseen the vacancy, at once produced their candidate, Stanislas Poniatowski, a Polish noble who had been Catherine's lover. Austria and France objected, but were not prepared to go to war, and, after a show of Russian military force and £300,000 in Russian bribes, Poniatowski was elected. Catherine and Frederick had also agreed that the constitutional anarchy that prevailed in Poland and Sweden, where the noble oligarchies had full powers to obstruct the executive, should be preserved. "There is there," wrote Catherine, "a happy anarchy which we can work at will." One unhappy feature of this anarchy was religious intolerance. The Catholic majority denied religious and political rights to the Christian minorities, mostly members of the Orthodox Church. The Dissidents, as they were called, appealed to Russia for justice, and Catherine took up their cause. She was already displeased with the Polish Diet which had attempted to reform the constitution by abolishing the veto and replacing it by majority decisions. The Russian troops, that had never been withdrawn after the election of the king, intervened: the leading reformers were sent "to populate Siberia", the old constitution was declared sacrosanct, the Dissidents were made eligible to all places in the Diet and Senate, and their monasteries and churches restored. The Catholic hierarchy and the Jesuits, encouraged by France, now fomented rebellion among the nobles. A group of them formed a federation at Bar, close to the Turkish frontier, and began a guerrilla war. The French sent Dumouriez with money and arms to help them, but nothing availed against the genius of the young Russian general, Suvorov, who drove the confederates over the Turkish frontier, where they were hotly pursued by Cossacks, who massacred many of them in the Turkish town of Balta. The Sultan, long provoked by the activities of Russian agents in his territories, worried by the Russian presence in Poland, and incited by France, declared war on Russia, "in defence of the liberties of Catholic Poland".

The Russian government was not yet diplomatically ready to fight the Turks. It had contemplated a smash-and-grab war when all conditions were favourable; but the matter was now complicated by the French support for Turkey and by the war-like preparations taking place in Austria, which was alarmed at a Russian advance on the Danube. Britain, it was thought, could be relied upon to neutralise French intervention, and Prussia could be used to appease Austria.

Frederick of Prussia, who had written *Anti-Machiavelli*, was quite willing to fish in troubled waters. He advised Austria to make a secret treaty with Turkey to oppose the Russian advance; he warned Russia that Austria was prepared to resist a Russian attack on Turkey, and that he would be unable to assist Russia because his country was exhausted; and finally he proposed that the three of them should come to terms on the Turkish question and seek their compensation in Poland. Maria Theresa, remembering how the Poles had helped to save Vienna from the Turks, shed tears at Poland's fate, but as Frederick observed, "the more she wept for Poland, the more she took of it".

By the Treaty of St. Petersburg, on August 5th, 1772, Russia, Austria and Prussia, "in order to put an end to the anarchy in Poland", agreed to partition among themselves a large part of Poland. Russia seized all the country east of the Dvina and the Dnieper, which anyway was largely Russian in character; Austria took Galicia and the city of Cracow; and Prussia annexed Posen and Polish Pomerania. Poland was in no position to resist and thus lost a third of her territory. While Austria, thus appeased, was digesting its meal, Russia felt free to continue the war against Turkey.

The North administration in Britain made no protest against this flagitious partition of Poland; nor did it show any disposition to intervene in the Turkish War. As is revealed by Sir George Macartney's letter, British acquiescence in Russian policies was ensured a few years before. Panin and other Russian ministers had convinced the unfortunate Macartney that all their actions were directed against the French and for the destruction of French influence in Denmark and Sweden. He was told that the commercial treaty with Britain would be concluded only if Britain signed a Treaty of Alliance, which contained a clause obliging Britain not only to support Russia in a war against Turkey but also to pay her a subsidy to help her to conduct that war. Macartney was willing that Britain should pay the subsidy in time of war, but thought the Russians unreasonable to ask for it in time of peace. Britain was also required to pay an annual subsidy to further Russian policy in Sweden, "for the total annihilation of the French interest there". In secret agreement with Russia, Britain was to organise a pro-English faction in Sweden, which, because "even the wisest men are imposed upon by a mere name", should appear as "the friends of liberty and independence". But nothing should be done to augment the power of the monarchy or to reduce the privileges of the oligarchy. In return for these services, Russia would drop the question of export duties on naval supplies, and lend Britain 15,000 Russian soldiers in the event of Spain attacking Portugal.

Macartney reveals that Denmark was induced to enter on a similar agreement, undertaking to pay Russia a subsidy of 500,000 roubles a year as a contribution to the proposed war against Turkey, to disengage herself from all her French connections, and "to enter into all the views of Russia in Sweden". The Russian plot for the Partition of Sweden was, however, foiled in 1772, by the *coup d'état* of Gustavus III, who overthrew the power of the Swedish oligarchy and entered into a firm alliance with France. Catherine, with the Turkish war on her hands and faced with a Cossack rebellion, had to abandon temporarily her designs on Sweden.

After Macartney's revelations, British conduct during the Russo-Turkish war of 1768–74 is no longer astonishing. In 1769 the Turks were routed on the Dniester, and the Russians occupied Jassy and Bucharest. The next year a Russian fleet left the Baltic, and, with English stores and two English admirals, Sir John Elphinstone and Sir John Greig, made its way through the North Sea, down the Channel, across the Bay of Biscay to the Eastern Mediterranean, where Admiral Orlov was waiting to support a Greek rebellion against the Turks. Orlov bungled the intended landing in Greece, but the Russian fleet, under its British commanders, met and completely destroyed the Turkish fleet at Tchesme, off Chios. On land the Russian armies overran the Crimea, captured the Turkish forts on the Danube and the Dniester, and occupied Moldavia and Wallachia. The Turks were forced to sue for peace, which was concluded at Kutchuk Kainardji in July 1774. The Crimea was declared independent; but Russia acquired Azov, Kertsch, commanding the straits between the Sea of Azov and the Black Sea, and Kinburn, at the mouth of the Dnieper. The Black Sea was thrown open to Russian shipping and trade, and Russia became the protector of all the Christians in Moldavia and Wallachia, thus giving her a permanent excuse for intervention.

The Russian successes against Turkey convinced the French foreign minister, D'Aiguillon, that the partition of her ally Sweden would be the next item on Catherine's agenda. He naïvely believed that as this would obviously be against British interests, he could count on British support in deterring the Empress. But he did not know the extent of British involvement in Russian schemes. When, therefore, he suggested to the British ambassador in Paris that Britain should join with France in sending a powerful fleet into the Baltic as a warning to Russia, he was told that if France sent a fleet into the Baltic, Britain would send one too, and then it would be "impossible to foresee the contingencies that might arise from accidental collision".

Britain had undoubtedly earned the gratitude of Russia; it was soon to discover that in the affairs of nations gratitude is a rare virtue.

12

The third and last of these letters published in the *Secret History* is to Lord Grantham, Secretary of State in the Shelborne

government, from Sir James Harris, who later became the Earl
of Malmesbury, then at St. Petersburg. It was written in August,
1782, when the fortunes of Britain were at their lowest. From
1779 she had stood alone against all Europe, actively at war with
France, Spain, Holland and the American colonies, and ham-
pered by the League of Armed Neutrality by which Russia,
Sweden, Denmark and Prussia joined with Spain, Holland and
France to prevent the British Navy from exercising the right of
searching their vessels for contraband of war. In 1781 the surrender of Cornwallis at Yorktown not only brought the American War to a virtual end but was disastrous to British prestige.
France and Spain were still besieging Gibraltar, and Minorca
was soon to be lost. In these circumstances the Shelborne
administration was anxious to negotiate as favourable a peace as
was possible, and Harris' task at St. Petersburg was to enlist
Russian support.

It was more difficult than London had thought. There had
been further shifts in the balance of Central Europe. In 1778,
Prussia and Austria had gone to war on the question of the
Bavarian succession. France and Russia stayed neutral, but
agreed to mediate; France, however, became involved in the
American War, and the task of mediation fell to Russia, which
backed up her peace plan by threatening to make war on Austria
unless the latter accepted her terms of settlement. The result
was the Peace of Teschen, by which Russia became the
arbiter of Europe. The result of Teschen was that Austria, no
longer having confidence in her alliance with France, turned to
Russia, which led Prussia to turn to France.

Harris, therefore, found himself obstructed at St. Petersburg,
not only by French intrigues with the *garçons perruquiers*, the
barbers' assistants, as Harris contemptuously calls Catherine's
pro-French ministers, but also by the King of Prussia, who "was
exerting his influence against us". The chief Prussian agent at
the court of Catherine was her minister, Count Nikita Panin,
who for many years had been paid by Berlin. Harris, therefore,
found Panin most uncooperative and even offensive. The
Russian minister was unimpressed by Harris' arguments and
went so far as to declare that Britain had brought her misfortunes on herself by her arrogant and obstinate ways, and should
expect neither help from her friends nor mercy from her

enemies, but should consent to any concession necessary to obtain peace. Harris was outraged, but fortunately "had temper enough not to give way to my feelings".

He fared little better with the Czarina and her favourite, Potemkin, who showed little inclination to listen to Harris' lectures on "the inseparable interests of Great Britain and Russia". The Empress was highly displeased, it appeared, with the conduct of the late North government in not acceding to her demands that Britain should surrender its maritime right of search. Harris, it seems, was prepared to agree even to that as "a well-timed act of complaisance". He had been instructed to oppose while appearing to acquiesce. Learning of this the Czarina was extremely irritated, and Harris sought to appease her by offering her Minorca, with the full consent of the North government. Catherine was compelled to reject the offer, first because it was opposed by France and Austria, who had got to hear of it, and second because Britain soon lost possession of it. An attempt by Harris to flatter the Empress by asking her to mediate between Britain and Holland was also spoilt by the North government which insisted in bringing in Austria as well.

Harris' position improved with the short-lived Rockingham ministry, in which Catherine's friend, Charles James Fox, was the main influence. She also looked favourably on the succeeding Shelbourne government, of which the Chancellor was the young William Pitt. She was soon to change her favourable opinion of Pitt.

13

Russia was preoccupied with projects other than picking British chestnuts out of the fire. In 1779, the Austrian Emperor, Joseph II, travelled to St. Petersburg in secret to meet Catherine, and the two of them agreed on a joint attack on Turkey with a view to partitioning that country. Russia was to have all the territory from the Bug to the Dniester, and an island in the Aegean; Rumania was to be independent under an Orthodox Christian prince; and Constantinople was to be independent under Catherine's grandson, appropriately named Constantine. Joseph, although receiving only a vague offer of some Danubian provinces and Mediterranean ports, expressed himself as very willing to carry out the Empress' wishes. Venetian claims were rejected out of hand. There was no mention of the Crimea, which in fact Catherine annexed in 1783.

In 1787, Turkey, determined to fight for her independence, declared war. Gustavus III, seeing an opportunity to recover Swedish power in the Baltic, also declared war and began to advance on St. Petersburg. Catherine blamed Pitt, who was now Prime Minister, for this untimely Swedish aggression; unjustly, for although Pitt had formed the Triple Alliance with Prussia and Holland it was directed against France rather than Russia. But the Russians knew that Pitt was one of the few politicians who saw danger to British interests in an unchecked Russian expansion to the East.

Pitt was soon to earn Catherine's further disfavour. In 1791, on the death of Joseph, Austria having no success in the war made peace with Turkey. Pitt now demanded in the House of Commons that Russia should do the same and return Oczakov (Odessa) to the Turks. There was, however, no need for Russian anxiety. The defence of Russia was undertaken by the Whig spokesmen, and Pitt faced a hostile house. Fox enthusiastically supported Russian plans "for raising her aggrandisement on the ruins of the Turkish Empire"; and Burke, the mouthpiece of the Cavendish family, praised Russia's attack on a nation of "destructive savages". Russia kept Oczakov. But Catherine was disturbed by the French Revolution, and wished to have her hands free for another project she had in mind. Accordingly, having already made peace with Sweden on the basis of the *status quo*, she consented to the Peace of Jassy in January, 1792, by which Turkey recognised the annexation of the Crimea, confirmed the provisions of the treaty of Kutchuk Kainardji, and consented to the extension of the Russian frontier to the Dniester.

Catherine had four years left of life to complete her last project, the destruction of Poland.

Since the first partition of 1772, Poland had to an extent reformed its constitution. The Czarina, free of the Turkish War, denounced the new constitution and invaded Poland to support the oligarchic opposition. Prussia, having been defeated by the French revolutionaries at Valmy, demanded compensation in Poland. Russia agreed. By the Second Partition Treaty of 1793, Prussia took Danzig, Posen, Thorn and the upper

Vistula, while Russia moved her frontier some 200 miles further west. A year later the Poles rebelled under Kosciuszko, but France was unable to support them, and the rebellion was crushed by Prussian and Russian troops. Austria was invited to join in and in 1795 the three brigands divided among them what was left of Poland. Apart from the short interlude of Napoleon's Grand Duchy, Poland disappeared from the map until 1919.

14

The energies released by Peter the Great in the Northern war had transformed semi-oriental Muscovy into a colossal world empire, the mistress of the Baltic and, after the fall of Napoleon, the arbiter of Europe. In the nineteenth century it had become "the northern spectre" which frightened Europe, the hammer of the Jacobins, the arch-enemy not only of revolution but of mild bourgeois liberalism. Yet its emergence as a super-power had been so imperceptible and so aided and abetted by those who should have been its natural enemies, that its significance was even then not fully appreciated by many in the West. "Even after world-wide achievements," wrote Marx, ". . . its very existence has never ceased to be treated like a matter of faith rather than like a matter of fact."

The power of the Czar was, however, very real to Marx and, indeed, to every branch of the revolutionary movement in Europe. It was only by destroying that power that the revolutionary movement could progress. The victims of Czarist imperialism, especially Poland, became the objects of revolutionary support. Thus, during the revolution of 1848, an enormous crowd of Paris workers staged a demonstration outside the Assembly building carrying the Polish eagle, the Irish harp and the Italian tricolour, the symbols of the nations oppressed by Russia, Britain and Austria. They cheered Blanqui when he said that the sword of France would not be sheathed until Poland had been set free, but when he continued to speak about the domestic problems of the French workers they interrupted him with the shout: "No! This is not what matters. Poland! Tell us about Poland!"

Thus the brutal solutions of the eighteenth century became the problems of the nineteenth. The energy released by the

French Revolution together with the dynastic upheavals brought
about by Napoleon had shattered the mystical belief in legitimacy. Kings had been executed, thrones had fallen and others
were tottering. Rebellion, either nationalist or social, was in the
very air that the crowned heads of Europe and their ministers
breathed. Characteristically they reacted unintelligently, seeking to destroy ideas by brute force, in the belief that the methods
of the eighteenth century would be effective in the new economic and political world of the nineteenth.

The Czar, the chief gendarme of the counter-revolution,
was the main target for the rebels. Yet in their obsession with
Czarist repression they tended to overlook Britain, the accessory
to it. Marx wrote the *Secret History* to show that it was un-
convincing for British politicians of the nineteenth century to
plead ignorance of Czarist motives and intentions. They had no
excuse, for the warnings had been ample. But the warnings had
fallen on deaf or unwilling ears. In *The Life of Lord Palmerston*
Marx continued the argument that the British leaders of
the nineteenth century were as pro-Russian as those of the
eighteenth.

LESTER HUTCHINSON

I

No. 1.   Mr. Rondeau to Horace Walpole.[1]

"Petersburg, 17th August, 1736. *

". . . I heartily wish . . . that the Turks could be brought to
condescend to make the first step, for this Court seems resolved
to hearken to nothing till that is done, to mortify the Porte, that
has on all occasions spoken of the Russians with the greatest
contempt, which the Czarina and her present Ministers cannot
bear. Instead of being obliged to Sir Everard Fawkner and Mr.
Thalman (the former the British, the latter the Dutch Ambassador at Constantinople), for informing them of the good
dispositions of the Turks, Count Oestermann[2] will not be persuaded that the Porte is sincere, and seemed very much surprised
that they had written to them (the Russian Cabinet) without
order of the King and the States-General, or without being
desired by the Grand Vizier, and that their letter had not been
concerted with the Emperor's Minister at Constantinople. . . .
I have shown Count Biron[3] and Count Oestermann the two
letters the Grand Vizier has written to the King, and at the
same time told these gentlemen that as there was in them several
hard reflections on this Court, I should not have communicated
them if they had not been so desirous to see them. Count Biron
said that was nothing, for they were used to be treated in this
manner by the Turks. I desired their Excellencies not to let the
Porte know that they had seen these letters, which would sooner
aggravate matters than contribute to make them up. . . ."

---

* This letter relates to the war against Turkey, commenced by the Empress Ann
in 1735. The British diplomatist at St. Petersburg is reporting about his endeavours
to induce Russia to conclude peace with the Turks. The passages omitted are irrelevant.

No. 2.   Sir George Macartney to the Earl of Sandwich.

"St. Petersburg, 1st (12th) *March*, 1765.

"Most Secret.*

". . . Yesterday M. Panin†[4] and the Vice-Chancellor, together with M. Osten, the Danish Minister, signed a treaty of alliance between this Court and that of Copenhagen. By one of the articles, a war with Turkey is made a *casus fœderis*; and whenever that event happens, Denmark binds herself to pay Russia a subsidy of 500,000 roubles per annum, by quarterly payments. Denmark also, by a most secret article, promises to disengage herself from all French connections, demanding only a limited time to endeavour to obtain the arrears due to her by the Court of France. At all events, she is immediately to enter into all the views of Russia in Sweden, and to act entirely, though not openly with her in that kingdom. Either I am deceived or M. Gross‡ has misunderstood his instructions, when he told your lordship that Russia intended to stop short, and leave all the burden of Sweden upon England. However desirous this Court may be that we should pay a large proportion of every pecuniary engagement, yet, I am assured, she will always CHOOSE to take the lead at Stockholm. Her design, her ardent wish, is to make a common cause with England and Denmark, for the total annihilation of the French interest there. This certainly cannot be done without a considerable expense; but Russia, at present, does not seem unreasonable enough to expect that WE SHOULD PAY THE WHOLE. It has been hinted to me that £1,500 per annum, on our part, would be sufficient to support our interest, and absolutely prevent the French from ever getting at Stockholm again.

"The Swedes, highly sensible of, and very much mortified at,

---

* England was at that time negotiating a commercial treaty with Russia.

† To this time it has remained among historians a point of controversy, whether or not Panin was in the pay of Frederick II of Prussia, and whether he was so behind the back of Catherine, or at her bidding. There can exist no doubt that Catherine II, in order to identify foreign Courts with Russian Ministers, allowed Russian Ministers ostensibly to identify themselves with foreign Courts. As to Panin in particular, the question is, however, decided by an authentic document which we believe has never been published. It proves that, having once become the man of Frederick II, he was forced to remain so at the risk of his honour, fortune and life.

‡ The Russian Minister at London.

D

the dependent situation they have been in for many years, are
extremely jealous of every Power that inter-meddles in their
affairs, and particularly so of their neighbours the Russians.
This is the reason assigned to me for this Court's desiring that
we and they should act upon SEPARATE bottoms, still preserving
between our respective Ministers a confidence without reserve.
That our first care should be, not to establish a faction under the
name of a Russian or of an English faction; but, as even the
wisest men are imposed upon by a mere name, to endeavour to
have OUR friends distinguished as the friends of liberty and
independence. At present we have a superiority, and the gen-
erality of the nation is persuaded how very ruinous their French
connections have been, and, if continued, how very destructive
they will be of their true interests. M. Panin does by no means
desire that the smallest change should be made in the constitution
of Sweden.* He wishes that the royal authority might be preserved without being augmented, and that the privileges of the
people should be continued without violation. He was not,
however, without his fears of the ambitious and intriguing
spirit of the Queen, but the great ministerial vigilance of Count
Oestermann has now entirely quieted his apprehensions on that
head.

"By this new alliance with Denmark, and by the success
in Sweden, which this Court has no doubt of, if properly seconded, M. Panin will, in some measure, have brought to bear his
grand scheme of uniting the Powers of the North.† Nothing,
then, will be wanted to render it entirely perfect, but the conclusion of a treaty alliance with Great Britain. I am persuaded
this Court desires it most ardently. The Empress has expressed
herself more than once, in terms that marked it strongly. Her
ambition is to form, by such an union, a certain counterpoise to
the family compact,‡ and to disappoint as much as possible, all
the views of the Courts of Vienna and Versailles, against which
she is irritated with uncommon resentment. I am not, however,
to conceal from your lordship that we can have no hope of any

* The oligarchic Constitution set up by the Senate after the death of Charles XII.
† Thus we learn from Sir George Macartney that what is commonly known as
Lord Chatham's "grand conception of the Northern Alliance," was in fact, Panin's
"grand scheme of uniting the Powers of the North." Chatham was duped into
fathering the Muscovite plan.
‡ The compact between the Bourbons of France and Spain concluded at Paris on
August, 1761.

such alliance, unless we agree, by some secret article, to pay a subsidy in case of a Turkish war, for no money will be desired from us, except upon an emergency of that nature. I flatter myself I have persuaded this Court of the unreasonableness of expecting any subsidy in time of peace, and that an alliance upon an equal footing will be more safe and more honourable for both nations. I can assure your lordship that a Turkish war's being a *casus fœderis*, inserted either in the body of the treaty or in a secret article, will be a *sine quâ non* in every negotiation we may have to open with this Court. The obstinacy of M. Panin upon that point is owing to the accident I am going to mention. When the treaty between the Emperor and the King of Prussia was in agitation, the Count Bestoucheff, who is a mortal enemy to the latter, proposed the Turkish clause, persuaded that the King of Prussia would never submit to it, and flattering himself with the hopes of blowing up that negotiation by his refusal. But this old politician, it seemed, was mistaken in his conjecture, for his Majesty immediately consented to the proposal on condition that Russia should make no alliance with any other Power but on the same terms.* This is the real fact, and to confirm it, a few days since, Count Solme, the Prussian Minister, came to visit me, and told me that if this Court had any intention of concluding an alliance with ours without such a clause, he had orders to oppose it in the strongest manner. Hints have been given me that if Great Britain were less inflexible in that article, Russia will be less inflexible in the article of export duties in the Treaty of Commerce, which M. Gross told your lordship this Court would never depart from. I was assured at the same time, by a person in the highest degree of confidence with M. Panin, that if we entered upon the Treaty of Alliance the Treaty of Commerce would go on with it *passibus æquis*; that then the latter would be entirely taken out of the hands of the College of Trade, where so many cavils and altercations had been made, and would be settled only between the Minister and myself, and that he was sure it would be concluded to our satisfaction, provided the Turkish clause was admitted into the Treaty of

---

* This was a subterfuge on the part of Frederick II. The manner in which Frederick was forced into the arms of the Russian Alliance is plainly told by M. Koch, the French professor of diplomacy and teacher of Talleyrand. "Frederick II," he says, "having been abandoned by the Cabinet of London, could not but attach himself to Russia." (See his *History of the Revolutions in Europe*.)

Alliance. I was told, also, that in case the Spaniards attacked Portugal, we might have 15,000 Russians in our pay to send upon that service. I must entreat your lordship on no account to mention to M. Gross the secret article of the Danish Treaty. . . . That gentleman, I am afraid, is no well-wisher to England."*

No. 3. Sir James Harris[5] to Lord Grantham.[6]

"Petersburg, 16 (27 August), 1782.

"(Private.)

". . . On my arrival here I found the Court very different from what it had been described to me. So far from any partiality to England, its bearings were entirely French. The King of Prussia (then in possession of the Empress' ear) was exerting his influence against us. Count Panin assisted him powerfully; Lacy and Corberon, the Bourbon Ministers, were artful and intriguing; Prince Potemkin had been wrought upon by them; and

---

* Horace Walpole characterises his epoch by the words—"*It was the mode of the times to be paid by one favour for receiving another.*" At all events, it will be seen from the text that such was the mode of Russia in transacting business with England. The Earl of Sandwich, to whom Sir George Macartney could dare to address the above despatch, distinguished himself, ten years later, in 1775, as First Lord of the Admiralty, in the North Administration, by the vehement opposition he made to Lord Chatham's motion for an equitable *adjustment of the American difficulties*. "He could not believe it (Chatham's motion) *the production of a British peer*; it appeared to him rather *the work of some American*." In 1777, we find Sandwich again blustering: "he would hazard every drop of blood, as well as the last shilling of the national treasure, rather than allow Great Britain to be defied, bullied, and dictated to, by her disobedient and rebellious subjects." Foremost as the Earl of Sandwich was in entangling England in war with her North American colonies, with France, Spain, and Holland, we behold him constantly accused in Parliament by Fox, Burke, Pitt, etc., of keeping the naval force inadequate to the defence of the country; of intentionally opposing small English forces where he knew the enemy to have concentrated large ones; of utter mismanagement of the service in all its departments, etc. (See debates of the House of Commons of 11th March, 1778; 31st March, 1778; February, 1779; Fox's motion of censure on Lord Sandwich; 9th April, 1779, address to the King for the dismissal of Lord Sandwich from his service on account of misconduct in service; 7th February, 1782, Fox's motion that there had been gross mismanagement in the administration of naval affairs during the year 1781.) On this occasion Pitt imputed to Lord Sandwich "all our naval disasters and disgraces". The ministerial majority against the motion amounted to only 22 in a House of 388. On the 22nd February, 1782, a similar motion against Lord Sandwich was only negatived by a majority of 19 in a House of 453. Such, indeed, was the character of the Earl of Sandwich's Administration that more than thirty distinguished officers quitted the naval service, or declared they could not act under the existing system. In point of fact, during his whole tenure of office, serious apprehensions were entertained of the consequences of the dissensions then prevalent in the navy. Besides, the Earl of Sandwich was openly accused, and, as far as circumstantial evidence goes, convicted of Peculation. (See debates of the House of Lords, 31st March, 1778; 9th April, 1779, and *seq.*) When the motion for his removal from office was negatived on April 9th 1779, thirty-nine peers entered their protest.

the whole tribe which surrounded the Empress—the Schuwal-offs, Stroganoffs, and Chernicheffs—were what they still are, *garçons perruquiers de Paris.* Events seconded their endeavours. The assistance the French affected to afford Russia in settling its disputes with the Porte, and the two Courts being immediately after united as mediators at the Peace of Teschen, contributed not a little to reconcile them to each other. I was, therefore, not surprised that all my negotiations with Count Panin, *from February,* 1778, *to July,* 1779, should be unsuccessful, as he meant to prevent, not to promote, an alliance. It was in vain we made concessions to obtain it. He ever started fresh difficulties; had ever fresh obstacles ready. A very serious evil resulted, in the meanwhile, from my apparent confidence in him. He availed himself of it to convey in his reports to the Empress, not the language I employed, and the sentiments I actually expressed, but the language and sentiments he wished I should employ and express. He was equally careful to conceal her opinions and feel-ings from me; and while he described England to her as obstinate, and overbearing, and reserved, he described the Empress to me as displeased, disgusted, and indifferent to our concerns; and he was so convinced that, by this double misrepresentation, he had shut up every avenue of success that, at the time when I presented to him the Spanish declaration, he ventured to say to me, ministeri-ally, '*That Great Britain had, by its own haughty conduct, brought down all its misfortunes on itself; that they were now at their height; that we must consent to any concession to obtain peace; and that we could expect neither assistance from our friends nor for-bearance from our enemies.*' I had temper enough not to give way to my feelings on this occasion. . . . I applied, without loss of time, to Prince Potemkin, and, by his means, the Empress *condescended* to see me alone at Peterhoff. I was so fortunate in this interview, as not only to efface all bad impressions she had against us, but by stating in its true light, our situation, and THE INSEPARABLE INTERESTS OF GREAT BRITAIN AND RUSSIA, to raise in her mind a decided resolution to assist us. *This resolution she declared to me in express words.* When this transpired—and Count Panin was the first who knew it—he became my implac-able and inveterate enemy. He not only thwarted by falsehoods and by a most undue exertion of his influence my public negotia-tions, but employed every means the lowest and most vindictive malice could suggest to depreciate and injure me personally; and from the very infamous accusations with which he charged me, had I been prone to fear, I might have apprehended the most infamous attacks at his hands. This relentless persecution still continues; it has outlived his Ministry. *Notwithstanding the positive assurances I had received from the Empress herself,* he found means, first to stagger, and afterwards to alter her resolutions. He was, indeed, very officiously assisted by his Prussian Majesty, who, at the time, was as much bent on oversetting our interest as he now seems eager to restore it. I was not, however, disheartened by this first disappointment, and, by redoubling my efforts, *I have twice more, during the course of my mission, brought the Empress to the verge (!) of standing forth our professed friend,* and, each time, my *expectations were grounded on assurances from her own mouth.* The first was when *our enemies conjured up the armed* neutrality;* the other WHEN MINORCA WAS OFFERED HER. Although, on the first of these occasions, I found the same opposition from the same quarter I had experienced before, yet I am compelled to say that the principal cause of my failure was attributable to the very awkward manner in which we replied to the famous neutral declaration of February, 1780. As I well knew from what quarter the blow would come, I was prepared to parry it. *My opinion was: 'If England feels itself strong enough to do without Russia, let it reject at once these new-fangled doctrines; but if its situation is such as to want assistance, let it yield to the necessity of the hour, recognise them as far as they relate to* RUSSIA ALONE, *and by a well-timed act of complaisance insure itself a powerful friend.'†* My opinion was *not* received; an ambiguous and trimming answer was given; *we seemed equally afraid to accept or dismiss them. I was instructed secretly to oppose, but avowedly to acquiesce in them,* and some unguarded expressions of one of its then con-

---

* Sir James Harris affects to believe that Catherine II[7] was not the author of, but a convert to, the armed neutrality of 1780. It is one of the grand stratagems of the Court of St. Petersburg to give to its own schemes the form of proposals suggested to and pressed on itself by foreign Courts. Russian diplomacy delights in those *quæ pro quo.* Thus the Court of Florida Bianca was made the responsible editor of the armed neutrality, and, from a report that vainglorious Spaniard addressed to Carlos III, one may see how immensely he felt flattered at the idea of having not only hatched the armed neutrality but allured Russia into abetting it.

† This same Sir James Harris, perhaps more familiar to the reader under the name of the Earl of Malmesbury, is extolled by English historians as the man who prevented England from surrendering the right of search in the Peace Negotiations of 1782–83.

fidential servants, made use of in speaking to Mr. Simolin, in direct contradiction to the temperate and cordial language that Minister had heard from Lord Stormont,[8] *irritated* the Empress to the last degree, and completed the *dislike* and *bad opinion* she entertained of that Administration.* Our enemies took advantage of these *circumstances.* . . . I SUGGESTED THE IDEA OF GIVING UP MINORCA TO THE EMPRESS, *because, as it was evident to me we should at the peace be compelled to make sacrifices, it seemed to me wiser to make them to our friends than to our enemies.* THE IDEA WAS ADOPTED AT HOME IN ITS WHOLE EXTENT,† *and*

* It might be inferred from this passage and similar ones occurring in the text, that Catherine II had caught a real Tartar in Lord North, whose Administration Sir James Harris is pointing at. Any such delusion will disappear before the simple statement that the first partition of Poland took place under Lord North's Administration, without any protest on his part. In 1773 Catherine's war against Turkey still continuing, and her conflicts with Sweden growing serious, France made preparations to send a powerful fleet into the Baltic. D'Aiguillon, the French Minister of Foreign Affairs, communicated this plan to Lord Stormont, then English Ambassador at Paris. In a long conversation, D'Aiguillon dwelt largely on the ambitious designs of Russia, and the common interest that ought to blend France and England into a joint resistance against them. In answer to this confidential communication, he was informed by the English Ambassador that, "if France sent her ships into the Baltic, they would instantly be followed by a British fleet; that the presence of two fleets would have no more effect than a neutrality; and however the British Court might desire to preserve the harmony now subsisting between England and France, it was impossible to foresee the contingencies that might arise from accidental collision." In consequence of these representations, D'Aiguillon countermanded the squadron at Brest, but gave new orders for the equipment of an armament at Toulon. "On receiving intelligence of these renewed preparations, the British Cabinet made instant and vigorous demonstrations of resistance; Lord Stormont was ordered to declare that every argument used respecting the Baltic applied equally to the Mediterranean. A memorial also was presented to the French Minister, accompanied by a demand that it should be laid before the King and Council. This produced the desired effect; the armament was countermanded, the sailors disbanded, and the chances of an extensive warfare avoided."

"*Lord North,*" says the complacent writer from whom we have borrowed the last lines, "*thus effectually served the cause of his ally* (Catherine II), *and facilitated the treaty of peace* (of Kutchuk-Kainardji) *between Russia and the Porte.*" Catherine II rewarded Lord North's good services, first by withholding the aid she had promised him in case of a war between England and the North American Colonies, and in the second place, by conjuring up and leading the armed neutrality against England. Lord North DARED NOT *repay, as he was advised by Sir James Harris,* this treacherous breach of faith by giving up to Russia, and to *Russia alone,* the maritime rights of Great Britain. Hence the irritation in the nervous system of the Czarina; the hysterical fancy she caught all at once of "entertaining a bad opinion" of Lord North, of "disliking" him, of feeling a "rooted aversion" against him, of being afflicted with "a total want of confidence," etc. In order to give the Shelburne Administration a warning example, Sir James Harris draws up a minute psychological picture of the feelings of the Czarina, and the disgrace incurred by the North Administration, for having wounded these same feelings. His prescription is very simple: surrender to Russia, as our friend, everything for asking which we would consider every other Power our enemy.

† It is then a fact that the English Government, not satisfied with having made Russia a Baltic power, strove hard to make her a Mediterranean power too. The

nothing could be more perfectly calculated to the meridian of this Court than the judicious instructions I received on this occasion from Lord Stormont. Why this project failed I am still at a loss to learn. *I never knew the Empress incline so strongly to any one measure as she did to this, before I had my full powers to treat, nor was I ever more astonished than when I found her shrink from her purpose when they arrived.* I imputed it at the same time, in my own mind, to the *rooted aversion she had for our Ministry,* and her *total want of confidence in them*; but I since am more strongly disposed to believe that she consulted the Emperor (of Austria) on the subject, and that he not only prevailed on her to decline the offer, but betrayed the secret to France, and that it thus became public. I cannot otherwise account for this rapid *change of sentiment in the Empress,* particularly as *Prince Potemkin*[9] (whatever he might be in other transactions) was certainly in this *cordial and sincere* in his support, and both from what I saw at the time, and from what has since come to my knowledge, *had its success at heart as much as myself.* You will observe, my lord, that *the idea of bringing the Empress forward as a friendly media-*

offer of the surrender of Minorca appears to have been made to Catherine II at the end of 1779, or the beginning of 1780, shortly after Lord Stormont's entrance into the North Cabinet—the same Lord Stormont we have seen thwarting the French attempts at resistance against Russia, and whom even Sir James Harris cannot deny the merit of having written *"instructions perfectly calculated to the meridian of the Court of St. Petersburg."* While Lord North's Cabinet, at the suggestion of Sir James Harris, offered Minorca to the *Muscovites,* the English Commoners and people were still trembling for fear lest the *Hanoverians* (?) should wrest out of their hands "one of the keys of the Mediterranean." On the 26th of October, 1775, the King, in his opening speech, had informed Parliament, amongst other things, that he had Sir James Graham's own words, when asked why they should not have kept up some blockade pending the settlement of the "plan," *"They did not take that responsibility upon themselves."* The responsibility of executing their orders! The despatch we have quoted is the only despatch read, except one of a later date. The despatch, said to be sent on the 5th of April, in which "the Admiral is ordered to use the *largest discretionary power* in blockading the Russian ports in the Black Sea," is not read, nor any replies from Admiral Dundas. The Admiralty sent *Hanoverian* troops to Gibraltar and Port Mahon (Minorca), to replace such British regiments as should be drawn from those garrisons for service in America. An amendment to the address was proposed by Lord John Cavendish, strongly condemning "the confiding *such important fortresses as Gibraltar and Port Mahon to foreigners."* After very stormy debates, in which the measure of entrusting Gibraltar and Minorca, *"the keys of the Mediterranean,"* as they were called, to *foreigners,* was furiously attacked, Lord North, acknowledging himself the adviser of the measure, felt obliged to bring in a *bill of indemnity.* However, these foreigners, these Hanoverians, were the English King's own subjects. Having virtually surrendered Minorca to Russia in 1780, Lord North was, of course, quite justified in treating, on November 22, 1781, in the House of Commons, "with utter scorn the insinuation that *Ministers were in the pay of France."*

Let us remark, *en passant,* that Lord North, one of the most base and mischievous Ministers England can boast of, perfectly mastered the art of keeping the House in perpetual laughter. So had Lord Sunderland. So has Lord Palmerston.

trix went hand-in-hand with the proposed cession of Minorca.[10]
As this idea has given rise to what has since followed, and
involved us in all the dilemmas of the present mediation, it will
be necessary for me to explain what my views then were, and to
exculpate myself from the blame of having placed my Court in
so embarrassing a situation, *my wish and intention was that she
should be sole mediatrix without an adjoint;* if you have perused
what passed between her and me, in December, 1780, your
lordship will readily perceive how very potent reasons I had to
imagine she would be a friendly and even a partial one.* I knew,
indeed, she was unequal to the task; but I knew, too, how
greatly *her vanity* would be flattered by this distinction, and was
well aware that when once engaged she would persist, and be
inevitably involved in our quarrel, particularly when it should
appear (and appear it would) that we had *gratified* her with
Minorca. The annexing to the mediation the other (Austrian)
Imperial Court entirely overthrew this plan. It not only afforded
her a pretence for not keeping her word, but piqued and mortified her; and it was under this impression that she made over the
whole business to the colleague we had given her, and ordered
her Minister at Vienna to subscribe implicitly to whatever the
Court proposed. Hence all the evils which have since arisen,
and hence those we at this moment experience. I myself could
never be brought to believe that the Court of Vienna, as long as
Prince Kaunitz[11] directs its measures, can mean England any
good or France any harm. It was not with that view that I
endeavoured to promote its influence here, but because *I found
that of Prussia in constant opposition to me;* and because I thought
that if I could by any means smite this, I should get rid of my
greatest obstacle. I was mistaken, and, by a singular fatality, the
Courts of Vienna and Berlin seem never to have agreed in

---

* Lord North having been supplanted by the Rockingham Administration, on
March 27, 1782 the celebrated Fox forwarded peace proposals to Holland through
the mediation of the *Russian* Minister. Now what were the consequences of the
Russian mediation so much vaunted by this Sir James Harris, the servile account
keeper of the Czarina's sentiments, humours, and feelings? While preliminary
articles of peace had been convened with France, Spain, and the American States, it
was found impossible to arrive at any such preliminary agreement with Holland.
Nothing but a simple cessation of hostilities was to be obtained from it. So powerful
proved the *Russian mediation*, that on the 2nd September, 1783, just one day before
conclusion of *definitive treaties* with America, France, and Spain, Holland condescended to accede to *preliminaries of peace*, and this not in consequence of the
Russian mediation, but through the influence of *France*.

anything but in the disposition to prejudice us here by turns.* The
proposal relative to Minorca was the last attempt I made to
induce the Empress to stand forth. I had exhausted my strength
and resources; the freedom with which I had spoken in my last
interview with her, though respectful, had *displeased*; and *from
this period to the removal of the late Administration*, I have been
reduced to act on the defensive. . . . . I have had more difficulty in
preventing the Empress from doing harm than I ever had in
attempting to engage her to do us good. It was to prevent evil,
that I inclined strongly for the acceptation of *her single mediation
between us and Holland, when her Imperial Majesty first offered
it.* The *extreme dissatisfaction* she expressed *at our refusal*
justified my opinion; and I TOOK UPON ME, when it was proposed
a second time, *to urge the necessity of its being agreed to* (ALTHOUGH
I KNEW IT TO BE IN CONTRADICTION OF THE SENTIMENTS OF MY
PRINCIPAL), since I firmly believed, had we again declined it, the
Empress would, in a *moment of anger*, have joined the Dutch
against us. As it is, *all has gone on well*; our *judicious* conduct has
transferred to them the *ill-humour* she originally was in with us,
and she now is as partial to our cause as she was before partial to
theirs. *Since the new Ministry in England, my road has been made
smoother*; the great and new path struck out by *your predecessor*,†
and which you, my lord, pursue, has operated a most advantageous
change in our favour upon the Continent. Nothing, indeed, but
events which come home to her, will, I believe, ever induce her
Imperial Majesty to take an active part; but there is now a
strong glow of friendship in our favour; she approves our measures;
she *trusts* our Ministry, and *she gives way to that predilection she
certainly has for our nation.* Our enemies know and feel this; it

---

* How much was England not prejudiced by the Courts of Vienna and Paris
thwarting the plan of the British Cabinet of ceding Minorca to Russia, and by
Frederick of Prussia's resistance against the great Chatham's scheme of a Northern
Alliance under Muscovite auspices.

† The predecessor is Fox. Sir James Harris establishes a complete scale of British
Administrations, according to the degree in which they enjoyed the favour of his
almighty Czarina. In spite of Lord Stormont, the Earl of Sandwich, Lord North, and
Sir James Harris himself; in spite of the partition of Poland, the bullying of D'Aiguillon, the treaty of Kutchuk-Kainardji, and the intended cession of Minorca—Lord
North's Administration is relegated to the bottom of the heavenly ladder; far above
it has climbed the Rockingham Administration, whose soul was Fox, notorious for
his subsequent intrigues with Catherine; but at the top we behold the Shelburne
Administration,[12] whose Chancellor of the Exchequer was the celebrated William
Pitt. As to Lord Shelburne himself, Burke exclaimed in the House of Commons, that
"if he was not a Catilina or Borgia in morals, it must not be ascribed to anything but
his understanding."

keeps them in awe. This is a succinct but accurate sketch of what has passed at this Court from the day of my arrival at Petersburg to the present hour. Several inferences may be deduced from it.* That the Empress is led by her passions, not by reason and argument; that her prejudices are very strong, easily acquired, and, when once fixed, irremovable; while, on the contrary, there is no sure road to her good opinion; that even when obtained, it is subject to perpetual fluctuations, and liable to be biassed by the most trifling incidents; that till she is fairly embarked in a plan, no assurances can be depended on; but that when once fairly embarked, she never retracts, and may be carried any length; that with very bright parts, an elevated mind, an uncommon sagacity, she wants *judgment, precision of idea, reflection, and* L'ESPRIT DE COMBINAISON (!!); that her Ministers are either ignorant of, or indifferent to, the welfare of the State, and act from a passive submission to her will, or from motives of party and private interests."†

4. (MANUSCRIPT) ACCOUNT OF RUSSIA DURING THE COMMENCEMENT OF THE REIGN OF THE EMPEROR PAUL, DRAWN UP BY THE REV. L. K. PITT, CHAPLAIN TO THE FACTORY OF ST. PETERSBURG, AND A NEAR RELATIVE OF WILLIAM PITT.‡

Extract.

"There can scarcely exist a doubt concerning the real sentiments of the late Empress of Russia on the great points which have, within the last few years, convulsed the whole system of European politics. She certainly felt from the beginning the fatal tendency of the new principles, but was not, perhaps, displeased to see every European Power exhausting itself in a struggle which raised, in proportion to its violence, her own importance. It is more than probable that the state of the newly acquired provinces in Poland was likewise

---

* Sir James Harris forgets deducing the main inference, that the Ambassador of England is the agent of Russia.

† In the eighteenth century, English diplomatists' despatches, bearing on their front the sacramental inscription, "Private," are despatches to be withheld from the King by the Minister to whom they are addressed. That such was the case may be seen from Lord Mahon's *History of England*.

‡ "To be burnt after my death." Such are the words prefixed to the manuscript by the gentleman whom it was addressed to.

a point which had considerable influence over the political conduct of Catherine. The fatal effects resulting from an apprehension of revolt in the late seat of conquest seem to have been felt in a very great degree by the combined Powers, who in the early period of the Revolution were so near reinstating the regular Government in France. The same dread of revolt in Poland, which divided the attention of the combined Powers and hastened their retreat, deterred likewise the late Empress of Russia from entering on the great theatre of war, until a combination of circumstances rendered the progress of the French armies a more dangerous evil than any which could possibly result to the Russian Empire from active operations. . . . The last words which the Empress was known to utter were addressed to her Secretary when she dismissed him on the morning on which she was seized: 'Tell Prince' (Zuboff), she said, 'to come to me at twelve, and to remind me of signing the Treaty of Alliance with England.' "

Having entered into ample considerations on the Emperor Paul's acts and extravagances, the Rev. Mr. Pitt continues as follows:

"When these considerations are impressed on the mind, the nature of the late secession from the coalition, and of the incalculable indignities offered to the Government of Great Britain, can alone be fairly estimated. . . . BUT THE TIES WHICH BIND HER (GREAT BRITAIN) TO THE RUSSIAN EMPIRE ARE FORMED BY NATURE, AND INVIOLABLE. United, these nations might almost brace the united world; divided, the strength and importance of each is FUNDAMENTALLY impaired. England has reason to regret with Russia that the imperial sceptre should be thus inconsistently wielded, but it is the sovereign of Russia alone who divides the Empires."

The reverend gentleman concludes his account by the words:

"As far as human foresight can at this moment penetrate, the despair of an enraged individual seems a more probable means to terminate the present scene of oppression than any more systematic combination of measures to restore the throne of Russia to its dignity and importance."

2

THE documents published in the first chapter extend from the reign of the Empress Ann to the commencement of the reign of the Emperor Paul, thus encompassing the greater part of the 18th century. At the end of that century it had become, as stated by the Rev. Mr. Pitt, the openly professed and orthodox dogma of English diplomacy, *"that the ties which bind Great Britain to the Russian Empire are formed by nature, and inviolable."*

In perusing these documents, there is something that startles us even more than their contents—viz., their form. All these letters are "confidential," "private," "secret," "most secret"; but in spite of secrecy, privacy, and confidence, the English statesmen converse among each other about Russia and her rulers in a tone of awful reserve, abject servility, and cynical submission, which would strike us even in the public despatches of Russian statesmen. To conceal intrigues against foreign nations secrecy is recurred to by Russian diplomatists. The same method is adopted by English diplomatists freely to express their devotion to a foreign Court. The secret despatches of Russian diplomatists are fumigated with some equivocal perfume. It is one part the *fumée de fausseté*, as the Duke of St. Simon[13] has it, and the other part that coquettish display of one's own superiority and cunning which stamps upon the reports of the French Secret Police their indelible character. Even the master despatches of Pozzo di Borgo[14] are tainted with this common blot of the *littérature de mauvais lieu.* In this point the English secret despatches prove much superior. They do not affect superiority but silliness. For instance, can there be anything more silly than Mr. Rondeau informing Horace Walpole that he has betrayed to the Russian Minister the letters addressed by the Turkish Grand Vizier to the King of England, but that he had told "at the same time those gentlemen that as there were several hard reflections on the Russian Court he should not have communicated them, *if they had not been so anxious to see them,*" and then told their excellencies not to tell the Porte that they had seen them (those letters)! At first view the infamy of the act is drowned in the silliness of the man. Or, take Sir George Macartney. Can there be anything more silly than his happiness that Russia seemed "reasonable" enough not to expect that England "should pay the WHOLE EXPENSES" for Russia's "choosing to take the lead at Stockholm"; or his "flattering himself" that he had "persuaded the Russian Court" not to be so "unreasonable" as to ask from England, in a time of peace, subsidies for a time of war against Turkey (then the ally of England); or his warning the Earl of Sandwich "not to mention" to the Russian Ambassador at London the secrets mentioned to himself by the Russian Chancellor at St. Petersburg? Or can there be anything more silly than Sir James Harris confidentially whispering into the ear of Lord Grantham that Catherine II was devoid of "judgment, precision of idea, reflection, and *l'esprit de combinaison*"?*

On the other hand, take the cool impudence with which Sir George Macartney informs his minister that because the Swedes were extremely jealous of, and mortified at, their dependence on Russia, England was directed by the Court of St. Petersburg to do its work at Stockholm, under the British colours of liberty and independence! Or Sir James Harris advising England to surrender to Russia Minorca and the right of search, and the monopoly of mediation in the affairs of the world—not in order to gain any material advantage, or even a formal engagement on the part of Russia, but only "a strong glow of friendship" from the Empress, and the transfer to France of her "ill humour."

The secret Russian despatches proceed on the very plain line that Russia knows herself to have no common interests whatever with other nations, but that every nation must be persuaded separately to have common interests with Russia to the exclusion of every other nation. The English despatches, on the contrary, never dare so much as hint that Russia has common interests with England, but only endeavour to convince England that she

* Or, to follow this affectation of silliness into more recent times, is there anything in diplomatic history that could match Lord Palmerston's proposal made to Marshal Soult (in 1839), to storm the Dardanelles, in order to afford the Sultan the support of the Anglo-French fleet against Russia?

has Russian interests. The English diplomatists themselves tell us that this was the single argument they pleaded, when placed face to face with Russian potentates.

If the English despatches we have laid before the public were addressed to private friends, they would only brand with infamy the ambassadors who wrote them. Secretly addressed as they are to the British Government itself, they nail it for ever to the pillory of history; and, instinctively, this seems to have been felt, even by Whig writers, because none has dared to publish them.

The question naturally arises from which epoch this Russian character of English diplomacy, become traditionary in the course of the 18th century, does date its origin. To clear up this point we must go back to the time of Peter the Great,[15] which, consequently, will form the principal subject of our researches. We propose to enter upon this task by reprinting some English pamphlets, written at the time of Peter I., and which have either escaped the attention of modern historians, or appeared to them to merit none. However, they will suffice for refuting the prejudice common to Continental and English writers, that the designs of Russia were not understood or suspected in England until at a later, and too late, epoch; that the diplomatic relations between England and Russia were but the natural offspring of the mutual material interests of the two countries; and that, therefore, in accusing the British statesmen of the 18th century of Russianism we should commit an unpardonable hysteron-proteron.[16] If we have shown by the English despatches that, at the time of the Empress Ann, England already betrayed her own allies to Russia, it will be seen from the pamphlets we are now about to reprint that, even before the epoch of Ann, at the very epoch of Russian ascendency in Europe, springing up at the time of Peter I., the plans of Russia were understood, and the connivance of British statesmen of these plans was denounced by English writers.

The first pamphlet we lay before the public is called *The Northern Crisis*. It was printed in London in 1716, and relates to the intended Dano-Anglo-Russian *invasion of Skana* (Schonen).[17]

During the year 1715 a northern alliance for the partition, not of Sweden proper, but of what we may call the Swedish

Empire, had been concluded between Russia, Denmark, Poland, Prussia, and Hanover. That partition forms the first grand act of modern diplomacy—the logical premiss to the partition of Poland. The partition treaties relating to Spain have engrossed the interest of posterity because they were the forerunners of the War of Succession, and the partition of Poland drew even a larger audience because its last act was played upon a contemporary stage. However, it cannot be denied that it was the partition of the Swedish Empire which inaugurated the modern era of international policy. The partition treaty not even pretended to have a pretext, save the misfortune of its intended victim. For the first time in Europe the violation of all treaties was not only made, but proclaimed the common basis of a new treaty. Poland herself, in the drag of Russia, and personated by that commonplace of immorality, Augustus II.,[18] Elector of Saxony and King of Poland, was pushed into the foreground of the conspiracy, thus signing her own death-warrant, and not even enjoying the privilege reserved by Polyphemus to Odysseus—to be last eaten. Charles XII. predicted her fate in the manifesto flung against King Augustus and the Czar, from his voluntary exile at Bender.[19] The manifesto is dated January 28, 1711.

The participation in this partition treaty threw England within the orbit of Russia, towards whom, since the days of the "Glorious Revolution," she had more and more gravitated. George I.,[20] as King of England, was bound to a defensive alliance with Sweden by the treaty of 1700. Not only as King of England, but as Elector of Hanover, he was one of the guarantees, and even of the direct parties to the treaty of Travendal, which secured to Sweden what the partition treaty intended stripping her of. Even his German electoral dignity he partly owed to that treaty. However, as Elector of Hanover he declared war against Sweden, which he waged as King of England.

In 1715 the confederates had divested Sweden of her German provinces, and to effect that end introduced the Muscovite on the German soil. In 1716 they agreed to invade Sweden proper —to attempt an armed descent upon Schonen—the southern extremity of Sweden now constituting the districts of Malmoe and Christianstadt. Consequently Peter of Russia brought with him from Germany a Muscovite army, which was scattered over Zealand,[21] thence to be conveyed to Schonen, under the protec-

tion of the English and Dutch fleets sent into the Baltic, on the
false pretext of protecting trade and navigation. Already in 1715,
when Charles XII. was besieged in Stralsund,[22] eight English
men-of-war, lent by England to Hanover, and by Hanover to
Denmark, had openly reinforced the Danish navy, and even
hoisted the Danish flag. In 1716 the British navy was commanded by his Czarish Majesty in person.

Everything being ready for the invasion of Schonen, there
arose a difficulty from a side where it was least expected.
Although the treaty stipulated only for 30,000 Muscovites,
Peter, in his magnanimity, had landed 40,000 on Zealand; but
now that he was to send them on the errand to Schonen, he all at
once discovered that out of the 40,000 he could spare but 15,000.
This declaration not only paralysed the military plan of the
confederates, it seemed to threaten the security of Denmark and
of Frederick IV., its king, as great part of the Muscovite army,
supported by the Russian fleet, occupied Copenhagen. One of
the generals of Frederick proposed suddenly to fall with the
Danish cavalry upon the Muscovites and to exterminate them,
while the English men-of-war should burn the Russian fleet.
Averse to any perfidy which required some greatness of will,
some force of character, and some contempt of personal danger,
Frederick IV. rejected the bold proposal, and limited himself to
assuming an attitude of defence. He then wrote a begging letter
to the Czar, intimating that he had given up his Schonen fancy,
and requested the Czar to do the same and find his way home: a
request the latter could not but comply with. When Peter at last
left Denmark with his army, the Danish Court thought fit to
communicate to the Courts of Europe a public account of the
incidents and transactions which had frustrated the intended
descent upon Schonen—and this document forms the starting
point of *The Northern Crisis.*

In a letter addressed to Baron Görtz,[23] dated from London,
January 23, 1717, by Count Gyllenborg,[24] there occur some
passages in which the latter, the then Swedish ambassador at the
Court of St. James's, seems to profess himself the author of *The
Northern Crisis,* the title of which he does not, however, quote.
Yet any idea of his having written that powerful pamphlet will
disappear before the slightest perusal of the Count's authenticated
writings, such as his letters to Görtz.

E

"THE NORTHERN CRISIS; OR IMPARTIAL REFLECTIONS ON
THE POLICIES OF THE CZAR; OCCASIONED BY MYNHEER
VON STOCKEN'S REASONS FOR DELAYING THE DESCENT
UPON SCHONEN. A TRUE COPY OF WHICH IS PREFIXED,
VERBALLY TRANSLATED AFTER THE TENOR OF THAT IN
THE GERMAN SECRETARY'S OFFICE IN COPENHAGEN,
OCTOBER 10, 1716. LONDON, 1716.

1.—*Preface*—— . . . 'Tis (the present pamphlet) not fit for
lawyers' clerks, but it is highly convenient to be read by those
who are proper students in the laws of nations; 'twill be but lost
time for any stock-jobbing, trifling dealer in Exchange-Alley to
look beyond the preface on't, but every merchant in England
(more especially those who trade to the Baltic) will find his
account in it. The Dutch (as the courants and postboys have
more than once told us) are about to mend their hands, if they
can, in several articles of trade with the Czar, and they have been
a long time about it to little purpose. Inasmuch as they are such
a frugal people, they are good examples for the imitation of our
traders; but if we can outdo them for once, in the means of pro-
jecting a better and more expeditious footing to go upon, for the
emolument of us both, let us, for once, be wise enough to set the
example, and let them, for once, be our imitators. This little
treatise will show a pretty plain way how we may do it, as to our
trade in the Baltic, at this juncture. I desire no little *coffee-house
politician* to meddle with it; but to give him even a dis-relish for
my company. I must let him know that he is not fit for mine.
Those who are even proficients in state science, will find in it
matter highly fit to employ all their powers of speculation, which
they ever before passed negligently by, and thought (too cursorily)
were not worth the regarding. No outrageous party-man will
find it all for his purpose; but every *honest Whig* and every *honest
Tory* may each of them read it, not only without either of their
disgusts, but with the satisfaction of them both. . . . 'Tis not fit,
in fine, for a mad, hectoring, Presbyterian Whig, or a raving,
fretful, dissatisfied, Jacobite Tory."

2.—THE REASONS HANDED ABOUT BY MYNHEER VON STOCKEN FOR DELAYING THE DESCENT UPON SCHONEN.

"There being no doubt, but most courts will be surprised that the descent upon Schonen has not been put into execution, notwithstanding the great preparations made for that purpose; and that all his Czarish Majesty's[25] troops, who were in Germany, were transported to Zealand, not without great trouble and danger, partly by his own gallies, and partly by his Danish Majesty's[26] and other vessels; and that the said descent is deferred till another time. His Danish Majesty hath therefore, in order to clear himself of all imputation and reproach, thought fit to order, that the following true account of this affair should be given to all impartial persons. Since the Swedes were entirely driven out of their *German* dominions, there was, according to all the rules of policy, and reasons of war, no other way left, than vigorously to attack the still obstinate King of Sweden, in the very heart of his country; thereby, with God's assistance, to force him to a lasting, good and advantageous peace for the allies. The King of Denmark and his Czarish Majesty were both of this opinion, and did, in order to put so good a design in execution, agree upon an interview, which at last (notwithstanding his Danish Majesty's presence, upon the account of Norway's being invaded, was most necessary in his own capital, and that the Muscovite ambassador, M. Dolgorouky, had given quite other assurances) was held at Ham and Horn, near Hamburgh, after his Danish Majesty had stayed there six weeks for the Czar. In this conference it was, on the 3rd of June, agreed between both their Majesties, after several debates, that the descent upon Schonen should positively be undertaken this year, and everything relating to the forwarding the same was entirely consented to. Hereupon his Danish Majesty made all haste for his return to his dominions, and gave orders to work day and night to get his fleet ready to put to sea. The transport ships were also gathered from all parts of his dominions, both with inexpressible charges and great prejudice to his subjects' trade. Thus, his Majesty (as the Czar himself upon his arrival at Copenhagen owned) did his utmost to provide all necessaries, and to forward the descent, upon whose success everything depended. It happened, however, in the meanwhile, and before the descent was agreed upon in the conference at Ham and Horn, that his Danish Majesty was obliged to secure his invaded and much oppressed kingdom of Norway, by sending thither a considerable squadron out of his fleet, under the command of Vice-Admiral Gabel, which squadron could not be recalled before the enemy had left that kingdom, without endangering a great part thereof; so that out of necessity the said Vice-Admiral was forced to tarry there till the 12th of July, when his Danish Majesty sent him express orders to return with all possible speed, wind and weather permitting; but this blowing for some time contrary, he was detained. . . . The Swedes were all the while powerful at sea, and his Czarish Majesty himself did not think it advisable that the remainder of the Danish, in conjunction with the men-of-war then at Copenhagen, should go to convoy the Russian troops from Rostock, before the above-mentioned squadron under Vice-Admiral Gabel was arrived. This happening at last in the month of August, the confederate fleet put to sea; and the transporting of the said troops hither to Zealand was put in execution, though with a great deal of trouble and danger, but it took up so much time that the descent could not be ready till September following. Now, when all these preparations, as well for the descent as the embarking the armies, were entirely ready, his Danish Majesty assured himself that the descent should be made within a few days, at farthest by the 21st of September. The Russian Generals and Ministers first raised some difficulties to those of Denmark, and afterwards, on the 17th September, declared in an appointed conference, that his Czarish Majesty, considering the present situation of affairs, was of opinion that neither forage nor provision could be had in Schonen, and that consequently the descent was not advisable to be attempted this year, but ought to be put off till next spring. It may be easily imagined how much his Danish Majesty was surprised at this; especially seeing the Czar, if he had altered his opinion, as to this design so solemnly concerted, might have declared it sooner, and thereby saved his Danish Majesty several tons of gold, spent upon the necessary preparations. His Danish Majesty did, however, in a letter dated the 20th of September, amply represent to the Czar, that although the season was very much advanced, the descent might, nevertheless, easily be undertaken with such a superior force, as to get a footing in Schonen, where being assured there had been a very plentiful harvest, he did not doubt but subsistence might be found; besides, that having an open communication with his own countries, it might easily be transported from thence. His Danish Majesty alleged also several weighty reasons why the descent was either to be made this year, or the thoughts of making it next spring entirely be laid aside. *Nor did he alone make these moving remonstrances to the Czar;* BUT HIS BRITISH MAJESTY'S MINISTER RESIDING HERE, AS WELL AS ADMIRAL NORRIS,[27] *seconded the same also in a very pressing manner;* AND BY EXPRESS ORDER OF THE KING, THEIR MASTER, *endeavoured to bring the Czar into their opinion, and to persuade him to go on with the descent*; but his Czarish Majesty declared by his answer, that he would adhere to the resolution that he had once taken concerning this delay of making the descent; but if his Danish Majesty was resolved to venture on the descent, that he then, according to the treaty made near Straelsund, would assist him only with the 15 battalions and 1,000 horse therein stipulated; that next spring he would comply with everything else, and neither could or would declare himself farther in this affair. Since then, his Danish Majesty could not, without running so great a hazard, undertake so great a work alone with his own army and the said 15 battalions; he desired, in another letter of the 23rd September, his Czarish Majesty would be pleased to add 13 battalions of his troops, in which case his Danish Majesty would still this year attempt the descent; but even this could not be obtained from his Czarish Majesty, who absolutely refused it by his ambassador on the 24th ditto: whereupon his Danish Majesty, in his letter of the 26th, declared to the Czar, that since things stood thus, he desired none of his troops, but that they might be all speedily transported out of his dominions; that so the transport, whose freight stood him in 40,000 rix dollars[28] per month, might be discharged, and his subjects eased of the intolerable contributions they now underwent. This he could not do less than agree to; and accordingly, all the Russian troops are already embarked, and intend for certain to go from here with the first favourable wind. It must be left to Providence and time, to discover what may have induced the Czar to a resolution so prejudicial to the Northern Alliance, and most advantageous to the common enemy.

If we would take a true survey of men, and lay them open in a proper light to the eye of our intellects, *we must* first *consider their natures* and then *their ends*; and by this method of examination, though their conduct is, seemingly, full of intricate mazes and perplexities, and winding round with infinite meanders of state-craft, we shall be able to dive into the deepest recesses, make our way through the most puzzling labyrinths, and at length come to the most abstruse means of bringing about the master secrets of their minds, and to unriddle their utmost mysteries. . . . The Czar . . . is, by nature, of a great and enterprising spirit, and of a genius thoroughly politic; and as for his ends, the manner of his own Government, where he sways arbitrary lord over the estates and honours of his people, must make him, if all the policies in the world could by far-distant aims promise him accession and accumulation of empire and wealth, be everlastingly laying schemes for the achieving of both with the extremest cupidity and ambition. Whatever ends of insatiate desire of opulency, and a boundless thirst for dominion, can ever put him upon, to satisfy their craving and voracious appetites, those must, most undoubtedly, be his.

The next questions we are to put to ourselves are these three:

1.   By what means can he gain these ends?

2.   How far from him, and in what place, can these ends be best obtained?

3.   And by what time, using all proper methods and succeeding in them, may he obtain these ends?

The possessions of the Czar were prodigious, vast in extent; the people all at his nod, all his downright arrant slaves, and all the wealth of the country his own at a word's command. But then the country, though large in ground, was not quite so in produce. Every vassal had his gun, and was to be a soldier upon call; but there was never a soldier among them, nor a man that understood the calling; and though he had all their wealth, they had no commerce of consequence, and little ready money; and consequently his treasury, when he had amassed all he could, very bare and empty. He was then but in an indifferent condition to satisfy those two natural appetites, when he had neither wealth to support a soldiery, nor a soldiery trained in the art of war. The first token this Prince gave of an aspiring genius, and of an ambition that is noble and necessary in a monarch who has a mind to flourish, was to believe none of his subjects more wise than himself, or more fit to govern. He did so, and looked upon his own proper person as the most fit to travel out among the other realms of the world and study politics for the advancing of his dominions. He then seldom pretended to any war-like dispositions against those who were instructed in the science of arms; his military dealings lay mostly with the Turks and Tartars, who, as they had numbers as well as he, had them likewise composed, as well as his, of a rude, uncultivated mob, and they appeared in the field like a raw, undisciplined militia. In this his Christian neighbours liked him well, insomuch as he was a kind of stay or stop-gap to the infidels. But when he came to look into the more polished parts of the Christian world, he set out towards it, from the very threshold, like a natural-born politician. He was not for learning the game by trying chances and venturing losses in the field so soon; no, he went upon the maxim *that it was, at that time of day, expedient and necessary for him to carry, like Samson, his strength in his head, and not in his arms*. He had then, he knew, but very few commodious places for commerce of his own, and those all situated in the *White Sea*, too remote, frozen up the most part of the year, and not at all fit for a fleet of men-of-war; but he knew of many more commodious ones of his neighbours in the Baltic, and within his reach whenever he could strengthen his hands to lay hold of them. He had a longing eye towards them; but with prudence seemingly turned his head another way, and secretly entertained the pleasant thought that he should come at them all in good time. Not to give any jealousy, he endeavours for no help from his neighbours to instruct his men in arms. That was like asking a skilful person, one intended to fight a duel with, to teach him first how to fence. *He went over to Great Britain*, where he knew that potent kingdom could, as yet, have no jealousies of his growth of power, and in the eye of which his vast extent of nation lay neglected and unconsidered and overlooked, as I am afraid it is to this very day. He was present at all our exercises, looked into all our laws, inspected our military, civil, and ecclesiastical regimen of affairs; yet this was the least he then wanted; this was the slightest part of his errand. But by degrees, when he grew familiar with our people, he visited our docks, pretending not to have any prospect of profit, but only to take a huge delight (the effect of curiosity only) to see our manner of building ships. He kept his court, as one may say, in our shipyard, so industrious was he in affording them his continual Czarish presence, and to his immortal glory for art and industry be it spoken, that the great Czar, by stooping often to the employ, could handle an axe with the best artificer of them all; and the monarch having a good mathematical head of his own, grew in some time a very expert royal shipwright. A ship or two for his diversion made and sent him, and then two or three more, and after that two or three more, would signify just nothing at all, if they were granted to be sold to him by the *Maritime Powers*[29] that could, at will, lord it over the sea. It would be a puny inconsiderable matter, and not worth the regarding. Well, but then, over and above this, he had artfully insinuated himself into the goodwill of many of our best workmen, and won their hearts by his good-natured familiarities and condescension among them. To turn this to his service, he offered many very large premiums and advantages to go and settle in his country, which they gladly accepted of. A little after he sends over some private ministers and officers to negotiate for more workmen, for land officers, and likewise for picked and chosen good seamen, who might be advanced and promoted to offices by going there. Nay, even to this day, any expert seaman that is upon our traffic to the port of Archangel, if he has the least spark of ambition and any ardent desire to be in office, he need but offer himself to the sea-service of the Czar, and he is a lieutenant immediately. Over and above this, that Prince has even found the way to take by force into his service out of our merchant ships as many of their ablest seamen as he pleased, giving the masters the same number of raw Muscovites in their place, whom they afterwards were forced in their own defence to make fit for their own use. Neither is this all; he had, during the last war, many hundreds of his subjects, both noblemen and common sailors, on board *ours, the French and the Dutch fleets*; and he has all along maintained, and still maintains numbers of them in *ours and the Dutch yards*.

But seeing he looked all along upon all these endeavours towards improving himself and his subjects as superfluous, whilst a seaport was wanting, where he might build a fleet of his own, and from whence he might himself export the products of his country, and import those of others; and finding the King of Sweden possessed of the most convenient ones, I mean Narva and Revel, which he knew that Prince never could nor would amicably part with, he at last resolved to wrest them out of his hands by force. His *Swedish* Majesty's tender youth seemed the the fittest time for this enterprise, but even then he would not run the hazard alone. He drew in other princes to divide the spoil with him. And the *Kings of Denmark and Poland* were weak enough to serve as instruments to forward the great and ambitious views of the Czar. It is true, he met with a mighty hard rub at his very first setting out; his whole army being entirely defeated by a handful of Swedes at Narva. But it was his good luck that his Swedish Majesty, instead of improving so great a victory against him, turned immediately his arms against the King of Poland, against whom he was personally piqued, and that so much the more, inasmuch as he had taken that Prince for one of his best friends, and was just upon the point of concluding with him the strictest alliance when he unexpectedly invaded the Swedish Livonia, and beseiged Riga. This was, in all respects, what the Czar could most have wished for; and foreseeing that the longer the war in Poland lasted, the more time should he have both to retrieve his first loss, and to gain Narva, he took care it should be spun out as great a length as possible; for which end he never sent the King of Poland succour enough to make him too strong for the King of Sweden; who, on the other hand, though he gained one signal victory after the other, yet never could subdue his enemy as long as he received continual re-inforcements from his hereditary country. And had not his Swedish Majesty, contrary to most people's expectations, marched directly into Saxony itself, and thereby forced the King of Poland to peace, the Czar would have had leisure enough in all conscience to bring his designs to greater maturity. This peace was one of the greatest disappointments the Czar ever met with, whereby he became singly engaged in the war. He had, however, the comfort of having beforehand taken *Narva*, and laid a foundation to his favourite town *Petersburg*, and to the seaport, the docks, and the vast magazines there; all which works, to what perfection they are now brought, let them tell who, with surprise, have seen them.

He (Peter) used all endeavours to bring matters to an accommodation. He proffered very advantageous conditions; *Petersburg* only, a trifle as he pretended, which he had set his heart upon, he would retain; and even for that he was willing some

other way to give satisfaction. But the King of Sweden was too
well acquainted with the importance of that place to leave it in
the hands of an ambitious prince, and thereby to give him an
inlet into the Baltic. This was the only time since the defeat at
Narva that the Czar's arms had no other end than that of self-
defence. They might, perhaps, even have fallen short therein,
had not the King of Sweden (through whose persuasion is still
a mystery), instead of marching the shortest way to Novogorod
and to Moscow, turned towards Ukrain, where his army, after
great losses and sufferings, was at last entirely defeated at Pul-
towa. As this was a fatal period to the Swedish successes, so how
great a deliverance it was to the Muscovites, may be gathered
from the Czar's celebrating every year, with great solemnity, the
anniversary of that day, from which his ambitious thoughts
began to soar still higher. The whole of *Livonia*, *Estland*, and
the best and greatest part of *Finland* was now what he demanded,
after which, though he might for the present condescend to give
peace to the remaining part of Sweden, he knew he could easily
even add that to his conquests whenever he pleased. The only
obstacle he had to fear in these his projects was from his northern
neighbours; but as the *Maritime Powers*, and even the neighbouring princes in Germany, were then so intent upon their war
against France, that they seemed entirely neglectful of that of the
North, so there remained only Denmark and Poland to be
jealous of. The former of these kingdoms had, ever since King
William,[30] of glorious memory, compelled it to make peace with
Holstein and, consequently, with Sweden, enjoyed an uninterrupted tranquillity, during which it had time, by a free trade and
considerable subsidies from the maritime powers to enrich itself,
and was in a condition, by joining itself to Sweden, as it was its
interest to do, to stop the Czar's progresses, and timely to prevent
its own danger from them. The other, I mean Poland, was now
quietly under the government of King Stanislaus, who, owing in
a manner his crown to the King of Sweden, could not, out of
gratitude, as well as real concern for the interest of his country,
fail opposing the designs of a too aspiring neighbour. The Czar
was too cunning not to find out a remedy for all this: he represented to the King of Denmark how low the King of Sweden
was now brought, and how fair an opportunity he had, during
that Prince's long absence, to clip entirely his wings, and to

aggrandise himself at his expense. In King Augustus he raised the long-hid resentment for the loss of the Polish Crown, which he told him he might now recover without the least difficulty. Thus both these Princes were immediately caught. The Danes declared war against Sweden without so much as a tolerable pretence, and made a descent upon Schonen, where they were soundly beaten for their pains. King Augustus re-entered Poland, where everything has ever since continued in the greatest disorder, and *that in a great measure owing to Muscovite intrigues.* It happened, indeed, that these new confederates, whom the Czar had only drawn in to serve his ambition, became at first more necessary to his preservation than he had thought; for the Turks having declared a war against him, they hindered the Swedish arms from joining with them to attack him; but that storm being soon over, through the Czar's wise behaviour and the avarice and folly of the Grand Vizier, he then made the intended use both of these his friends, as well as of them he afterwards, through hopes of gain, persuaded into his alliance, which was to lay all the burden and hazard of the war upon them, in order entirely to weaken them, together with Sweden, whilst *he was preparing to swallow the one after the other.* He has put them on one difficult attempt after the other; their armies have been considerably lessened by battles and long sieges, whilst his own were either employed in easier conquests, and more profitable to him, or kept at the vast expense of neutral princes—near enough at hand to come up to demand a share of the booty without having struck a blow in getting it. His behaviour has been as cunning at sea, where his fleet has always kept out of harm's way and at a great distance whenever there was any likelihood of an engagement between the Danes and the Swedes. He hoped that when these two nations had ruined one another's fleets, his might then ride master in the Baltic. All this while he had taken care to make his men improve, by the example of foreigners and under their command, in the art of war. . . . His fleets will soon considerably outnumber the Swedish and the Danish ones joined together. He need not fear their being a hindrance from his giving a finishing stroke to this great and glorious undertaking. Which done, *let us look to ourselves; he will then most certainly become our rival, and as dangerous to us as he is now neglected.* We then may, perhaps though too late, call to mind what our own ministers and merchants have told us of his designs of carrying on alone all the northern trade, and of getting all that from Turkey and Persia into his hands through the rivers which he is joining and making navigable from the Caspian, or the Black Sea, to his Petersburg. *We shall then wonder at our blindness that we did not suspect his designs* when we heard the prodigious works he has done at Petersburg and Revel; of which last place, the *Daily Courant*, dated November 23, says:

HAGUE, *Nov.* 17.

The captains of the men-of-war of the States, who have been at Revel, advise that the Czar has put that port and the fortifications of the place into such a condition of defence that it may pass for one of the most considerable fortresses, not only of the Baltic, but even of Europe.

Leave we him now, as to his sea affairs, commerce and manufactures, and other works both of his policy and power, and let us view him in regard to his proceedings in this last campaign, especially as to that so much talked of descent, he, in conjunction with his allies, was to make upon Schonen, and we shall find that even therein he has acted with his usual cunning. There is no doubt but the King of Denmark was the first that proposed this descent. He found that nothing but a speedy end to a war he had so rashly and unjustly begun, could save his country from ruin and from the bold attempts of the King of Sweden, either against Norway, or against Zealand and Copenhagen. To treat separately with that prince was a thing he could not do, as foreseeing that he would not part with an inch of ground to so unfair an enemy; and he was afraid that a Congress for a general peace, supposing the King of Sweden would consent to it upon the terms proposed by his enemies, would draw the negotiations out beyond what the situation of his affairs could bear. He invites, therefore, all his confederates to make a home thrust at the King of Sweden, by a descent into his country, where, having defeated him, as by the superiority of the forces to be employed in that design he hoped they should, they might force him to an immediate peace on such terms as they themselves pleased. I don't know how far the rest of his confederates came into that project; but neither the *Prussian* nor the *Hanoverian* Court appeared *openly* in that project, *and how far our English fleet, under Sir John Norris, was to have forwarded it, I have nothing to say, but leave others to judge out of the King of Denmark's own declaration:* but the Czar came readily into it. He got thereby a new pretence to carry the war one campaign more at other people's expense; to march his troops into the Empire again, and to have them quartered and maintained, first in Mecklenburg[31] and then in Zealand. In the meantime he had his eyes upon *Wismar,* and upon a Swedish island called *Gotland.* If, by surprise, he could get the first out of the hands of his confederates, he then had a good seaport, whither to transport his troops when he pleased into *Germany,* without asking the King of *Prussia's* leave for a free passage through his territories; and if, by a sudden descent, he could dislodge the *Swedes* out of the other, he then became master of the best port in the Baltic. He miscarried, however, in both these projects; for Wismar was too well guarded to be surprised; and he found his confederates would not give him a helping hand towards conquering Gotland. After this he began to look with another eye upon the descent to be made upon Schonen. He found it equally contrary to his interest, whether it succeeded or not. For if he did, and the King was thereby forced to a general peace, he knew his interests therein would be least regarded; having already notice enough of his confederates being ready to sacrifice them, provided they got their own terms. If he did not succeed, then, besides the loss of the flower of an army he had trained and disciplined with so much care, as he very well foresaw that the English fleet would hinder the King of Sweden from attempting anything against Denmark; so he justly feared the whole shock would fall upon him, and he be thereby forced to surrender all he had taken from Sweden. These considerations made him entirely resolved not to make one of the descent; but he did not care to declare it till as late as possible: first, that he might the longer have his troops maintained at the Danish expense; secondly, that it might be too late for the King of Denmark to demand the necessary troops from his other confederates, and to make the descent without him; and, lastly, that by putting the Dane to a vast expense in making necessary preparations, he might still weaken him more, and, therefore, make him now the more dependent on him, and hereafter a more easy prey.

Thus he very carefully dissembles his real thoughts, till just when the descent was to be made, and then he, all of a sudden, refuses joining it, and defers it till next spring, with this averment, *that he will then be as good as his word.* But mark him, as some of our newspapers tell us, under this restriction, *unless he can get an advantageous peace of Sweden.* This passage, together with the common report we now have of his treating a separate peace with the King of Sweden, is a new instance of his cunning and policy. He has there two strings to his bow, of which one must serve his turn. There is no doubt but the Czar knows that an accommodation between him and the King of Sweden must be very difficult to bring about. For as he, on the one side, should never consent to part with those seaports, for the getting of which he began this war, and which are absolutely necessary towards carrying on his great and vast designs; so the King of Sweden would look upon it as directly contrary to his interest to yield up these same seaports, if possibly he could hinder it. But then again, the Czar is so well acquainted with the great and heroic spirit of his Swedish Majesty, that he does not question his yielding, rather in point of interest than nicety of honour. From hence it is, he rightly judges, that his Swedish Majesty must be less exasperated against him who, though he began an unjust war, has very often paid dearly for it, and carried it on all along through various successes than against some confederates; that taking an opportunity of his Swedish Majesty's misfortunes, fell upon him in an ungenerous manner, and made a partition treaty of his provinces. The Czar, still more to accommodate himself to the genius of his great enemy, unlike his confederates, who, upon all occasions, spared no reflections and even very unbecoming ones (bullying memorials and hectoring manifestoes), spoke all along with the utmost civility of his brother Charles as he calls him, maintains him to be the greatest general in Europe, and even publicly avers, he will more trust a word from him than the greatest assurances, oaths, nay, even treaties with his confederates. These kind of civilities may, perhaps, make a deeper impression upon the noble mind of the King of Sweden, and he be persuaded rather to sacrifice a real interest to a generous enemy, than to gratify, in things of less moment, those by whom he has been ill, and even inhumanly used. But if this should not succeed, the Czar is still a gainer by having made his confederates uneasy at these his separate negotiations; and as we find by the newspapers, the more solicitous to keep him ready to their confederacy, which must cost them very large proffers and promises. In the meantime he leaves the Dane and the Swede securely bound up together in war, and weakening one another as fast as they can, and he turns towards the Empire and views the Protestant Princes there; and, under many specious pretences, not only marches and counter-marches about their several territories his troops that came back from Denmark, but makes also slowly advance towards Germany those whom he has kept this great while in Poland, under pretence to help the King against his dissatisfied subjects, whose commotions all the while he was the greatest fomenter of. He considers the Emperor is in war with the Turks, and therefore has found, by too successful experience, how little his Imperial Majesty is able to show his authority in protecting the members of the Empire. His troops remain in Mecklenburg, notwithstanding their departure is highly insisted upon. His replies to all the demands on that subject are filled with such reasons as if he would give new laws to the Empire.

Now let us suppose that the King of Sweden should think it more honourable to make a peace with the Czar, and to carry the force of his resentment against his less generous enemies, what a stand will then the princes of the empire, even those that unadvisedly drew in 40,000 Muscovites, to secure the tranquillity of that empire against 10,000 or 12,000 Swedes,—I say what stand will they be able to make against him while the Emperor is already engaged in war with the Turks? and the Poles, when they are once in peace among themselves (if after the miseries of so long a war they are in a condition to undertake anything) are by treaty obliged to join their aids against that common enemy of Christianity.

Some will say I make great and sudden rises from very small beginnings. My answer is, that I would have such an objector look back and reflect why I show him, from such a speck of entity, at his first origin, growing, through more improbable and almost insuperable difficulties, to such a bulk as he has already attained to, and *whereby, as his advocates, the Dutch themselves own, he is grown too formidable for the repose, not only of his neighbours, but of Europe in general.*

But then, again, they will say he has no pretence either to make a peace with the Swedes separately from the Dane or to make war upon other princes, some of whom he is bound in alliance with. Whoever thinks these objections not answered must have considered the Czar neither as to his nature or to his ends. The Dutch own further, *that he made war against Sweden without any specious pretence*. He that made war without any specious pretence may make a peace without any specious pretence, and make a new war without any specious pretence for it too. His Imperial Majesty (of Austria), like a wise Prince, when he was obliged to make war with the Ottomans, made it, as in policy, he should, powerfully. But, in the meantime, may not the Czar, who is a wise and potent Prince too, follow the example upon the neighbouring Princes round him that are Protestants? If he should, I tremble to speak it, it is not impossible, but in this age of Christianity *the Protestant religion should, in a great measure, be abolished*; and that among the Christians, the *Greeks* and *Romans* may once more come to be the only Pretenders for Universal Empire. The pure possibility carries with it warning enough for the Maritime Powers, and all the other Protestant Princes, to mediate a peace for Sweden, and strengthen his arms again, without which no preparations can put them sufficiently upon their guard; and this must be done early and betimes, *before the King of Sweden, either out of despair or revenge, throws himself into the Czar's hands*. For 'tis a certain maxim (which all Princes ought, and the Czar seems at this time to observe too much for the repose of Christendom) that a wise man must not stand for ceremony, and only *turn* with opportunities. No, he must even *run* with them. For the Czar's part, I will venture to say so much in his commendation, that he will hardly suffer himself to be overtaken that way. He seems to act just as the tide serves. There is nothing which contributes more to the making our undertakings prosperous than the taking of times and opportunities; for time carrieth with it the seasons of opportunities of business. If you let them slip, all your designs are rendered unsuccessful.

In short, things seem now come to that *crisis* that peace should as soon as possible be procured to the Swede, with such advantageous articles as are consistent with the nicety of his honour to accept, and with the safety of the Protestant interest, that he should have offered to him, which can be scarce less than all the possessions which he formerly had in the Empire. As in all other things, so in politics, a long-tried certainty must be preferred before an uncertainty, tho' grounded on ever so probable suppositions. Now can there be anything more certain, than that the provinces Sweden has had in the Empire, were given to it to make it nearer at hand and the better able to secure the Protestant interest which, together with the liberties of the Empire it just then had saved? Can there be anything more certain than that kingdom has, by those means, upon all occasions, secured that said interest now near four-score years? Can there be anything more certain than, as to his present Swedish Majesty, that I may use the words of a letter her late Majesty, Queen Anne, wrote to him (Charles XII.), and *in the time of a Whig Ministry too*, viz.: 'That, as a true Prince, hero and Christian, the chief end of his endeavours has been the promotion of the fear of God among men: and that without insisting on his own particular interest.'

On the other hand, is it not very uncertain whether those princes, who, by sharing among them the Swedish provinces in the Empire, are now going to set up as protectors of the Protestant interests there, exclusive of the Swedes, will be able to do it? *Denmark* is already so low, and will in all appearance be so much lower still before the end of the war, that very little assistance can be expected from it in a great many years. In *Saxony*, the prospect is but too dismal under a Popish prince, so that there remain only the two illustrious houses of Hanover and Brandenburg of all the Protestant princes, powerful enough to lead the rest. Let us therefore only make a parallel between what now happens in the Duchy of Mecklenburg, and what may happen to the Protestant interest, and we shall soon find how we may be mistaken in our reckoning. That said poor Duchy has been most miserably ruined by the Muscovite troops, and it is still so; the Electors of Brandenburg and Hanover are obliged, both as directors of the circle of Lower Saxony, as neighbours, and Protestant Princes, to rescue a fellow state of the Empire, and a Protestant country, from so cruel an oppression of a foreign Power. But, pray, what have they done? The Elector of Brandenburg, cautious lest the Muscovites might on one side invade his electorate, and on the other side from Livonia and Poland, his kingdom of Prussia; and the Elector of Hanover having the same wise caution as to his hereditary countries, have not upon this, though very pressing occasion, thought it for their interest, to use any other means than

F

representations. But pray with what success? The Muscovites are still in Mecklenburg, and if at last they march out of it, it will be when the country is so ruined that they cannot there subsist any longer.

It seems the King of Sweden should be restored to all that he has lost on the side of the Czar; and this appears the *joint interest of both the Maritime Powers*. This may they please to undertake: *Holland*, because it is a maxim there that the Czar grows too great, and must not be suffered to settle in the Baltic, and that Sweden must not be abandoned; *Great Britain*, because, if the Czar compasses his vast and prodigious views, he will, by the ruin and conquest of Sweden, become our nearer and more dreadful neighbour. Besides, we are bound to it by a treaty concluded in the year 1700, between King William and the present King of Sweden, by virtue of which King William assisted the King of Sweden, when in more powerful circumstances, with all that he desired, with great sums of money, several hundred pieces of cloth, and considerable quantities of gunpowder.

But *some Politicians (whom nothing can make jealous of the growing strength and abilities of the Czar) though they are even foxes and vulpones in the art, either will not see or pretend they cannot see* how the Czar can ever be able to make so great a progress in power as to hurt us here in our island. To them it is easy to repeat the same answer a hundred times over, if they would be so kind as to take it at last, viz., *that what has been may be again*; and that they did not see how he could reach the height of power, which he has already arrived at, after, I must confess, a very incredible manner. Let those *incredulous* people look narrowly into the *nature* and the *ends* and the *designs* of this great monarch; they will find that they are laid very deep, and that his plans carry in them a prodigious deal of prudence and foresight, and his ends are at the long run brought about by a kind of magic in policy; and will they not after that own that we ought to fear everything from him? As he desires that the designs with which he labours may not prove abortive, so he does not assign them a certain day of their birth, but leaves them to the natural productions of fit times and occasions, like those curious artists in China, who temper the mould this day of which a vessel may be made a hundred years hence.

There is another sort of short-sighted politicians among us, who have more of cunning court intrigue and immediate state-craft in them than of true policy and concern for their country's interest. These gentlemen pin entirely their faith upon other people's sleeves; ask as to everything that is proposed to them, how it is liked at Court? what the opinion of their party is concerning it? and if the contrary party is for or against it? Hereby they rule their judgment, and it is enough for their cunning leaders to brand anything with *Whiggism* or *Jacobitism*, for to make these people, without any further inquiry into the matter, blindly espouse it or oppose it. This, it seems, is at present the case of the subject we are upon. Anything said or written in favour of Sweden and the King thereof, is immediately said to come from a *Jacobite* pen, and thus reviled and rejected, without being read or considered. Nay, I have heard gentlemen go so far as to maintain publicly, and with all the vehemence in the world, that the King of Sweden was a Roman Catholic, and that the Czar was a good Protestant. This, indeed, is one of the greatest misfortunes our country labours under, and till we begin to see with our own eyes, and inquire ourselves into the truth of things, we shall be led away, God knows whither, at last. The serving of Sweden according to our treaties and real interest has nothing to do with our party causes. Instead of seeking for and taking hold of any pretence to undo Sweden, we ought openly to assist it. Could our Protestant succession have a better friend or a bolder champion?

I shall conclude this by shortly recapitulating what I have said. That since the Czar has not only replied to the King of Denmark entreating the contrary, but also answered our Admiral Norris, that he would persist in his resolution to delay the descent upon Schonen, and is said by other newspapers to resolve not to make it then, if he can have peace with Sweden; every Prince, and we more particularly, ought to be jealous of his having some such design as I mention in view, and consult how to prevent them, and to clip, in time, his too aspiring wings, which cannot be effectually done, first, without the Maritime Powers please to begin to keep him in some check and awe, and 'tis to be hoped a certain potent nation, that has helped him forward, can, in some measure, bring him back, and may then speak to this great enterpriser in the language of a countryman in Spain, who coming to an image enshrined, the first making whereof he could well remember, and not finding all the respectful usage he expected,—'You need not,' quoth he, 'be so proud, for we have known you from a plum-tree.' The next only way is to restore, by a peace, to the King of Sweden what he has lost; that checks his (the Czar's) power immediately, and on that side nothing else can. I wish it may not at last be found true, that those who have been fighting against the King have, in the main, been fighting against themselves. If the Swede ever has his dominions again, and lowers the high spirit of the Czar, still he may say by his neighbours, as an old Greek hero did, whom his countrymen constantly sent into exile whenever he had done them a service, but were forced to call him back to their aid, whenever they wanted success. 'These people,' quoth he, 'are always using me like the palm-tree. They will be breaking my branches continually, and yet, if there comes a storm, they run to me, and can't find a better place for shelter.' But if he has them not, I shall only exclaim a phrase out of Terence's 'Andria':

> Hoccine credibile est aut memorabile
> Tanta vecordia innata cuiquam ut siet,
> Ut malis gaudeant ?[32]

4. POSTSCRIPT.—I flatter myself that this little history is of that curious nature, and on matters hitherto so unobserved, that I consider it, with pride, as a valuable New Year's gift to the present world; and that posterity will accept it, as the like, for many years after, and read it over on that anniversary, and call it their *Warning Piece*. I must have my *Exegi-Monumentum*[33] as well as others."

3

To understand a limited historical epoch, we must step beyond
its limits, and compare it with other historical epochs. To judge
Governments and their acts, we must measure them by their own
times and the conscience of their contemporaries. Nobody will
condemn a British statesman of the 17th century for acting on a
belief in witchcraft, if he find Bacon himself ranging demonology
in the catalogue of science. On the other hand, if the Stanhopes,
the Walpoles, the Townshends, etc., were suspected, opposed,
and denounced in their own country by their own contemporaries
as tools or accomplices of Russia, it will no longer do to shelter
their policy behind the convenient screen of prejudice and
ignorance common to their time. At the head of the historical
evidence we have to sift, we place, therefore, long-forgotten
English pamphlets printed at the very time of Peter I. These
preliminary *pièces des procès* we shall, however, limit to three
pamphlets, which, from three different points of view, illustrate
the conduct of England towards Sweden. The first, the *Northern
Crisis* (given in Chapter II.), revealing the general system of
Russia, and the dangers accruing to England from the Russifica-
tion of Sweden; the second, called *The Defensive Treaty*, judg-
ing the acts of England by the Treaty of 1700; and the third,
entitled *Truth is but Truth, however it is Timed*, proving that the
new-fangled schemes which magnified Russia into the paramount
Power of the Baltic were in flagrant opposition to the traditionary policy England had pursued during the course of a whole
century.

The pamphlet called *The Defensive Treaty* bears no date of
publication. Yet in one passage it states that, for reinforcing the
Danish fleet, eight English men-of-war were left at Copenhagen
"the year before last," and in another passage alludes to the
assembling of the confederate fleet for the Schonen expedition as
having occurred *"last summer."* As the former event took place

in 1715, and the latter towards the end of the summer of 1716, it is evident that the pamphlet was written and published in the earlier part of the year 1717. The Defensive Treaty between England and Sweden, the single articles of which the pamphlet comments upon in the form of queries, was concluded in 1700 between William III. and Charles XII., and was not to expire before 1719. Yet, during almost the whole of this period, we find England continually assisting Russia and waging war against Sweden, either by secret intrigue or open force, although the treaty was never rescinded nor war ever declared. This fact is perhaps even less strange than the *conspiration de silence* under which modern historians have succeeded in burying it, and among them historians by no means sparing of censure against the British Government of that time, for having, without any previous declaration of war, destroyed the Spanish fleet in the Sicilian waters. But then, at least, England was not bound to Spain by a defensive treaty. How, then, are we to explain this contrary treatment of similar cases? The piracy committed against Spain was one of the weapons which the Whig Ministers, seceding from the Cabinet in 1717, caught hold of to harass their remaining colleagues. When the latter stepped forward in 1718, and urged Parliament to declare war against Spain, Sir Robert Walpole rose from his seat in the Commons, and in a most virulent speech denounced the late ministerial acts "as contrary to the laws of nations, and a breach of solemn treaties." "Giving sanction to them in the manner proposed," he said, "could have no other view than to screen ministers, who were conscious of having done something amiss, and who, having begun a war against Spain, would now make it the Parliament's war." The treachery against Sweden and the connivance at the plans of Russia, never happening to afford the ostensible pretext for a family quarrel amongst the Whig rulers (they being rather unanimous on these points), never obtained the honours of historical criticism so lavishly spent upon the Spanish incident.

How apt modern historians generally are to receive their cue from the official tricksters themselves, is best shown by their reflections on the commercial interests of England with respect to Russia and Sweden. Nothing has been more exaggerated than the dimensions of the trade opened to Great Britain by the huge market of the Russia of Peter the Great, and his immediate successors. Statements bearing not the slightest touch of criticism have been allowed to creep from one book-shelf to another, till they became at last historical household furniture, to be inherited by every successive historian, without even the *beneficium inventarii*. Some incontrovertible statistical figures will suffice to blot out these hoary common-places.

BRITISH COMMERCE FROM 1697–1700.

	£
Export to Russia	58,884
Import from Russia . .	112,252
Total . . .	171,136
Export to Sweden. . . .	57,555
Import from Sweden . . .	212,094
Total . . .	269,649

During the same period the total

	£
Export of England amounted to .	3,525,906
Import	3,482,586
Total . . .	7,008,492

In 1716, after all the Swedish provinces in the Baltic, and on the Gulfs of Finland and Bothnia, had fallen into the hands of Peter I., the

	£
Export to Russia was . . .	113,154
Import from Russia . . .	197,270
Total . . .	310,424
Export to Sweden. . . .	24,101
Import from Sweden . . .	136,959
Total . . .	161,060

At the same time, the total of English exports and imports together reached about £10,000,000. It will be seen from these figures, when compared with those of 1697–1700, that the increase in the Russian trade is balanced by the decrease in the Swedish trade, and that what was added to the one was subtracted from the other.

In 1730, the

		£
Export to Russia was	. .	46,275
Import from Russia	. .	258,802
Total . . .		305,077

Fifteen years, then, after the consolidation in the meanwhile of the Muscovite settlement on the Baltic, the British trade with Russia had fallen off by £5,347. The general trade of England reaching in 1730 the sum of £16,329,001, the Russian trade amounted not yet to $\frac{1}{53}$rd of its total value. Again, thirty years later, in 1760, the account between Great Britain and Russia stands thus:

		£
Import from Russia (in 1760).		536,504
Export to Russia		39,761
Total .	.	576,265

while the general trade of England amounted to £26,361,760. Comparing these figures with those of 1706, we find that the total of the Russian commerce, after nearly half a century, has increased by the trifling sum of only £265,841. That England suffered positive loss by her new commercial relations with Russia under Peter I. and Catherine I. becomes evident on comparing, on the one side, the export and import figures, and on the other, the sums expended on the frequent naval expeditions to the Baltic which England undertook during the lifetime of Charles XII., in order to break down his resistance to Russia, and, after his death, on the professed necessity of checking the maritime encroachments of Russia.

Another glance at the statistical data given for the years 1697, 1700, 1716, 1730, and 1760, will show that the British *export* trade to Russia was continually falling off, save in 1716, when

Russia engrossed the whole Swedish trade on the eastern coast of the Baltic and the Gulf of Bothnia, and had not yet found the opportunity of subjecting it to her own regulations. From £58,884, at which the British exports to Russia stood during 1697–1700, when Russia was still precluded from the Baltic, they had sunk to £46,275 in 1730, and to £39,761 in 1760, showing a decrease of £19,123, or about ⅓rd of their original amount in 1700. If, then, since the absorption of the Swedish provinces by Russia, the British market proved expanding for Russia raw produce, the Russian market, on its side, proved straitening for British manufacturers, a feature of that trade which could hardly recommend it at a time when the Balance of Trade doctrine ruled supreme. To trace the circumstances which produced the increase of the Anglo-Russian trade under Catherine II. would lead us too far from the period we are considering.

On the whole, then, we arrive at the following conclusions: During the first sixty years of the eighteenth century the total Anglo-Russian trade formed but a very diminutive fraction of the general trade of England, say less than $\frac{1}{45}$th. Its sudden increase during the earliest years of Peter's sway over the Baltic did not at all affect the general balance of British trade, as it was a simple transfer from its Swedish account to its Russian account. In the later times of Peter I., as well as under his immediate successors, Catherine I. and Anne, the Anglo-Russian trade was positively declining; during the whole epoch, dating from the final settlement of Russia in the Baltic provinces, the export of British manufactures to Russia was continually falling off, so that at its end it stood one-third lower than at its beginning, when that trade was still confined to the port of Archangel. Neither the contemporaries of Peter I., nor the next British generation reaped any benefit from the advancement of Russia to the Baltic. In general the Baltic trade of Great Britain was at that time trifling in regard of the capital involved, but important in regard of its character. It afforded England the raw produce for its maritime stores. That from the latter point of view the Baltic was in safer keeping in the hands of Sweden than in those of Russia, was not only proved by the pamphlets we are reprinting, but fully understood by the British Ministers themselves. Stanhope writing, for instance, to Townshend on October 16th, 1716:

"It is certain that if the Czar be let alone three years, he will be absolute master in those seas."*

If, then, neither the navigation nor the general commerce of England was interested in the treacherous support given to Russia against Sweden, there existed, indeed, one small fraction of British merchants whose interests were identical with the Russian one—the Russian Trade Company. It was this gentry that raised a cry against Sweden. See, for instance:

"Several grievances of the English merchants in their trade into the dominions of the King of Sweden, whereby it does appear how dangerous it may be for the English nation to depend on Sweden only for the supply of the naval stores, when they might be amply furnished with the like stores from the dominions of the Emperor of Russia."

"The case of the merchants trading to Russia" (a petition to Parliament), etc.

It was they who in the years 1714, 1715, and 1716, regularly assembled twice a week before the opening of Parliament, to draw up in public meetings the complaints of the British merchantmen against Sweden. On this small fraction the Ministers relied; they were even busy in getting up its demonstrations, as may be seen from the letters addressed by Count Gyllenborg to Baron Görtz, dated 4th of November and 4th of December, 1716, wanting, as they did, but the shadow of a pretext to drive their "mercenary Parliament," as Gyllenborg calls it, where they liked. The influence of these British merchants trading to Russia was again exhibited in the year 1765, and our own times have witnessed the working for his interest, of a Russian merchant at the head of the Board of Trade, and of a Chancellor of the Exchequer in the interest of a cousin engaged in the Archangel trade.

The oligarchy which, after the "glorious revolution," usurped wealth and power at the cost of the mass of the British people, was, of course, forced to look out for allies, not only abroad, but also at home. The latter they found in what the French would

* In the year 1657, when the Courts of Denmark and Brandenburg intended engaging the Muscovites to fall upon Sweden, they instructed their Minister so to manage the affair that the Czar might by no means get any footing in the Baltic, because "they did not know what to do with so troublesome a neighbour." (See Puffendorf's *History of Brandenburg*.)

call *la haute bourgeoisie*, as represented by the Bank of England, the money-lenders, State creditors, East India and other trading corporations, the great manufacturers, etc. How tenderly they managed the material interests of that class may be learned from the whole of their domestic legislation—Bank Acts, Protectionist enactments, Poor Regulations, etc. As to their *foreign policy*, they wanted to give it the appearance at least of being altogether regulated by the mercantile interest, an appearance the more easily to be produced, as the exclusive interest of one or the other small fraction of that class would, of course, be always identified with this or that Ministerial measure. The interested fraction then raised the commerce and navigation cry, which the nation stupidly re-echoed.

At that time, then, there devolved on the Cabinet, at least, the *onus* of inventing *mercantile pretexts*, however futile, for their measures of foreign policy. In our own epoch, British Ministers have thrown this burden on foreign nations, leaving to the French, the Germans, etc., the irksome task of discovering the *secret* and *hidden* mercantile springs of their actions. Lord Palmerston, for instance, takes a step apparently the most damaging to the material interests of Great Britain. Up starts a State philosopher, on the other side of the Atlantic, or of the Channel, or in the heart of Germany, who puts his head to the rack to dig out the mysteries of the mercantile Machiavellism of "perfide Albion," of which Palmerston is supposed the unscrupulous and unflinching executor. We will, *en passant*, show, by a few modern instances, what desperate shifts those foreigners have been driven to, who feel themselves obliged to interpret Palmerston's acts by what they imagine to be the English commercial policy. In his valuable *Histoire Politique et Sociale des Principautés Danubiennes*, M. Elias Regnault, startled by the Russian conduct, before and during the years 1848–49 of Mr. Colquhoun, the British Consul at Bucharest, suspects that England has some secret material interest in keeping down the trade of the Principalities. The late Dr. Cunibert, private physician of old Milosh, in his most interesting account of the Russian intrigues in Servia, gives a curious relation of the manner in which Lord Palmerston, through the instrumentality of Colonel Hodges, betrayed Milosh[34] to Russia by feigning to support him against her. Fully believing in the personal integrity of Hodges, and the patriotic zeal of Palmerston, Dr. Cunibert is found to go a step further than M. Elias Regnault. He suspects England of being interested in putting down Turkish commerce generally. General Mieroslawski, in his last work on Poland, is not very far from intimating that mercantile Machiavellism instigated England to sacrifice her own *prestige* in Asia Minor, by the surrender of Kars.[35] As a last instance may serve the present lucubrations of the Paris papers, hunting after the secret springs of commercial jealousy, which induce Palmerston to oppose the cutting of the Isthmus of Suez canal.[36]

To return to our subject. The mercantile pretext hit upon by the Townshends,[37] Stanhopes,[38] etc., for the hostile demonstrations against Sweden, was the following. Towards the end of 1713, Peter I had ordered all the hemp and other produce of his dominions, destined for export, to be carried to St. Petersburg instead of Archangel. Then the Swedish Regency, during the absence of Charles XII, and Charles XII himself, after his return from Bender, declared all the Baltic ports, occupied by the Russians, to be blockaded. Consequently, English ships, breaking through the blockade, were confiscated. The English Ministry then asserted that British merchantmen had the right of trading to those ports according to Article XVII of the Defensive Treaty of 1700, by which English commerce, with the exception of contraband of war, was allowed to go on with ports of the enemy. The absurdity and falsehood of this pretext being fully exposed in the pamphlet we are about to reprint, we will only remark that the case had been more than once decided against commercial nations, not bound, like England, by treaty to defend the integrity of the Swedish Empire. In the year 1561, when the Russians took Narva, and laboured hard to establish their commerce there, the Hanse towns, chiefly Lübeck, tried to possess themselves of this traffic. Eric XIV, then King of Sweden, resisted their pretensions. The city of Lübeck represented this resistance as altogether new, as they had carried on their commerce with the Russians time out of mind, and pleaded the common right of nations to navigate in the Baltic, provided their vessels carried no contraband of war. The King replied that he did not dispute the Hanse towns the liberty of trading with Russia, but only with Narva, which was no Russian port. In the year 1579 again, the Russians having broken the suspension of arms with Sweden, the Danes likewise claimed the navigation to Narva, by virtue of their treaty, but King John was as firm in maintaining the contrary, as was his brother Eric.

In her open demonstrations of hostility against the King of Sweden as well as in the false pretence on which they were founded, England seemed only to follow in the track of Holland, which declaring the confiscation of its ships to be piracy, had issued two proclamations against Sweden in 1714.

In one respect, the case of the States-General was the same as that of England. King William had concluded the Defensive Treaty as well for Holland as for England. Besides, Article XVI, in the Treaty of Commerce, concluded between Holland and Sweden in 1703, expressly stipulated that no navigation ought to be allowed to the ports blocked up by either of the confederates. The then common Dutch cant that "there was no hindering traders from carrying their merchandise where they will," was the more impudent as, during the war, ending with the Peace of Ryswick, the Dutch Republic had declared all France to be blocked up, forbidden the neutral Powers all trade with that kingdom, and caused all their ships that went there or came thence to be brought up without any regard to the nature of their cargoes.

In another respect, the situation of Holland was different from that of England. Fallen from its commercial and maritime grandeur, Holland had then already entered upon its epoch of decline. Like Genoa and Venice, when new roads of commerce had dispossessed them of their old mercantile supremacy, it was forced to lend out to other nations its capital, grown too large for the vessels of its own commerce. Its fatherland had begun to lie there where the best interest for its capital was paid. Russia, therefore, proved an immense market, less for the commerce than for the outlay of capital and men. To this moment Holland has remained the banker of Russia. At the time of Peter they supplied Russia with ships, officers, arms and money, so that his fleet, as a contemporary writer remarks, ought to have been called a Dutch rather than a Muscovite one. They gloried in having sent the first European merchant ship to St. Petersburg, and returned the commercial privileges they had obtained from Peter, or hoped to obtain from him, by that fawning meanness which characterises their intercourse with

Japan. Here, then, was quite another solid foundation than in England for the Russianism of statesmen, whom Peter I had entrapped during his stay at Amsterdam and the Hague in 1697, whom he afterwards directed by his ambassadors, and with whom he renewed his personal influence during his renewed stay at Amsterdam in 1716–17. Yet, if the paramount influence England exercised over Holland during the first *decennia* of the eighteenth century be considered, there can remain no doubt that the proclamations against Sweden by the States-General would never have been issued, if not with the previous consent and at the instigation of England. The intimate connection between the English and Dutch Governments served more than once the former to put up precedents in the name of Holland, which they were resolved to act upon in the name of England. On the other hand, it is no less certain that the Dutch statesmen were employed by the Czar to influence the British ones. Thus Horace Walpole, the brother of the "Father of Corruption," the brother-in-law of the Minister, Townshend, and the British Ambassador at the Hague during 1715–16, was evidently inveigled into the Russian interest by his Dutch friends. Thus, as we shall see by-and-by, Theyls, the Secretary to the Dutch Embassy at Constantinople, at the most critical period of the deadly struggle between Charles XII and Peter I, managed affairs at the same time for the Embassies of England and Holland at the Sublime Porte. This Theyls, in a print of his, openly claims it as a merit with his nation to have been the devoted and rewarded agent of Russian intrigue.

4

"The Defensive Treaty concluded in the year 1700, *between his late Majesty, King William, of ever-glorious memory, and his present Swedish Majesty, King Charles XII. Published at the earnest desire of several members of both Houses of Parliament.*

'Nec rumpite fœdera pacis,
Nec regnis præferte fidem.'[39]

"*Article* I. Establishes between the Kings of Sweden and England 'a sincere and constant friendship for ever, a league and good correspondence, so that they shall never mutually or separately molest one another's kingdoms, provinces, colonies, or subjects, wheresoever situated, *nor shall they suffer or agree that this should be done by others, etc.*'

"*Article* II. 'Moreover, each of the Allies, his heirs and successors, shall be obliged to take care of, and promote, as much as in him lies, the profit and honour of the other, to detect and give notice to his other ally (as soon as it shall come to his own knowledge) of all imminent dangers, conspiracies, and hostile designs formed against him, to withstand them as much as possible, and to prevent them both by advice and assistance; and therefore *it shall not be lawful for either of the Allies, either by themselves or any other whatsoever, to act, treat, or endeavour anything to the prejudice or loss of the other*, his lands or dominions whatsoever or wheresoever, whether by land or sea; that one shall in no wise favour the other's foes, either rebels or enemies, to the prejudice of his Ally,' etc.

"*Query* I. How the words marked in italics agree with our present conduct, when our fleet acts in conjunction with the enemies of Sweden, *the Czar commands our fleet, our Admiral enters into Councils of War, and is not only privy to all their designs, but together with our own Minister at Copenhagen (as* the King of Denmark has himself owned it in a public declaration), *pushed on the Northern Confederates to an enterprise entirely destructive to our Ally Sweden, I mean the descent designed last summer upon Schonen?*

"*Query* II. In what manner we also must explain that passage in the first article by which it is stipulated that one Ally shall not either by themselves or any other whatsoever, act, treat, or endeavour anything to the loss of the other's lands and dominions; to justify in particular our leaving in the year 1715, even when the season was so far advanced as no longer to admit of our usual pretence of conveying and protecting our trade, which was then got already safe home, eight men-of-war in the Baltic, with orders to join in one line of battle with the Danes, whereby we made them so much superior in number to the Swedish fleet, that it could not come to the relief of Straelsund, and whereby *we chiefly occasioned Sweden's entirely losing its German Provinces,* and even the *extreme danger his Swedish Majesty ran in his own person,* in crossing the sea, before the surrender of the town.

"*Article* III. By a special defensive treaty, the Kings of Sweden and England mutually oblige themselves, 'in a strict alliance, to defend one another mutually, as well as their kingdoms, territories, provinces, states, subjects, possessions, as their rights and liberties of navigation and commerce, as well in the Northern, Deucalidonian, Western, and Britannic Sea, commonly called the Channel, the Baltic, the Sound; as also of the privileges and prerogatives of each of the Allies belonging to them, by virtue of treaties and agreements, as well as by received customs, the laws of nations, hereditary right, against any aggressors or invaders and molesters in Europe by sea or land, etc.'

"*Query.* It being by the law of nations an indisputable right and prerogative of any king or people, in case of a great necessity or threatening ruin, to use all such means they themselves shall judge most necessary for their preservation; it having moreover been a constant prerogative and practice of the Swedes, for these several hundred years, in case of a war with their most dreadful enemies the Muscovites, to hinder all trade with them in the Baltic; and since it is also stipulated in this article that amongst other things, *one Ally ought to defend the prerogatives belonging to the other, even by received customs, and the law of nations:* how come we now the King of Sweden stands more than ever in need of using that prerogative, not only to dispute it, but also to take thereof a pretence for an open hostility against him?

"*Articles* IV, V, VI, *and* VII. fix the strength of the auxiliary forces England and Sweden are to send each other in case the territory of either of these powers should be invaded, or its navigation 'molested or hindered' in one of the seas enumerated in Article III. The invasion of the *German* provinces of Sweden is expressly included as a *casus fœderis.*

"*Article* VIII. stipulates that that Ally who is not attacked shall first act the part of a pacific mediator; but, the mediation having proved a failure, 'the aforesaid forces shall be sent without delay; nor shall the confederates desist before the injured party shall be satisfied in all things.'

"*Article* IX. That Ally that requires the stipulated 'help, has to choose whether he will have the above-named army either all or any, either in soldiers, ships, ammunition, or money.'

"*Article* X. Ships and armies serve under 'the command of him that required them.'

"*Article* XI. 'But if it should happen that the above-mentioned forces should not be proportionable to the danger, as supposing that perhaps the aggressor should be assisted by the forces of some other confederates of his, then one of the Allies, after previous request, shall be obliged to help the other that is injured, with greater forces, such as he shall be able to raise with safety and convenience, both by sea and land. . . .'

"*Article* XII. 'It shall be lawful for either of the Allies and their subjects to bring their men-of-war into one another's harbours, and to winter there.' Peculiar negotiations about this point shall take place at Stockholm, but 'in the meanwhile, the articles of treaty concluded at London, 1661, relating to the navigation and commerce shall remain, in their full force, as much as if they were inserted here word for word.'

"*Article* XIII. '. . . The subjects of either of the Allies . . . shall no way, either by sea or land, serve them (the enemies of either of the Allies), either as mariners or soldiers, and therefore it shall be forbid them upon severe penalty.'

"*Article* XIV. 'If it happens that either of the confederate kings . . . should be engaged in a war against a common enemy,

G

or be molested by any other neighbouring king . . . in his own kingdoms or provinces . . . to the hindering of which, he that requires help may by the force of this treaty himself be obliged to send help: then that Ally so molested shall not be obliged to send the promised help. . . .'

"*Query* I. Whether in our conscience we don't think the King of Sweden most unjustly attacked by all his enemies; whether consequently we are not convinced that we owe him the assistance stipulated in these Articles; whether he has not demanded the same from us, and why it has hitherto been refused him?

"*Query* II. These articles, setting forth in the most expressing terms, in what manner Great Britain and Sweden ought to assist one another, can either of these two Allies take upon him to prescribe to the other who requires his assistance a way of lending him it not expressed in the treaty; and if that other Ally does not think it for his interest to accept of the same, but still insists upon the performance of the treaty, can he from thence take a pretence, not only to withhold the stipulated assistance, but also to use his Ally in a hostile way, and to join with his enemies against him? If this is not justifiable, as even common sense tells us it is not, how can the reason stand good, which we allege amongst others, for using the King of Sweden as we do, *id est*, that demanding a literal performance of his alliance with us, *he would not accept the treaty of neutrality for his German provinces*, which we proposed to him some years ago, a treaty which, not to mention its partiality in favour of the enemies of Sweden, and that it was calculated only for our own interest, and for to prevent all disturbance in the empire, whilst we were engaged in a war against France, the King of Sweden had so much less reason to rely upon, as he was to conclude it with those very enemies, that had every one of them broken several treaties in beginning the present war against him, and as it was to be guaranteed by those powers, who were also every one of them guarantees of the broken treaties, without having performed their guarantee?

"*Query* III. How can we make the words in the 7th Article, *that in assisting our injured Ally we shall not desist before he shall be satisfied in all things*, agree with our endeavouring, to the contrary, to help the enemies of that Prince, though all unjust aggressors, not only to take one province after the other from him, but also to remain undisturbed possessors thereof, blaming all along the King of Sweden for not tamely submitting thereunto?

"*Query* IV. The treaty concluded in the year 1661, between Great Britain and Sweden, being in the 11th Article confirmed, and the said treaty forbidding expressly one of the confederates *either himself or his subjects to lend or to sell to the other's enemies, men-of-war or ships of defence;* the 13th Article of this present treaty forbidding also expressly the subjects of either of the Allies *to help anyways the enemies of the other, to the inconvenience and loss of such an Ally;* should we not have accused the Swedes of the most notorious breach of this treaty, had they, during our late war with the French, lent them their own fleet, the better to execute any design of theirs against us, or had they, notwithstanding our representations to the contrary, suffered their subjects to furnish the French with ships of 50, 60, and 70 guns! Now, if we turn the tables, and remember upon how many occasions our fleet has of late been entirely subservient to the designs of the enemies of Sweden, even in most critical times, and that *the Czar of Muscovy has actually above a dozen English-built ships* in his fleet, will it not be very difficult for us to excuse in ourselves what we should most certainly have blamed, if done by others?

"*Article* XVII. The obligation shall not be so far extended as that all friendship and mutual commerce with the enemies of that Ally (that requires the help) shall be taken away; for supposing that one of the confederates should send his auxiliaries, and should not be engaged in the war himself, it shall then be lawful for the subjects to trade and commerce with that enemy of that Ally that is engaged in the war, also directly and safely to merchandise with such enemies, for all goods not expressly forbid and called contraband, as in a special treaty of commerce hereafter shall be appointed.

"*Query* I. This Article being the only one out of twenty-two whose performance we have now occasion to insist upon from the Swedes, the question will be whether we ourselves, in regard to Sweden, have performed all the other articles as it was our part to do, and whether in demanding of the King of Sweden the executing of this Article, we have promised that we would also do our duty as to all the rest; if not, may not the Swedes say that we complain unjustly of the breach of one single Article, when we ourselves may perhaps be found guilty of having in the most material points either not executed or even acted against the whole treaty?

"*Query* II. Whether the liberty of commerce one Ally is, by virtue of this Article, to enjoy with the other's enemies, ought to have no limitation at all, neither as to time nor place; in short, whether it ought even to be extended so far as to destroy the very end of this Treaty, which is the promoting the safety and security of one another's kingdoms?

"*Query* III. Whether in case the French had in the late wars made themselves masters of Ireland or Scotland, and either in new-made seaports, or the old ones, endeavoured by trade still more firmly to establish themselves in their new conquest, we, in such a case, should have thought the Swedes our true allies and friends, had they insisted upon this Article to trade with the French in the said seaports taken from us, and to furnish them there with several necessaries of war, nay, even with armed ships, whereby the French might the easier have annoyed us here in England?

"*Query* IV. Whether, if we had gone about to hinder a trade so prejudicial to us, and in order thereunto brought up all Swedish ships going to the said seaports, we should not highly have exclaimed against the Swedes, had they taken from thence a pretence to join their fleet with the French, to occasion the losing of any of our dominions and even to encourage the invasion upon us, have their fleet at hand to promote the same?

"*Query* V. Whether upon an impartial examination this would not have been a case exactly parallel to that we insist upon, as to a free Trade to the seaports the Czar has taken from Sweden, and to our present behaviour, upon the King of Sweden's hindering the same?

"*Query* VI. Whether we have not ever since Oliver Cromwell's time till 1710, in all our wars with France and Holland, without any urgent necessity at all, brought up and confiscated Swedish ships, though not going to any prohibited ports, and that to a far greater number and value, than all those the Swedes have now taken from us, and whether the Swedes have ever taken a pretence from thence to join with our enemies, and to send whole squadrons of ships to their assistance?

"*Query* VII. Whether, if we inquire narrowly into the state of commerce, as it has been carried on for these many years, we shall not find that the trade of the above-mentioned places was not so very necessary to us, at least not so far as to be put into the balance with the preservation of a Protestant confederate nation, much less to give us a just reason *to make war against that nation, which, though not declared, has done it more harm than the united efforts of all its enemies?*

"*Query* VIII. Whether, if it happened two years ago, that this trade became something more necessary to us than formerly, it is not easily proved, that it was occasioned only by the Czar's forcing us out of our old channel of trade to Archangel, and bringing us to Petersburg, and our complying therewith. So that all the inconveniences we laboured under upon that account ought to have been laid to the Czar's door, and not to the King of Sweden's?

"*Query* IX. Whether the Czar did not in the very beginning of 1715 again permit us to trade our old way to Archangel, and whether our Ministers had not notice there of a great while before our fleet was sent that year to protect our *trade to Petersburg*, which by this alteration in the Czar's resolution was become as unnecessary for us as before?

"*Query* X. Whether the King of Sweden had not declared, that if we would forbear trading to *Petersburg*, etc., which he looked upon as ruinous to his kingdom, he would in no manner disturb our trade, neither in the Baltic nor anywhere else; but that in case we would not give him this slight proof of our friendship, he should be excused if the innocent came to suffer with the guilty?

"*Query* XI. Whether, by our insisting upon the trade to the ports prohibited by the King of Sweden, which besides it being unnecessary to us, hardly makes one part in ten of that we carry on in the Balitic, we have not drawn upon us the hazards that our trade has run all this while, been ourselves the occasion of our great expenses in fitting out fleets for its protection, and by our joining with the enemies of Sweden, fully justified his Swedish Majesty's resentment; had it ever gone so far as to seize and confiscate without distinction all our ships and effects, wheresoever he found them, either within or without his kingdoms?

"*Query* XII. If we were so tender of our trade to the northern ports in general, ought we not in policy rather to have considered the hazard that trade runs by the approaching ruin of Sweden, and *by the Czar's becoming the whole and sole master of the Baltic, and all the naval stores we want from thence*? Have we not also suffered greater hardships and losses in the said trade from the Czar, than that amounting only to sixty odd thousand pounds (whereof, by the way, two parts in three may perhaps be disputable), which provoked us first to send twenty men-of-war in the Baltic with order to attack the Swedes wherever they met them? And yet, did not this very Czar, this very aspiring and dangerous prince, *last summer command the whole confederate fleet*, as it was called, *of which our men-of-war made the most considerable part? The first instance that ever was of a Foreign Potentate having the command given him of the English fleet, the bulwark of our nation*: and did not our said men-of-war afterwards convey his (the Czar's) transport ships and troops on board of them, in their return from Zealand, *protecting them from the Swedish fleet*, which else would have made a considerable havoc amongst them?

"*Query* XIII. Suppose now, we had, on the contrary, taken hold of the great and many complaints our merchants have made of the ill-usage they meet from the Czar, to have sent our fleet to show our resentment against that prince, to prevent his great and pernicious designs even to us, *to assist Sweden pursuant to this Treaty*, and effectually to restore the peace in the North, would not that have been more for our interest, more necessary, more honourable and just, and more according to our Treaty; and would not the several 100,000 pounds these our Northern expeditions have cost the nation, have been thus better employed?

"*Query* XIV. If the preserving and securing our trade against the Swedes has been the only and real object of all our measures, as to the Northern affairs, how come we the year before the last to leave eight men-of-war in the Baltic and at Copenhagen, when we had no more trade there to protect, and how came Admiral Norris last summer, although he and the Dutch together made up the number of twenty-six men-of-war, and consequently were too strong for the Swedes, to attempt anything against our trade under their convoy; yet to lay above two whole months of the best season in the Sound, without convoying our and the Dutch merchantmen to the several ports they were bound for, whereby they were kept in the Baltic so late that their return could not but be very hazardous, as it even proved, both to them and our men-of-war themselves? Will not the world be apt to think that the hopes of forcing the King of Sweden to an inglorious and disadvantageous peace, by which the Duchies of Bremen and Verden ought to be added to the Hanover dominions, or that some other such view, foreign, if not contrary, to the true and old interest of Great Britain, had then a greater influence upon all these our proceedings than *the pretended care of our trade*?

"*Article* XVIII. 'For as much as it seems convenient for the preservation of the liberty of navigation and commerce in the Baltic Sea, that a firm and exact friendship should be kept between the Kings of Sweden and Denmark; and whereas the former Kings of Sweden and Denmark did oblige themselves mutually, not only by the public Articles of Peace made in the camp of Copenhagen, on the 27th of May, 1660, and by the ratifications of the agreement interchanged on both sides, sacredly and inviolably to observe all and every one of the clauses comprehended in the said agreement, but also declared together to . . . Charles II, King of Great Britain . . . a little before the treaty concluded between England and Sweden in the year 1665, that they would stand sincerely . . . to all . . . of the Articles of the said peace . . . whereupon Charles II, with the approbation and consent of both the forementioned Kings of Sweden and Denmark, took upon himself a little after the Treaty concluded between England and Sweden, 1st March, 1665, to wit 9th October, 1665, guarantee of the same agreements . . . Whereas an instrument of peace between . . . the Kings of Sweden and Denmark happened to be soon after these concluded at Lunden in Schonen, in 1679, which contains an express transaction, and repetition and confirmation of the Treaties concluded at Roskild, Copenhagen, and Westphalia; therefore . . . the King of Great Britain binds himself by the force of this Treaty . . . that if either of the Kings of Sweden and Denmark shall consent to the violation, either of all the agreements, or one or more articles comprehended in them, and consequently if either of the Kings shall to the prejudice of the person, provinces, territories, islands, goods, dominions and rights of the other, which by the force of the agreements so often repeated, and made in the camp of Copenhagen, on the 27th of May, 1660, as also of those made in the . . . peace at Lunden in Schonen in 1679, were attributed to every one that was interested and comprehended in the words of the peace, should either by himself or by others, presume, or secretly design or attempt, or by open molestations, or by any injury, or by any violence of arms, attempt anything; that then the . . . King of Great Britain . . . shall first of all, by his interposition, perform all the offices of a friend and princely ally, which may serve towards the keeping inviolable all the frequently mentioned agreements, and of every article comprehended in them, and consequently towards the preservation of peace between both kings; that afterwards if the King, who is the beginner of such prejudice or any molestation or injury, contrary to all agreements, and contrary to any articles comprehended in them, shall refuse after being admonished . . . then the King of Great Britain . . . shall . . . assist him that is injured as by the present agreements between the Kings of Great Britain and Sweden in such cases is determined and agreed.'

"*Query.* Does not this article expressly tell us how to remedy the disturbances our trade in the Baltic might suffer, in case of a misunderstanding betwixt the Kings of Sweden and Denmark, by obliging both these Princes to keep all the Treaties of Peace, that have been concluded between them from 1660–70, and in case either of them should in an hostile manner act against the said Treaties, by assisting the other against the aggressor? How comes it then that we don't make use of so just a remedy against an evil we are so great sufferers by? Can anybody, though ever so partial, deny but the King of Denmark, though seemingly a sincere friend to the King of Sweden, from the peace of Travendahl[40] till he went out of Saxony against the Muscovites, fell very unjustly upon him immediately after, taking ungenerously advantage of the fatal battle of Pultava? Is not then the King of Denmark the violator of all the above-mentioned Treaties, and consequently the true author of the disturbances our trade meets with in the Baltic? Why in God's name don't we, according to this article, assist Sweden against him, and why do we, on the contrary, declare openly against the injured King of Sweden, send hectoring and threatening memorials to him, upon the least advantage he has over his enemies, as we did last summer upon his entering Norway, and even order our fleets to act openly against him in conjunction with the Danes?

"*Article* XIX. There shall be 'stricter confederacy and union between the above-mentioned Kings of Great Britain and Sweden, for the future, *for the defence and preservation of the Protestant, Evangelic, and reformed religion.*'

"*Query* I. How do we, according to this article, join with Sweden to *assert, protect, and preserve the Protestant religion*? Don't we suffer that nation, which has always been a bulwark to the said religion, most unmercifully to be torn to pieces? . . . *Don't we ourselves give a helping hand towards its destruction?* And why all this? Because our merchants have lost their ships to the value of sixty odd thousand pounds. *For this loss, and nothing else, was the pretended reason why, in the year* 1715, *we sent our fleet in the Baltic, at the expense of* £200,000; and as to what our merchants have suffered since, suppose we attribute it to our threatening memorials as well as open hostilities against the King of Sweden, must we not even then own that that Prince's resentment has been very moderate?

"*Query* II. How can other Princes, and especially our fellow Protestants, think us sincere in what we have made them believe as to our zeal in spending millions of lives and money for to secure the Protestant interest only in one single branch of it, *I mean the Protestant succession here,* when they see that that succession has hardly taken place, before we, only for sixty odd thousand pounds (for let us always remember that this paltry sum was the first pretence for our quarrelling with Sweden) go about to undermine the very foundation of that interest in general, by helping, as we do, entirely to sacrifice Sweden, the old and sincere protector of the Protestants, to its neighbours, of which some are professed Papists, some worse, and some, at least, but lukewarm Protestants?

"*Article* XX. 'Therefore, that a reciprocal faith of the Allies and their perseverance in this agreement may appear . . . both the fore-mentioned kings mutually oblige themselves, and declare that . . . they will not depart a little from the genuine and common sense of all and every article of this treaty under any pretences of friendship, profit, former treaty, agreement, and promise, or upon any colour whatsoever: but that they will most fully and readily, either by themselves, or ministers, or subjects, put in execution whatsoever they have promised in this treaty . . . without any hesitation, exception, or excuse. . . .'

"*Query* I. Inasmuch as this article sets forth that, at the time of concluding of the treaty, we were under no engagement contrary to it, and that it were highly unjust should we afterwards, and while this treaty is in force, which is eighteen years after the day it was signed, have entered into any such engagements, how can we justify to the world our late proceedings against the King of Sweden, which naturally seem the consequences of a treaty either of our own making with the enemies of that Prince, *or of some Court or other that at present influences our measures*?

"*Query* II. The words in this article . . . how in the name of honour, faith, and justice, do they agree with the *little and pitiful pretences* we now make use of, not only for not assisting Sweden, pursuant to this treaty, *but even for going about so heartily as we do to destroy it*?

"*Article* XXI. 'This defensive treaty shall last for eighteen years, before the end of which the confederate kings may . . . again treat.'

"*Ratification of the abovesaid treaty*. 'We, having seen and considered this treaty, have approved and confirmed the same in all and every particular article and clause as by the present. We do approve the same for us, our heirs, and successors; assuring and promising our princely word that we shall perform and observe sincerely and in good earnest all those things that are therein contained, for the better confirmation whereof we have ordered our great seal of England to be put to these presents, which were given at our palace of Kensington, 25th of February, in the year of our Lord 1700, and in the 11th year of our reign (Gulielmus Rex).'*

"*Query*. How can any of us that declares himself for the late happy revolution, and that is a true and grateful lover of King William's for ever-glorious memory . . . yet bear with the least patience, that the said treaty should (that I may again use the words of the 20th article) be *departed from, under any pretence of profit, or upon any colour whatsoever*, especially so insignificant

---

* The treaty was concluded at the Hague on the 6th and 16th January, 1700, and ratified by William III on February 5th, 1700.

and trifling a one as that which has been made use of for two years together to employ our ships, our men, and our money, *to accomplish the ruin of Sweden*, that same Sweden whose defence and preservation this great and wise monarch of ours has so solemnly promised, and which he always looked upon to be of the utmost necessity for to secure the Protestant interest in Europe?"

5

BEFORE entering upon an analysis of the pamphlet headed, *"Truth is but truth, as it is timed,"* with which we shall conclude the *Introduction* to the Diplomatic Revelations, some preliminary remarks on the general history of Russian politics appear opportune.

The overwhelming influence of Russia has taken Europe at different epochs by surprise, startled the peoples of the West, and been submitted to as a fatality, or resisted only by convulsions. But alongside the fascination exercised by Russia, there runs an ever-reviving scepticism, dogging her like a shadow, growing with her growth, mingling shrill notes of irony with the cries of agonising peoples, and mocking her very grandeur as a histrionic attitude taken up to dazzle and to cheat. Other empires have met with similar doubts in their infancy; Russia has become a colossus without outliving them. She affords the only instance in history of an immense empire, the very existence of whose power, even after world-wide achievements, has never ceased to be treated like a matter of faith rather than like a matter of fact. From the outset of the eighteenth century to our days, no author, whether he intended to exalt or to check Russia, thought it possible to dispense with first proving her existence.

But whether we be spiritualists or materialists with respect to Russia—whether we consider her power as a palpable fact, or as the mere vision of the guilt-stricken consciences of the European peoples—the question remains the same: "How did this power, or this phantom of a power, contrive to assume such dimensions as to rouse on the one side the passionate assertion, and on the other the angry denial of its threatening the world with a rehearsal of Universal Monarchy?" At the beginning of the eighteenth century Russia was regarded as a mushroom creation extemporised by the genius of Peter the Great. Schloezer thought it a discovery to have found out that she possessed a past; and in modern times, writers, like Fallmerayer, unconsciously following in the track beaten by Russian historians, have deliberately asserted that the northern spectre which frightens the Europe of the nineteenth century already overshadowed the Europe of the ninth century. With them the policy of Russia begins with the first Ruriks, and has, with some interruptions indeed, been systematically continued to the present hour.

Ancient maps of Russia are unfolded before us, displaying even larger European dimensions than she can boast of now: her perpetual movement of aggrandisement from the ninth to the eleventh century is anxiously pointed out; we are shown Oleg[41] launching 88,000 men against Byzantium, fixing his shield as a trophy on the gate of that capital, and dictating an ignominious treaty to the Lower Empire; Igor making it tributary; Sviataslaff glorying, "the Greeks supply me with gold, costly stuffs, rice, fruits and wine; Hungary furnishes cattle and horses; from Russia I draw honey, wax, furs, and men"; Vladimir conquering the Crimea and Livonia, extorting a daughter from the Greek Emperor, as Napoleon did from the German Emperor, blending the military sway of a northern conqueror with the theocratic despotism of the Porphyrogeniti,[42] and becoming at once the master of his subjects on earth, and their protector in heaven.

Yet, in spite of the plausible parallelism suggested by these reminiscences, the policy of the first Ruriks[43] differs fundamentally from that of modern Russia. It was nothing more nor less than the policy of the German barbarians inundating Europe— the history of the modern nations beginning only after the deluge has passed away. The Gothic period of Russia in particular forms but a chapter of the Norman conquests. As the empire of Charlemagne precedes the foundation of modern France, Germany, and Italy, so the empire of the Ruriks precedes the foundation of Poland, Lithuania, the Baltic Settlements, Turkey and Muscovy itself. The rapid movement of aggrandisement was not the result of deep-laid schemes, but the natural off-spring of the primitive organisation of Norman conquest— vassalship without fiefs, or fiefs consisting only in tributes— the necessity of fresh conquests being kept alive by the uninterrupted influx of new Varangian adventurers, panting for glory and plunder. The chiefs, becoming anxious for repose,

were compelled by the Faithful Band to move on, and in Russian,
as in French Normandy, there arrived the moment when the
chiefs despatched on new predatory excursions their uncon-
trollable and insatiable companions-in-arms with the single view
to get rid of them. Warfare and organisation of conquest on the
part of the first Ruriks differ in no point from those of the
Normans in the rest of Europe. If Slavonian tribes were sub-
jected not only by the sword, but also by mutual convention,
this singularity is due to the exceptional position of those tribes,
placed between a northern and eastern invasion, and embracing
the former as a protection from the latter. The same magic
charm which attracted other northern barbarians to the Rome
of the West attracted the Varangians to the Rome of the East.
The very migration of the Russian capital—Rurik fixing it
at Novgorod, Oleg removing it to Kiev, and Sviataslaff attempting to establish it in Bulgaria—proves beyond doubt that the
invader was only feeling his way, and considered Russia as a
mere halting-place from which to wander on in search of an
empire in the South. If modern Russia covets the possession of
Constantinople to establish her dominion over the world, the
Ruriks were, on the contrary, forced by the resistance of Byzantium, under Zimiskes, definitively to establish their dominion
in Russia.

It may be objected that victors and vanquished amalgamated
more quickly in Russia than in any other conquest of the northern
barbarians, that the chiefs soon commingled themselves with the
Slavonians—as shown by their marriages and their names. But
then, it should be recollected that the Faithful Band, which
formed at once their guard and their privy council, remained
exclusively composed of Varangians; that Vladimir, who marks
the summit, and Yaroslav, who marks the commencing decline
of Gothic Russia, were seated on her throne by the arms of the
Varangians. If any Slavonian influence is to be acknowledged in
this epoch, it is that of Novgorod, a Slavonian State, the traditions, policy and tendencies of which were so antagonistic to
those of modern Russia that the one could found her existence
only on the ruins of the other. Under Yaroslav the supremacy
of the Varangians is broken, but simultaneously with it disappears the conquering tendency of the first period, and the
decline of Gothic Russia begins. The history of that decline,

more still than that of the conquest and formation, proves the exclusively Gothic character of the Empire of the Ruriks.

The incongruous, unwieldy, and precocious Empire heaped together by the Ruriks, like the other empires of similar growth, is broken up into appanages, divided and sub-divided among the descendants of the conquerors, dilacerated by feudal wars, rent to pieces by the intervention of foreign peoples. The paramount authority of the Grand Prince vanishes before the rival claims of seventy princes of the blood. The attempt of Andrew of Susdal at recomposing some large limbs of the empire by the removal of the capital from Kiev to Vladimir proves successful only in propagating the decomposition from the South to the centre. Andrew's third successor resigns even the last shadow of supremacy, the title of Grand Prince, and the merely nominal homage still offered him. The appanages to the South and to the West become by turns Lithuanian, Polish, Hungarian, Livonian, Swedish. Kiev itself, the ancient capital, follows destinies of its own, after having dwindled down from a seat of the Grand Princedom to the territory of a city. Thus, the Russia of the Normans completely disappears from the stage, and the few weak reminiscences in which it still outlived itself, dissolve before the terrible apparition of Genghis Khan. The bloody mire of Mongolian slavery, not the rude glory of the Norman epoch, forms the cradle of Muscovy, and modern Russia is but a metamorphosis of Muscovy.

The Tartar[44] yoke lasted from 1237 to 1462—more than two centuries; a yoke not only crushing, but dishonouring and withering the very soul of the people that fell its prey. The Mongol Tartars established a rule of systematic terror, devastation and wholesale massacre forming its institutions. Their numbers being scanty in proportion to their enormous conquests, they wanted to magnify them by a halo of consternation, and to thin, by wholesale slaughter, the populations which might rise in their rear. In their creations of desert they were, besides, led by the same economical principle which has depopulated the Highlands of Scotland and the Campagna di Roma—the conversion of men into sheep, and of fertile lands and populous abodes into pasturage.

The Tartar yoke had already lasted a hundred years before Muscovy emerged from its obscurity. To entertain discord among the Russian princes, and secure their servile submission, the Mongols had restored the dignity of the Grand Princedom. The strife among the Russian princes for this dignity was, as a modern author has it, "an abject strife—the strife of slaves, whose chief weapon was calumny, and who were always ready to denounce each other to their cruel rulers; wrangling for a degraded throne, whence they could not move but with plundering, parricidal hands—hands filled with gold and stained with gore; which they dared not ascend without grovelling, nor retain but on their knees, prostrate and trembling beneath the scimitar of a Tartar, always ready to roll under his feet those servile crowns, and the heads by which they were worn." It was in this infamous strife that the Moscow branch won at last the race. In 1328 the crown of the Grand Princedom, wrested from the branch of Tver by dint of denunciation and assassination, was picked up at the feet of Usbeck Khan by Yury, the elder brother of Ivan Kalita. Ivan I Kalita[45], and Ivan III[46] surnamed the Great, personate Muscovy rising by means of the Tartar yoke, and Muscovy getting an independent power by the disappearance of the Tartar rule. The whole policy of Muscovy, from its first entrance into the historical arena, is resumed in the history of these two individuals.

The policy of Ivan Kalita was simply this: to play the abject tool of the Khan, thus to borrow his power, and then to turn it round upon his princely rivals and his own subjects. To attain this end, he had to insinuate himself with the Tartars by dint of cynical adulation, by frequent journeys to the Golden Horde, by humble prayers for the hand of Mongol princesses, by a display of unabounded zeal for the Khan's interest, by the unscrupulous execution of his orders, by atrocious calumnies against his own kinsfolk, by blending in himself the characters of the Tartar's hangman, sycophant, and slave-in-chief. He perplexed the Khan by continuous revelations of secret plots. Whenever the branch of Tver betrayed a velleité of national independence, he hurried to the Horde to denounce it. Wherever he met with resistance, he introduced the Tartar to trample it down. But it was not sufficient to act a character: to make it acceptable, gold was required. Perpetual bribery of the Khan and his grandees was the only sure foundation upon which to raise his fabric of deception and usurpation. But how was the slave to

get the money wherewith to bribe the master? He persuaded
the Khan to instal him his tax-gatherer throughout all the Russian
appanages. Once invested with this function, he extorted money
under false pretences. The wealth accumulated by the dread
held out of the Tartar name, he used to corrupt the Tartars themselves. By a bribe he induced the primate to transfer his episcopal
seat from Vladimir to Moscow, thus making the latter the capital
of the empire, because the religious capital, and coupling the
power of the Church with that of his throne. By a bribe he
allured the Boyards of the rival princes into treason against their
chiefs, and attracted them to himself as their centre. By the joint
influence of the Mahometan Tartar, the Greek Church, and
the Boyards, he unites the princes holding appanages into a
crusade against the most dangerous of them—the prince of
Tver; and then having driven his recent allies by bold attempts
at usurpation into resistance against himself, into a war for the
public good, he draws not the sword but hurries to the Khan.
By bribes and delusion again, he seduces him into assassinating
his kindred rivals under the most cruel torments. It was the
traditional policy of the Tartar to check the Russian princes
the one by the other, to feed their dissensions, to cause their
forces to equiponderate and to allow none to consolidate himself.
Ivan Kalita converts the Khan into the tool by which he rids
himself of his most dangerous competitors, and weighs down
every obstacle to his own usurping march. He does not conquer the appanages, but surreptitiously turns the rights of the
Tartar conquest to his exclusive profit. He secures the succession of his son through the same means by which he had raised
the Grand Princedom of Muscovy, that strange compound of
princedom and serfdom. During his whole reign he swerves not
once from the line of policy he had traced to himself; clinging to
it with a tenacious firmness, and executing it with methodical
boldness. Thus he becomes the founder of the Muscovite power,
and characteristically his people call him Kalita—that is, the
purse, because it was the purse and not the sword with which he
cut his way. The very period of his reign witnesses the sudden
growth of the Lithuanian power which dismembers the Russian
appanages from the West, while the Tartar squeezes them into
one mass from the East. Ivan, while he dared not repulse the one
disgrace, seemed anxious to exaggerate the other. He was not to

be seduced from following up his ends by the allurements of glory, the pangs of conscience, or the lassitude of humiliation. His whole system may be expressed in a few words: the machiavellism of the usurping slave. His own weakness—his slavery—he turned into the mainspring of his strength.

The policy traced by Ivan I. Kalita is that of his successors; they had only to enlarge the circle of its application. They followed it up laboriously, gradually, inflexibly. From Ivan I. Kalita, we may, therefore, pass at once to Ivan III, surnamed the Great.

At the commencement of his reign (1462–1505) Ivan III. was still a tributary to the Tartars; his authority was still contested by the princes holding appanages; Novgorod, the head of the Russian republics, reigned over the north of Russia; Poland-Lithuania was striving for the conquest of Muscovy; lastly, the Livonian knights were not yet disarmed. At the end of his reign we behold Ivan III. seated on an independent throne, at his side the daughter of the last emperor of Byzantium, at his feet Kasan, and the remnant of the Golden Horde flocking to his court; Novgorod and the other Russian republics enslaved—Lithuania diminished, and its king a tool in Ivan's hands—the Livonian knights vanquished. Astonished Europe, at the commencement of Ivan's reign, hardly aware of the existence of Muscovy, hemmed in between the Tartar and the Lithuanian, was dazzled by the sudden appearance of an immense empire on its eastern confines, and Sultan Bajazet himself, before whom Europe trembled, heard for the first time the haughty language of the Muscovite. How, then, did Ivan accomplish these high deeds? Was he a hero? The Russian historians themselves show him up a confessed coward.

Let us shortly survey his principal contests, in the sequence in which he undertook and concluded them—his contests with the Tartars, with Novgorod, with the princes holding appanages, the lastly with Lithuania-Poland.

Ivan rescued Muscovy from the Tartar yoke, not by one bold stroke, but by the patient labour of about twenty years. He did not break the yoke, but disengaged himself by stealth. Its overthrow, accordingly, has more the look of the work of nature than the deed of man. When the Tartar monster expired at last, Ivan appeared at its deathbed like a physician, who prognosticated and speculated on death rather than like a warrior who imparted it. The character of every people enlarges with its enfranchisement from a foreign yoke; that of Muscovy in the hands of Ivan seems to diminish. Compare only Spain in its struggles against the Arabs with Muscovy in its struggles against the Tartars.

At the period of Ivan's accession to the throne, the Golden Horde had long since been weakened, internally by fierce feuds, externally by the separation from them of the Nogay Tartars, the eruption of Timour Tamerlane, the rise of the Cossacks, and the hostility of the Crimean Tartars. Muscovy, on the contrary, by steadily pursuing the policy traced by Ivan Kalita, had grown to a mighty mass, crushed, but at the same time compactly united by the Tartar chain. The Khans, as if struck by a charm, had continued to remain instruments of Muscovite aggrandisement and concentration. By calculation they had added to the power of the Greek Church, which, in the hand of the Muscovite grand princes, proved the deadliest weapon against them.

In rising against the Horde, the Muscovite had not to invent but only to imitate the Tartars themselves. But Ivan did not rise. He humbly acknowledged himself a slave of the Golden Horde. By bribing a Tartar woman he seduced the Khan into commanding the withdrawal from Muscovy of the Mongol residents. By similar and imperceptible and surreptitious steps he duped the Khan into successive concessions, all ruinous to his sway. He thus did not conquer, but filch strength. He does not drive, but manœuvre his enemy out of his strongholds. Still continuing to prostrate himself before the Khan's envoys, and to proclaim himself his tributary, he eludes the payment of the tribute under false pretences, employing all the stratagems of a fugitive slave who dare not front his owner, but only steal out of his reach. At last the Mongol awakes from his torpor, and the hour of battle sounds. Ivan, trembling at the mere semblance of an armed encounter, attempts to hide himself behind his own fear, and to disarm the fury of his enemy by withdrawing the object upon which to wreak his vengeance. He is only saved by the intervention of the Crimean Tartars, his allies. Against a second invasion of the Horde, he ostentatiously gathers together such disproportionate forces that the mere rumour of their number parries the attack. At the third invasion, from the midst of 200,000 men, he absconds a disgraced deserter. Reluctantly dragged back, he attempts to haggle for conditions of slavery, and at last pouring into his army his own servile fear, he involves it in a general and disorderly flight. Muscovy was then anxiously awaiting its irretrievable doom, when it suddenly hears that by an attack on their capital made by the Crimean Khan, the Golden Horde has been forced to withdraw, and has, on its retreat, been destroyed by the Cossacks and Nogay Tartars. Thus defeat was turned into success, and Ivan had overthrown the Golden Horde, not by fighting it himself, but by challenging it through a feigned desire of combat into offensive movements, which exhausted its remnants of vitality and exposed it to the fatal blows of the tribes of its own race whom he had managed to turn into his allies. He caught one Tartar with another Tartar. As the immense danger he had himself summoned proved unable to betray him into one single trait of manhood, so his miraculous triumph did not infatuate him even for one moment. With cautious circumspection he dared not incorporate Kasan with Muscovy, but made it over to sovereigns belonging to the family of Menghi-Ghirei, his Crimean ally, to hold it, as it were, in trust for Muscovy. With the spoils of the vanquished Tartar, he enchained the victorious Tartar. But if too prudent to assume, with the eye-witnesses of his disgrace, the airs of a conqueror, this imposter did fully understand how the downfall of the Tartar empire must dazzle at a distance—with what halo of glory it would encircle him, and how it would facilitate a magnificent entry among the European Powers. Accordingly he assumed abroad the theatrical attitude of the conqueror, and, indeed, succeeded in hiding under a mask of proud susceptibility and irritable haughtiness the obtrusiveness of the Mongol serf, who still remembered kissing the stirrup of the Khan's meanest envoy. He aped in more subdued tone the voice of his old masters, which terrified his soul. Some standing phrases of modern Russian diplomacy, such as the magnanimity, the wounded dignity of the master, are borrowed from the diplomatic instructions of Ivan III.

After the surrender of Kasan, he set out on a long-planned expedition against Novgorod, the head of the Russian republics. If the overthrow of the Tartar yoke was, in his eyes, the first condition of Muscovite greatness, the overthrow of Russian freedom was the second. As the republic of Viatka had declared itself neutral between Muscovy and the Horde, and the republic of Tskof, with its twelve cities, had shown symptoms of disaffection, Ivan flattered the latter and affected to forget the former, meanwhile concentrating all his forces against Novgorod the Great, with the doom of which he knew the fate of the rest of the Russian republics to be sealed. By the prospect of sharing in this rich booty, he drew after him the princes holding appanages, while he inveigled the boyards by working upon their blind hatred of Novgorodian democracy. Thus he contrived to march three armies upon Novgorod and to overwhelm it by disproportionate force. But then, in order not to keep his word to the princes, not to forfeit his immutable "Vos non vobis," at the same time apprehensive, lest Novgorod should not yet have become digestible from the want of preparatory treatment, he thought fit to exhibit a sudden moderation; to content himself with a ransom and the acknowledgement of his suzerainty; but into the act of submission of the republic he smuggled some ambiguous words which made him its supreme judge and legislator. Then he fomented the dissensions between the patricians and plebeians raging as well in Novogorod as at Florence. Of some complaints of the plebeians he took occasion to introduce himself again into the city, to have its nobles, whom he knew to be hostile to himself, sent to Moscow loaded with chains, and to break the ancient law of the republic that "none of its citizens should ever be tried or punished out of the limits of its own territory." From that moment he became supreme arbiter. "Never," say the annalists, "never since Rurik had such an event happened; never had the grand princes of Kiev and Vladimir seen the Novgorodians come and submit to them as their judges. Ivan alone could reduce Novgorod to that degree of humiliation." Seven years were employed by Ivan to corrupt the republic by the exercise of his judicial authority. Then, when he found its strength worn out, he thought the moment ripe for declaring himself. To doff his own mask of moderation, he wanted, on the part of Novgorod, a breach of the peace. As he had simulated calm endurance, so he simulated now a sudden burst of passion. Having bribed an envoy of the republic to address him during a public audience with the name of sovereign, he claimed, at once, all the rights of a despot—the self-annihilation of the republic.

*As he had foreseen, Novgorod answered his usurpation with an insurrection, with a massacre of the nobles, and the surrender to Lithuania. Then this Muscovite contemporary of Machiavelli complained with the accent and the gesture of moral indignation. "It was the Novgorodians who sought him for their sovereign; and when, yielding to their wishes, he had at last assumed that title, they disavowed him, they had the impudence to give him the lie formally in the face of all Russia; they had dared to shed the blood of their compatriots who remained faithful, and to betray heaven and the holy land of the Russians by calling into its limits a foreign religion and domination." As he had, after his first attack on Novgorod, openly allied himself with the plebeians against the patricians, so he now entered into a secret conspiracy with the patricians against the plebeians. He marched the united forces of Muscovy and its feudatories against the republic. On its refusal of unconditional submission, he recurred to the Tartar reminiscence of vanquishing by consternation. During a whole month he drew straighter and straighter around Novgorod a circle of fire and devastation, holding the sword all the while in suspense, and quietly watching till the republic, torn by factions, had run through all the phases of wild despair, sullen despondency, and resigned impotence. Novgorod was enslaved. So were the other Russian republics.

It is curious to see how Ivan caught the very moment of victory to forge weapons against the instruments of that victory. By the union of the domains of the Novgorod clergy with the crown, he secured himself the means of buying off the boyards, henceforth to be played off against the princes, and of endowing the followers of the boyards, henceforth to be played off against the boyards. It is still worthy of notice what exquisite pains were always taken by Muscovy as well as by modern Russia to execute republics. Novgorod and its colonies lead the dance; the republic of the Cossacks follows; Poland closes it. To understand the Russian mastication of Poland, one must study the execution of Novgorod, lasting from 1178 till 1528.

* The paragraphs from here to the end of the chapter were omitted in the pamphlet published by Swan Sonnenschein in 1899. The text is here reproduced from *The Free Press*, February 25, 1857.

Ivan seemed to have snatched the chain with which the Mongols crushed Muscovy only to bind with it the Russian republics. He seemed to enslave these republics only to republicanise the Russian princes. During twenty-three years he had recognised their independence, borne with their petulance, and stooped even to their outrages. Now, by the overthrow of the Golden Horde, and by the downfall of the republics, he had grown so strong, and the princes, on the other hand, had grown so weak by the influence which the Muscovite wielded over their boyards, that the mere display of force on the part of Ivan sufficed to decide the contest. Still, at the outset, he did not depart from his method of circumspection. He singled out the prince of Tver, the mightiest of the Russian feudatories, to be the first object of his operations. He began by driving him to the offensive and into an alliance with Lithuania, then denounced him as a traitor, then terrified him into successive concessions destructive of the prince's means of defence, then played upon the false position in which these concessions placed him with respect to his own subjects, and then left this system to work out its consequences. It ended in the abandonment of the contest by the prince of Tver and his flight into Lithuania. Tver united with Muscovy—Ivan pushed forward with terrible vigour in the execution of his long-meditated plan. The other princes underwent their degradation into simple governors almost without resistance. There remained still two brothers of Ivan. The one was persuaded to renounce his appanage; the other, enticed to the Court and put off his guard by hypocritical demonstrations of fraternal love, was assassinated.

We have now arrived at Ivan's last great contest—that with Lithuania. Beginning with his accession to the throne, it ended only some years before his death. During thirty years he confined this contest to a war of diplomacy, fomenting and improving the internal dissensions between Lithuania and Poland, drawing over disaffected Russian feudatories of Lithuania, and paralysing his foe by stirring up foes against him; Maximilian of Austria, Mathias Corvinus, of Hungary; and above all, Stephen, the gospodar of Moldavia, whom he had attached to himself by marriage; lastly, Menghi-Ghirei, who proved as powerful a tool against Lithuania as against the Golden Horde. On the death of king Casimir, however, and the accession of the weak Alexander, when the thrones of Lithuania and Poland became temporarily disjoined; when those two countries had crippled each other's forces in mutual strife; when the Polish nobility, lost in its efforts to weaken the royal power on the one hand, and to degrade the kmetons and citizens on the other, deserted Lithuania, and suffered it to recede before the simultaneous incursions of Stephen of Moldavia and of Menghi-Ghirei; when thus the weakness of Lithuania had become palpable; then Ivan understood the opportunity had ripened for putting out his strength, and that condition exuberated for a successful explosion on his part. Still he did not go beyond a theatrical demonstration of war—the assemblage of overwhelming forces. As he had completely foreseen, the feigned desire of combat now sufficed to make Lithuania capitulate. He extorted the acknowledgement by treaty of the encroachments, surreptitiously made in king Casimir's time, and plagued Alexander at the same time with his alliance and with his daughter. The alliance he employed to forbid Alexander the defence against attacks instigated by the father-in-law, and the daughter to kindle a religious war between the intolerant Catholic king and his persecuted subjects of the Greek confession. Amidst this turmoil he ventured at last to draw the sword, and seized the Russian appanages under Lithuanian sway as far as Kiev and Smolensk.

The Greek religion generally proved one of his most powerful means of action. But to lay claim to the inheritance of Byzantium, to hide the stigma of Mongolian serfdom under the mantle of the Porphyrogeniti, to link the upstart throne of Muscovy to the glorious empire of St. Vladimir, to give in his own person a new temporal head to the Greek Church, whom of all the world should Ivan single out? The Roman Pope. At the Pope's court there dwelt the last princess of Byzantium. From the Pope Ivan embezzled her by taking an oath to apostatise—an oath which he ordered his own primate to release him from.

A simple substitution of names and dates will prove to evidence that between the policy of Ivan III., and that of modern Russia, there exists not similarity but sameness. Ivan III., on his part, did but perfect the traditionary policy of Muscovy, bequeathed by Ivan I, Kalita. Ivan Kalita, the Mongolian slave, acquired greatness by wielding the power of his greatest foe, the Tartar, against his minor foes, the Russian princes. He could not wield the power of the Tartar but under false pretences. Forced to dissemble before his masters the strength he really gathered, he had to dazzle his fellow-serfs with a power he did not own. To solve his problem he had to elaborate all the ruses of the most abject slavery into a system, and to execute that system with the patient labour of the slave. Open force itself could enter as an intrigue only into a system of intrigues, corruption and underground usurpation. He could not strike before he had poisoned. Singleness of purpose became with him duplicity of action. To encroach by the fraudulent use of a hostile power, to weaken that power by the very act of using it, and to overthrow it at last by the effects produced through its own instrumentality—this policy was inspired to Ivan Kalita by the peculiar character both of the ruling and the serving race. His policy remained still the policy of Ivan III.

It is yet the policy of Peter the Great, and of modern Russia, whatever changes of name, seat, and character the hostile power used may have undergone. Peter the Great is indeed the inventor of modern Russian policy, but he became so only by divesting the old Muscovite method of encroachment of its merely local character and its accidental admixtures, by distilling it into an abstract formula, by generalising its purpose, and exalting its object from the overthrow of certain given limits of power to the aspiration of unlimited power. He metamorphosed Muscovy into modern Russia by the generalisation of its system, not by the mere addition of some provinces.

To resume. It is in the terrible and abject school of Mongolian slavery that Muscovy was nursed and grew up. It gathered strength only by becoming a virtuoso in the craft of serfdom. Even when emancipated, Muscovy continued to perform its traditional part of the slave as master. At length Peter the Great coupled the political craft of the Mongol slave with the proud aspiration of the Mongol master, to whom Genghiz Khan had, by will, bequeathed his conquest of the earth.

6

ONE feature characteristic of the Slavonic race must strike every observer. Almost everywhere it confined itself to an inland country, leaving the sea-borders to non-Slavonic tribes. Finno-Tartaric tribes held the shores of the Black Sea. Lithuanians and Fins those of the Baltic and White Sea. Wherever they touched the sea-board, as in the Adriatic and part of the Baltic, the Slavonians had soon to submit to foreign rule. The Russian people shared this common fate of the Slavonian race. Their home, at the time they first appear in history, was the country about the sources and upper course of the Volga and its tributaries, the Dnieper, Don, and Northern Dwina. Nowhere did their territory touch the sea except at the extremity of the Gulf of Finland. Nor had they before Peter the Great proved able to conquer any maritime outlet beside that of the White Sea, which, during three-fourths of the year, is itself enchained and immovable. The spot where Petersburg now stands had been for a thousand years past contested ground between Fins, Swedes, and Russians. All the remaining extent of coast from Polangen, near Memel, to Torrea, the whole coast of the Black Sea, from Akerman to Redut Kaleh, has been conquered later on. And, as if to witness the anti-marine peculiarity of the Slavonic race, of all this line of coast, no portion of the Baltic coast has really adopted Russian nationality. Nor has the Circassian and Mingrelian east coast of the Black Sea. It is only the coast of the White Sea, as far as it was worth cultivating, some portion of the northern coast of the Black Sea, and part of the coast of the Sea of Azof, that have really been peopled with Russian inhabitants, who, however, despite the new circumstances in which they are placed, still refrain from taking to the sea, and obstinately stick to the land-lopers' traditions of their ancestors.

From the very outset, Peter the Great broke through all the traditions of the Slavonic race. "It is water that Russia wants."

These words he addressed as a rebuke to Prince Cantemir are inscribed on the title-page of his life. The conquest of the Sea of Azof was aimed at in his first war with Turkey, the conquest of the Baltic in his war against Sweden, the conquest of the Black Sea in his second war against the Porte, and the conquest of the Caspian Sea in his fraudulent intervention in Persia. For a system of local encroachment, land was sufficient; for a system of universal aggression, water had become indispensable. It was but by the conversion of Muscovy from a country wholly of land into a sea-bordering empire, that the traditional limits of the Muscovite policy could be superseded and merged into that bold synthesis which, blending the encroaching method of the Mongol slave with the world-conquering tendencies of the Mongol master, forms the life-spring of modern Russian diplomacy.

It has been said that no great nation has ever existed, or been able to exist, in such an inland position as that of the original empire of Peter the Great; that none has ever submitted thus to see its coasts and the mouths of its rivers torn away from it; that Russia could no more leave the mouth of the Neva, the natural outlet for the produce of Northern Russia, in the hands of the Swedes, than the mouths of the Don, Dnieper, and Bug, and the Straits of Kertch, in the hands of nomadic and plundering Tartars; that the Baltic provinces, from their very geographical configuration, are naturally a corollary to whichever nation holds the country behind them; that, in one word, Peter, in this quarter, at least, but took hold of what was absolutely necessary for the natural development of his country. From this point of view, Peter the Great intended, by his war against Sweden, only rearing a Russian Liverpool, and endowing it with its indispensable strip of coast.

But then, one great fact is slighted over, the *tour de force* by which he transferred the capital of the Empire from the inland centre to the maritime extremity, the characteristic boldness with which he erected the new capital on the first strip of Baltic coast he conquered, almost within gunshot of the frontier, thus deliberately giving his dominions an *eccentric centre*. To transfer the throne of the Czars from Moscow to Petersburg was to place it in a position where it could not be safe, even from insult, until the whole coast from Libau to Tornea was subdued—a work not completed till 1809, by the conquest of Finland. "St. Petersburg

is the window from which Russia can overlook Europe," said
Algarotti.[47] It was from the first a defiance to the Europeans, an
incentive to further conquest to the Russians. The fortifications
in our own days of Russian Poland are only a further step in the
execution of the same idea. Modlin, Warsaw, Ivangorod, are
more than citadels to keep a rebellious country in check. They
are the same menace to the west which Petersburg, in its
immediate bearing, was a hundred years ago to the north. They
are to transform Russia into Panslavonia, as the Baltic provinces
were to transform Muscovy into Russia.

Petersburg, the *eccentric centre* of the empire, pointed at once
to a periphery still to be drawn.

It is, then, not the mere conquest of the Baltic provinces
which separates the policy of Peter the Great from that of his
ancestors, but it is the transfer of the capital which reveals the
true meaning of his Baltic conquests. Petersburg was not like
Muscovy, the centre of a race, but the seat of a government; not
the slow work of a people, but the instantaneous creation of a
man; not the medium from which the peculiarities of an inland
people radiate, but the maritime extremity where they are lost;
not the traditional nucleus of a national development, but the
deliberately chosen abode of a cosmopolitan intrigue. By the
transfer of the capital, Peter cut off the natural ligaments which
bound up the encroaching system of the old Muscovite Czars
with the natural abilities and aspirations of the great Russian
race. By planting his capital on the margin of a sea, he put to
open defiance the anti-maritime instincts of that race, and
degraded it to a mere weight in his political mechanism. Since the
16th century Muscovy had made no important acquisitions but
on the side of Siberia, and to the 16th century the dubious conquests made towards the west and the south were only brought
about by direct agency on the east. By the transfer of the capital,
Peter proclaimed that he, on the contrary, intended working on
the east and the immediately neighbouring countries through the
agency of the west. If the agency through the east was narrowly
circumscribed by the stationary character and the limited
relations of Asiatic peoples, the agency through the west became
at once illimited and universal from the movable character and
the all-sided relations of Western Europe. The transfer of the
capital denoted this intended change of agency, which the con-

quest of the Baltic provinces afforded the means of achieving, by securing at once to Russia the supremacy among the neighbouring Northern States; by putting it into immediate and constant contact with all points of Europe; by laying the basis of a material bond with the maritime Powers, which by this conquest became dependent on Russia for their naval stores; a dependence not existing as long as Muscovy, the country that produced the great bulk of the naval stores, had got no outlets of its own; while Sweden, the Power that held these outlets, had not got the country lying behind them.

If the Muscovite Czars, who worked their encroachments by the agency principally of the Tartar Khans, were obliged to *tartarize* Muscovy, Peter the Great, who resolved upon working through the agency of the west, was obliged to *civilize* Russia. In grasping upon the Baltic provinces, he seized at once the tools necessary for this process. They afforded him not only the diplomatists and the generals, the brains with which to execute his system of political and military action on the west, they yielded him, at the same time, a crop of bureaucrats, schoolmasters, and drill-sergeants, who were to drill Russians into that varnish of civilization that adapts them to the technical appliances of the Western peoples, without imbuing them with their ideas.

Neither the Sea of Azof, nor the Black Sea, nor the Caspian Sea, could open to Peter this direct passage to Europe. Besides, during his lifetime still Taganrog, Azof, the Black Sea, with its new-formed Russian fleets, ports, and dockyards, were again abandoned or given up to the Turk. The Persian conquest, too, proved a premature enterprise. Of the four wars which fill the military life of Peter the Great, his first war, that against Turkey, the fruits of which were lost in a second Turkish war, continued in one respect the traditionary struggle with the Tartars. In another respect, it was but the prelude to the war against Sweden, of which the second Turkish war forms an episode and the Persian war an epilogue. Thus the war against Sweden, lasting during twenty-one years, almost absorbs the military life of Peter the Great. Whether we consider its purpose, its results, or its endurance, we may justly call it *the* war of Peter the Great. His whole creation hinges upon the conquest of the Baltic coast.

Now, suppose we were altogether ignorant of the details of

his operations, military and diplomatic. The mere fact that the conversion of Muscovy into Russia was brought about by its transformation from a half-Asiatic inland country into the paramount maritime Power of the Baltic, would it not enforce upon us the conclusion that England, the greatest maritime Power of that epoch—a maritime Power lying, too, at the very gates of the Baltic, where, since the middle of the 17th century, she had maintained the attitude of supreme arbiter—that England must have had her hand in this great change, that she must have proved the main prop or the main impediment of the plans of Peter the Great, that during the long protracted and deadly struggle between Sweden and Russia she must have turned the balance, that if we do not find her straining every nerve in order to save the Swede we may be sure of her having employed all the means at her disposal for furthering the Muscovite? And yet, in what is commonly called history, England does hardly appear on the plan of this grand drama, and is represented as a spectator rather than as an actor. Real history will show that the Khans of the Golden Horde were no more instrumental in realizing the plans of Ivan III. and his predecessors than the rulers of England were in realizing the plans of Peter I. and his successors.

The pamphlets which we have reprinted, written as they were by English contemporaries of Peter the Great, are far from concurring in the common delusions of later historians. They emphatically denounce England as the mightiest tool of Russia. The same position is taken up by the pamphlet of which we shall now give a short analysis, and with which we shall conclude the introduction to the diplomatic revelations. It is entitled, *"Truth is but Truth as it is timed; or, our Ministry's present measures against the Muscovite vindicated,* etc., etc. Humbly dedicated to the House of C., London, 1719."

The former pamphlets we have reprinted, were written at, or shortly after, the time when, to use the words of a modern admirer of Russia, "Peter traversed the Baltic Sea as master at the head of the combined squadrons of all the northern Powers, England included, which gloried in sailing under his orders." In 1719, however, when *Truth is but Truth* was published, the face of affairs seemed altogether changed. Charles XII. was dead, and the English Government now pretended to side with Sweden, and to wage war against Russia. There are other circumstances connected with this anonymous pamphlet which claim particular notice. It purports to be an extract from a relation, which, on his return from Muscovy, in August, 1715, its author, by order of George I., drew up and handed over to Viscount Townshend, then Secretary of State.

"It happens," says he, "to be an advantage that at present I may own to have been the first so happy to foresee, or honest to forewarn our Court here, of the absolute necessity of our then breaking with the Czar, and shutting him out again of the Baltic." "My relation discovered his aim as to other States, and even to the German Empire, to which, although an inland Power, he had offered to annex Livonia as an Electorate so that he could but be admitted as an elector. It drew attention to the Czar's then contemplated assumption of the title of Autocrator. Being head of the Greek Church he would be owned by the other potentates as head of the Greek Empire. I am not to say how reluctant we would be to acknowledge that title, since we have already made an ambassador treat him with the title of Imperial Majesty, which the Swede has never yet condescended to."

For some time attached to the British Embassy in Muscovy, our author, as he states, was later on "*dismissed the service, because the Czar desired it,*" having made sure that

"I had given our Court such light into his affairs as is contained in this paper; for which I beg leave to appeal to the King, and to vouch the Viscount Townshend, who heard his Majesty give that vindication." "And yet, notwithstanding all this, I have been for these five years past kept soliciting for a very long arrear still due, and whereof I contracted the greatest part in executing a commission for her late Majesty."

The anti-Muscovite attitude, suddenly assumed by the Stanhope Cabinet, our author looks to in rather a sceptic mood.

"I do not pretend to foreclose, by this paper, the Ministry of that applause due to them from the public, when they shall satisfy us as to what the motives were which made them, till but yesterday, straiten the Swede in everything, although then our ally as much as now; or strengthen, by all the ways they could, the Czar, although under no tie, but barely that of amity with Great Britain. . . . At the minute I write this I learn that the gentleman who brought the Muscovites, not yet three years ago, as a royal navy, not under our protection, on their first appearance in the Baltic, is again authorised by the persons now in power, to give the Czar a second meeting in these seas. For what reason or to what good end?"

The gentleman hinted at is Admiral Norris, whose Baltic campaign against Peter I. seems, indeed, to be the original pattern upon which the recent naval campaigns of Admirals Napier and Dundas were cut out.

The restoration to Sweden of the Baltic provinces is required by the commercial as well as the political interest of Great Britain. Such is the pith of our author's argument:

"Trade is become the very life of our State; and what food is to life, naval stores are to a fleet. The whole trade we drive with all the other nations of the earth, at best, is but lucrative; this, of the north, is indispensably needful, and may not be improperly termed the *sacra embole* of Great Britain, as being its chiefest foreign vent, for the support of all our trade, and our safety at home. As woollen manufactures and minerals are the staple commodoties of Great Britain, so are likewise naval stores those of Muscovy, as also of all those very provinces in the Baltic which the Czar has so lately wrested from the crown of Sweden. Since those provinces have been in the Czar's possession, Pernan is entirely waste. At Revel we have not one British merchant left, and all the trade which was formerly at Narwa is now brought to Petersburg. . . . The Swede could never possibly engross the trade of our subjects, because those seaports in his hands were but so many thoroughfares from whence these commodities were uttered, the places of their produce or manufacture lying behind those ports, in the dominions of the Czar. But, if left to the Czar, these Baltic ports are no more thoroughfares, but peculiar magazines from the inland countries of the Czar's own dominions. Having already Archangel in the White Sea, to leave him but any seaport in the Baltic were to put no less in his hands than the *two keys of the general magazines of all the naval stores of Europe*; it being known that Danes, Swedes, Poles, and Prussians have but single and distinct branches of those commodities in their several dominions. If the Czar should thus engross 'the supply of what we cannot do without,' where then is our fleet? Or, indeed, where is the security for all our trade to any part of the earth besides?"

If, then, the interest of British commerce requires to exclude the Czar from the Baltic, "the interest of our State ought to be no less a spur to quicken us to that attempt. By the interest of our State I would be understood to mean neither the party measures of a Ministry, nor any foreign motives of a court, but precisely what is, and ever must be, the immediate concern, either for the safety, ease, dignity, or emolument of the Crown, as well as the common weal of Great Britain." With respect to the Baltic, it has "from the earliest period of our naval power" always been considered a fundamental interest of our State: first, to prevent the rise there of any new maritime Power; and, secondly, to maintain the balance of power between Denmark and Sweden.

> "One instance of the wisdom and foresight of our *then truly British statesmen* is the peace at Stalboa, in the year 1617. James the First was the mediator of that treaty, by which the Muscovite was obliged to give up all the provinces which he then was possessed of in the Baltic, and to be barely an inland Power on this side of Europe."

The same policy of preventing a new maritime Power from starting in the Baltic was acted upon by Sweden and Denmark.

> "Who knows not that the Emperor's attempt to get a seaport in Pomerania weighed no less with the great Gustavus than any other motive for carrying his arms even into the bowels of the house of Austria? What befel, at the times of Charles Gustavus,[48] the crown of Poland itself, who, besides it being in those days by far the mightiest of any of the northern Powers, had then a long stretch of coast on, and some ports in, the Baltic? The Danes, though then in alliance with Poland, would never allow them, even for their assistance against the Swedes, to have a fleet in the Baltic, but destroyed the Polish ships wherever they could meet them."

As to the maintenance of the balance of power between the established maritime States of the Baltic, the tradition of British policy is no less clear. "When the Swedish power gave us some uneasiness there by threatening to crush Denmark," the honour of our country was kept up by retrieving the then inequality of the balance of power.

The Commonwealth of England sent in a squadron to the Baltic which brought on the treaty of Roskild (1658), afterwards

confirmed at Copenhagen (1660). The fire of straw kindled by
the Danes in the times of King William III. was as speedily
quenched by George Rock in the treaty of Copenhagen.

Such was the hereditary British policy.

> "It never entered into the mind of the politicians of those
> times in order to bring the scale again to rights, to find out
> the happy *expedient of raising a third naval Power* for framing
> a juster balance in the Baltic. . . . Who has taken this counsel
> against Tyre, the crowning city, whose merchants are princes,
> whose traffickers are the honourables of the earth? *Ego
> autem neminem nomino, quare irasci mihi nemo poterit, nisi qui ante
> de se noluerit confiteri.*[49] Posterity will be under some difficulty
> to believe that this could be the *work of any of the persons now
> in power* . . . that *we* have opened *St. Petersburg to the Czar
> solely at our own expense, and without any risk to him.* . . ."

The safest line of policy would be to return to the treaty of
Itolbowa, and to suffer the Muscovite no longer "to nestle in the
Baltic." Yet, it may be said, that in "the present state of affairs"
it would be "difficult to retrieve the advantage we have lost by
not curbing, when it was more easy, the growth of the Muscovite
power." A middle course may be thought more convenient.

> "If we should find it consistent with the welfare of our
> State that the Muscovite have an inlet into the Baltic, as
> having, of all the princes of Europe, a country that can be
> made most beneficial to its prince, by uttering its produce to
> foreign markets. In this case, it were but reasonable to expect,
> on the other hand, that in return for our complying so far
> with his interest, for the improvement of his country, his
> Czarish Majesty, on his part, should demand nothing that
> may tend to the disturbance of another; and, therefore,
> contenting himself with ships of trade, should demand none
> of war."

> "We should thus preclude his hopes of being ever more
> than an inland Power," but "obviate every objection of
> using the Czar worse than any Sovereign Prince may expect.
> I shall not for this give an instance of a Republic of Genoa,
> or another in the Baltic itself, of the Duke of Courland; but
> will assign Poland and Prussia, who, though both now
> crowned heads, have ever contented themselves with the
> freedom of an open traffic, without insisting on a fleet. Or the
> treaty of Falczin, between the Turk and Muscovite, by which

Peter was forced not only to restore Asoph, and to part with all his men-of-war in those parts, but also to content himself with the bare freedom of traffic in the Black Sea. Even an inlet in the Baltic for trade is much beyond what he could morally have promised himself not yet so long ago on the issue of his war with Sweden."

If the Czar refuse to agree to such "a healing temperament," we shall have "nothing to regret but the time we lost to exert all the means that Heaven has made us master of, to reduce him to a peace advantageous to Great Britain." War would become inevitable. In that case

"it ought no less to animate our Ministry to pursue their present measures, than fire with indignation the breast of every honest Briton that a Czar of Muscovy, who owes his naval skill to our instructions, and his grandeur to our forbearance, should so soon deny to Great Britain the terms which so few years ago he was fain to take up with from the Sublime Porte."

"'Tis every way our interest to have the Swede restored to those provinces which the Muscovite has wrested from that crown in the Baltic. *Great Britain can no longer hold the balance in that sea,*" since she "*has raised the Muscovite to be a maritime Power there.* . . . Had we performed the articles of our alliance made by King William with the crown of Sweden, that gallant nation would ever have been a bar strong enough against the Czar coming into the Baltic. . . . Time must confirm us, that the Muscovite's *expulsion from the Baltic* is *now* the principal end of our Ministry."

SUPPLEMENTARY NOTES

1. Walpole, Horace, 4th earl of Orford, 1717–97. Third son of Sir Robert Walpole. Held many sinecures in his father's government. Author of the terror novel *The Castle of Otranto*. His letters and reminiscences are a source of information on Georgian England.

2. Oestermann, Count Andrei Ivanovich, 1686–1747. Russian diplomat in service of Peter I, Catherine I and Anne. Vice-chancellor under Catherine I. Exiled to Siberia by Elizabeth.

3. Biron, Count Ernst Johann, 1690–1772. Real name Bühren, but assumed name and arms of French ducal family, de Biron. Made Duke of Courland, 1737. Regent of Russia on death of Empress Anne, 1740. Exiled to Siberia. 1762 released by Peter III and recovered dukedom.

4. Panin, Count Nikita Petrovitch, 1721–89. Minister of Foreign Affairs under Catherine II. Believed to have been in the pay of Frederick II of Prussia.

5. Harris, Sir James, 1st earl of Malmesbury, 1746–1820. British ambassador to St. Petersburg, 1777–82.

6. Grantham, Thomas Robinson, 2nd baron, 1738–86. Secretary of State, 1782–3.

7. Catherine II, Empress of Russia, called the Great, 1729–96. Of German birth, married the future Peter III, whom, with the help of her lover Grigori Orlov, she deposed and succeeded in 1762. Reactionary at home she followed an imperialist foreign policy. She secured the major share in the Polish partitions of 1772, 1793 and 1795, annexed the Crimea, 1783, and in two wars against Turkey, 1767–74, 1787–92, made Russia dominant in Near East.

8. Stormont, David Murray, Earl of Mansfield, Viscount, 1727–96. British ambassador to France 1772–78. Lord President of the Council in the Portland government, 1783.

9. Potemkin, Prince Grigori Alexandrovich, 1739–91. Favourite and minister of Catherine II, to whom he was thought to be secretly married. Born near Smolensk of Polish

family. Reaped the credit of Suvorov's victories against the Turks.

10. Minorca. Second largest of Balearic Islands. Frequently changed hands in eighteenth century. British 1708–56, French 1756–63, British 1763–82, occupied by French and Spanish 1782 recovered by Britain 1798, acquired by Spain 1802. Offered by Lord North's government to Russia in 1779.

11. Kaunitz, Wenzel Anton, Fürst von, 1711–94. Austrian chancellor and foreign minister under Maria Theresa, Joseph II and Leopold II. Formed the coalition against Prussia which led to the Seven Years War and secured a share of Poland for Austria in the partition of 1772.

12. The Shelburne Government of 1782.

13. St. Simon, Louis de Rouvroy, duc de, 1675–1755. Author of memoirs on the court of Louis XIV.

14. Pozzo di Borgo, Count Carlo Andrea, 1764–1842. Russian diplomat, born in Corsica. Supported British occupation of Corsica in 1794. Replaced Paoli in authority. Driven into exile by the French reconquest of the island, he entered the Russian service in 1804. Encouraged the Czar Alexander I to oppose Napoleon. Russian ambassador to France after 1814.

15. Peter I, the Great, Czar of Russia, 1672–1725. Founder of the Russian Empire. His objects were Westernisation and expansion towards the Baltic and the Black Sea. Victor in the Northern War, 1700–21, he made Russia instead of Sweden the dominant power in the Baltic. Moved the capital from Moscow to his new city of St. Petersburg, "the window of Europe", 1713. Introduced many administrative reforms, founded hospitals and encouraged trade, but further enslaved the serfs.

16. *Hysteron-proteron*, putting the cart before the horse.

17. Skana (Schonen), Scania or Skane, province of South Sweden, chief city Malmo. Ceded by Denmark to Sweden by the Treaty of Copenhagen, 1660.

18. Augustus II, the Strong, 1670–1733, elector of Saxony and king of Poland. Elected king of Poland with Russian support. Ally of Russia and Denmark against Sweden in Northern War. Deposed by Charles XII of Sweden in 1704, but recovered crown after Russian victories.

19. Bender, town in Bessarabia, conquered by Turks in 1538. Refuge of Charles XII of Sweden, 1709–13.

20. George I, 1660–1727, elector of Hanover, king of Great Britain and Ireland, 1714–27. Great-grandson of James I of England.

21. Zealand, largest island of Denmark, between Kattegat and Baltic Sea, separated from Sweden by the Sound (Oresund). Chief city, the capital Copenhagen.

22. Stralsund, a Hansa port and fort in Pomerania in the Baltic opposite Rügen. Taken by Sweden in 1648. Charles XII failed to relieve it, 1715, but Sweden retained possession until 1815 when it passed to Prussia. After the war of 1939–45, Stralsund was incorporated in Mecklenburg, now in the German Democratic Republic.

23. Görtz, Georg Heinrich, baron von, 1668–1719. Born in Holstein. Chief minister of Charles XII of Sweden, 1714. Negotiated peace with the Russians on the Aland Islands, 1718. With the approval of Peter the Great conspired with exiled Jacobites for the Stuart restoration in England. Executed 1718.

24. Gyllenborg, Carl, count of, 1679–1746. Swedish ambassador in England. Had his house searched and was arrested in London in 1716 because of his intrigues with the Jacobites. President of the Swedish chancellery in 1739, and was largely responsible for the Russo-Swedish war of 1741–43, in which Sweden lost Viborg.

25. *Czarish Majesty*, Peter I.

26. *Danish Majesty*, Frederick IV of Denmark and Norway, 1671–1730.

27. Norris, Sir John, Admiral, 1660–1749. British commander-in-chief, Mediterranean, 1710–11, and the Baltic, 1715–27. Lord of Admiralty, 1718–30.

28. Rix-dollar. Continental silver coin in sixteenth–nineteenth centuries, ranging in value from 2s. 3d. to 4s. 6d.

29. *Maritime Powers*, Britain and Holland.

30. William III, king of England, Scotland and Ireland, 1650–1702.

31. Mecklenburg, Grand Duchy of. Chief cities Schwerin, Rostock, Wismar, Stralsund. In 1716, its Grand Duke, Karl Leopold, married Peter the Great's niece and put his country entirely at the disposal of the Russian army. Now in the German Democratic Republic.

32. "Now can you believe it, can you understand it, that any-

one should be born with so much stupidity in him that he would take pleasure in wickedness?" Terence, *Andria*.

33. *Exegi monumentum (aere perennius)*. "I have completed a monument more lasting than one of bronze." Horace, *Odes*. III. XXX.

34. Milosh, prince of Serbia, 1780–1860. Led war of liberation 1815. Prince, 1817. Abdicated 1839. Creator of modern Serbia.

35. Kars, former Turkish city in Armenia, surrendered by British garrison to the Russians in 1855 during the Crimean War.

36. Suez Canal, cut 1859–69 by Ferdinand de Lesseps. British government at first hostile suspecting an extension of French imperialism in Egypt and the East.

37. Townshend, Charles, 2nd Viscount, 1674–1738. Brother-in-law of Robert Walpole. Secured Hanoverian Succession, 1709. Secretary of State 1714–16. Crushed Jacobite rebellion of 1715.

38. Stanhope, James, 1st Earl, 1673–1721. Secretary of State 1714–17 under George I. His grandson, Charles, 3rd earl, 1753–1816, brother-in-law of William Pitt the younger.

39. "Neither break peace-treaties, nor prefer allegiance to kingdoms." Silius, *Lip*. II.

40. The Treaty of Travendahl, 1700, between Denmark and Sweden. Denmark agreed to renounce its claim to Holstein, and to abandon its alliance with Russia and Saxony.

41. Oleg, prince of Kiev, raided Constantinople in 907. His successor Igor made two military expeditions in 941 and 944 to the Byzantine Empire, which resulted in a trade agreement, improved by his son Svyatoslav I. (Sviataslaff) who conquered Bulgaria and threatened Constantinople until defeated by the deputy Byzantine emperor, John Zimisces. Svyatoslav's son Vladimir I also threatened Constantinople but made peace after marrying the emperor's daughter and adopting orthodox Christianity in 989.

42. *Porphyrogeneti*, born in the purple, that is born to a member of the imperial family.

43. Rurik, leader of Scandinavian merchant-warriors called Varangians who invaded Russia in the ninth century. Rurik founded the state of Novgorod in 862, died 879.

44. Tartars, collective name of nomadic tribes which under Mongol leadership overran large parts of Asia and Russia in the thirteenth century. Their host was called the Golden Horde because of the splendour of the court of their leader Batu, died 1255, grandson of Jenghiz Khan.

45. Ivan I, Kalita (the Purse), Grand Prince of Moscow, 1328–40.

46. Ivan III, the Great, 1440–1505, Grand Prince of Moscow. Expanded the Moscovite state and freed Muscovy from the Tartar yoke. Conquered Kazan and Astrakan.

47. Algarotti, Francesco, Count, 1712–64. Italian philosopher. Friend of Frederick II of Prussia and Voltaire. Wrote *Newtonian Philosophy for Ladies.*

48. Charles Gustavus, Charles X, King of Sweden, 1654–60. By the Treaty of Roskilde obliged the Danes to surrender all the territory that they held in Southern Sweden.

49. "But I name no one, so that no one will be angry with me, other than he who might refuse to express himself openly before the event."

THE STORY OF THE LIFE OF LORD PALMERSTON

INTRODUCTION

I

HENRY JOHN TEMPLE, the third Viscount Palmerston, is one of the most controversial figures in British political history. First as Foreign Secretary and then as Prime Minister, he dominated British politics for thirty years, running the affairs of state as though they were his own private business, arrogantly indifferent to the views of the Queen, the cabinet and parliament. Driven by a restless energy, almost it seemed by a craving for personal excitement, he embarked on a reckless diplomacy, which more than once brought Britain to the verge of an unnecessary war. He considered, said Marx, that the movement of history itself was a pastime expressly invented for his own private satisfaction. He was therefore unpredictable and often inconsistent in action, and evasive, untruthful and irrelevant in explanation. He was widely distrusted and disliked by contemporary politicians both in England and abroad. His strength rested on the people, by whom, with one or two setbacks, he was regarded as a hero. Possessing a great talent for acting, he appeared as the embodiment of insular prejudice and arrogance, a John Bull who knew how to keep foreigners in their place. They enjoyed his airs of a Regency buck, his cavalier treatment of foreign diplomats, his habit of ordering out the fleet to enforce his will on Europe; above all they believed him to be the champion of liberalism and constitutionalism, he said so often enough, and the arch-enemy of the absolutist powers, who were also misled on similar lines. They did not pause to consider that, in the words of Marx, "Poles, Italians, Hungarians, Germans, found him in office whenever they were crushed". Metternich, the Czar and other European absolutists, who relied on the gallows, the bludgeon and the secret police, failed to understand Palmerston, who was shrewder than them all. He was a classic example of a phenomenon which has become quite common in Britain, the reactionary waving a progressive and liberal banner.

Marx was very conscious of the deceptive role played by

Palmerston. *The Story of the Life of Lord Palmerston* was written
not as a biography but as a polemic to counteract "this astonishing confidence in a man so false and hollow" and "the ease with
which people are imposed on by brilliant abilities". It was "new
evidence of the necessity of taking off the mask from this wily
enemy of the progress of human freedom". Instead of being the
champion of constitutionalism he was in reality "the unflinching
and persevering advocate of Russian interests".

Marx stated his case with his usual acumen but, as will be
seen below, there were also others, less gifted, who had similar
views.

2

The period between 1815 and 1848 was one of change and
revolt. A new social order had come into being but was not yet
stabilised, with the result that it was an age of conspiracy, riot
and rebellion on one side and brutal police repression on the other.
The impact of the French Revolution accompanied by the Industrial Revolution and the Napoleonic upheaval had shattered the
economic and social forms of the eighteenth century and had
created a powerful industrial capitalist class, which in its own
expanding interests had to oppose the diehards of the anachronistic
aristocratic order. In this conflict with the entrenched oligarchies, the monied classes advocated Constitutionalism as opposed
to Absolutism. The European bourgeoisie was liberal in sentiment, demanding government by legal constitution rather than
by despotic edicts. The ideological conflict of the time was
therefore between constitutionalism and absolutism, much as a
hundred years later it was between democracy and fascism.

But middle-class liberalism was strictly bounded by its own
interests. In demanding electoral reform and constitutional rule
they were well aware of the danger of opening the gates to the
working class. In abolishing sixty-five "rotten boroughs" the
Great Reform Bill of 1832 in Britain gave the same number of
seats in the Commons to the new industrial centres such as
Manchester, Birmingham, Leeds and Sheffield, hitherto unrep-
resented, and laid a heavy property qualification on voting.
When sixteen years later the Chartists tried to obtain free and
universal suffrage, the liberal middle class rushed to the support
of the reactionary old Duke of Wellington, and more than

200,000 of them volunteered as special constables. In France there was also an age qualification: no man could vote under thirty or become a deputy under forty.

The working class was degraded rather than uplifted by the Industrial Revolution, which had destroyed not only their cottage industry but also their skill. The demand now was for unskilled workers, including women and children, to work the machines. The system of apprenticeship fell into disuse together with the trade guilds. Driven off the land by the enclosures and off the roads by the savage vagrancy acts, the new working class clustered in the manufacturing towns, herded in slums, working long hours for little money and at the mercy of their employers, as a result of the Combination Act of 1799 which forbade trade unions. Their distress was augmented by the passing of the Corn Law in 1815 which forbade the importation of foreign corn until the price of English wheat rose to £4 a quarter. Discontent expressed itself in machine-breaking, riots and plots, all of which frightened the government into believing that they were on the verge of a Jacobin revolution, the Tower of London replacing the Bastille. A Radical Party was formed which canalised public anger into agitation for the Reform Bill, and the Government of Lord Liverpool, which included Sidmouth, Castlereagh and Palmerston, suspended Habeas Corpus and brought in the six repressive measures, under which men were hanged or transported to Australia. The repression was however ineffective, and it was the Whigs who prevented a revolutionary situation developing in England by forcing the Reform Bill through Parliament and introducing some industrial and penal reforms. But the Whigs shared with the Tories the same fear and mistrust of the "mob", as they referred to the poor, and refused to take any step towards enfranchising the working man until 1867.

The Whigs stood as much for "Peace and Order" as the Czar, the Emperor of Austria and the King of Prussia: they differed only in their methods of achieving them. Whereas the absolutists lacked imagination and relied on the bayonet and censorship, the Whigs preferred the subtler and more liberal method imposed by the needs of a rising industrial capitalism of being a wolf in sheep's clothing. For that reason the British government had been lukewarm to the Holy Alliance of Russia, Prussia and

Austria, dedicated to the crushing of Jacobinism and rebellion generally. It was, said Castlereagh, "a piece of sublime mysticism and nonsense", and his successor as Foreign Secretary, Canning, described the sacred alliance as nothing more than a system of repression and espionage, "a European Areopagus". Metternich, the Austrian Chancellor, was the inspiration of the Alliance, and the self-appointed counter-revolutionary policeman of Europe. His hatred and fear of the people was obsessive. "I am so sick," he said, "of the word fraternity that if I had a brother I would call him cousin." To him and Czar Nicholas the faintest breath of liberalism was a preliminary to the sounding the tocsins in the sections and the surge of the *sansculottes* on to the palaces and estates of the noble and wealthy. To Palmerston this rigid attitude was ridiculous, and as Foreign Secretary he scandalised the diplomats by sending letters critical of Metternich to the British ambassador in Vienna through the ordinary post, thus ensuring that Metternich via the censors should read them. His object was to "play the good genius at his ear to whisper to him sounder and saner principles".

Metternich imposed his counter-revolutionary will not only on the Habsburg Empire and Italy but on the whole of Germany. The "fatal theory" of popular sovereignty was threatening the thrones of the thirty-eight monarchs who had subscribed to the German Bund of 1815. In 1819 he took the opportunity provided by the assassination of Kotzebue, an agent and spy of the Holy Alliance, to induce the Diet to issue the Carlsbad decrees which imposed a severe censorship on the press, put the universities under strict control, and dissolved the radical students' association, the *Burschenschaften*. A federal secret police was also created to exercise control over revolutionary activities in all the individual states of the Bund.

Similar repression took place in France after the assassination of the Duc de Berry in 1820. Individual liberty and the freedom of the press were suspended, and a new electoral law introduced the double vote, reserving the final ballot for the wealthiest taxpayers. The resultant plots and insurrections were forerunners of the Revolution of 1830.

The middle classes were not indifferent to these draconic measures. In their own trade and manufacturing interests, they required a more liberal atmosphere in which the powers of government should cease to be arbitrary but be controlled constitutionally by an assembly in which the middle classes would have the dominant voice. In Germany and Italy they were tending towards republicanism in their opposition to the customs duties imposed by a multitude of petty states which hindered the free movement of trade. But they were cautious in their approach, fearing that a discontented people might get out of hand and attack all privileges including their own. Meantime the politicians of the opposition groomed themselves to lead the masses, should revolution break out, lest the working class should produce its own leaders. Thus Lafayette, having betrayed the first Revolution, was ready at hand to lead the revolutionaries of 1830 into the open arms of Louis Philippe, whom another ardent champion of the people, Thiers, the butcher of the Paris Commune of 1871, described as "a prince devoted to the cause of the revolution".

The frustration of intellectual youth, seeking to free itself from clerical and monarchial traditions, expressed itself in Gothic despair. In their dream world of wild and weird landscapes illuminated by ghostly moonlight, they relived the *Sorrows of Werther* and the gloomy epics of Ossian. In the arts it was the age of Romanticism, which drove some to suicide and others to rebellion. From this romanticism sprang many conspiratorial societies, the *Carbonari*, the *Amis de la Verité*, the *Chevaliers de la Liberté* and the *Burschenschaften*. Their activities were all strictly "cloak and dagger"; they had no contact with the mass of the people, and no plans for popular insurrection. In France, in alliance with resentful Bonapartist officers, they staged military insurrections at Belfort, Saumur, La Rochelle and Colmar. In Russia the rising of the Decembrists in 1825 was engineered by young officers and students, and students played the major part in the Polish rebellion of 1830. The *Carbonari*, an international secret society, largely composed of young aristocrats, officers and students, was behind General Riego's rising in Spain in 1820, and in the same year promoted a number of insurrections in Naples and Piedmont. Modelled on the *Carbonari* was Auguste Blanqui's *Société des Saisons*, a genuine revolutionary organisation which, however, had, in the words of Engels, "the fantastic idea of overturning an entire society by the action of a small conspiracy". Yet it must be stated that the majority of these esoteric conspirators were ready enough to risk their lives with the people in any spontaneous rising.

At the same time as the conspiracies, men began to formulate their ideas of a society based on justice and reason. Some like Buonarotti were disciples of Babeuf and extreme Jacobinism; others like Sismondi, St. Simon, Fourier and Owen, the "Utopians", conscientiously examined the social and economic causes of injustice and sought idealistically to remedy them; and in Germany Hegel and the Neo-Hegelians who applied the dialectic principle to history finally produced Marx and scientific socialism, which began to be known as communism. In 1841 the German socialist, Moses Hess, wrote to the writer Auerbach, "You can rely on making the acquaintance of the greatest, I might even say, the only living philosopher . . . Marx. . . . He is quite young, not more than twenty-four, and he is destined to give the death-blow to the religion and politics of the Middle Ages." Six years later the Communist League was formed, and a year later the famous *Manifesto*, drafted by Marx and Engels, boldly served notice on "pope and czar; Metternich and Guizot; French radicals and German police" that the communist aim was the "forcible overthrow of all existing social conditions".

The same period saw the rise of the anarchists, the disciples of Stirner in Germany and of Proudhon in France, who differed from the socialists in that they saw the state itself as an evil, no matter how it was controlled.

But to the secret police of the Holy Alliance there was little difference between anarchism, socialism, radicalism, liberalism and nationalism; they were all impertinent and dangerous manifestations of free thought and republicanism, and had to be suppressed.

In England, the Ultras, as Continental reactionaries were called, received little support except from High Tories like the Duke of Wellington. The English Revolution of 1649 had made profound and lasting changes. The monarchy was not absolute, and parliament, however corrupt and unrepresentative, was jealous of its privileges. Capitalism, first merchant and then industrial, was more firmly entrenched than anywhere else in the world and finally determined the policies followed by the ruling oligarchy established by the revolution of 1688. As was clearly demonstrated in 1830, when Wellington and the Tories were thrown out for opposing the Reform Bill, no aristocratic government could continue long in office unless its policy was in tune with the commercial and political interests of the capitalist class. To the latter the stultifying procedures of the Holy Alliance would lead to commercial petrefaction and political stagnation.

The British attitude was not, however, intended to encourage dangerous revolutionary sentiment abroad, but to check it and divert it into more acceptable channels. The methods of Metternich and the Czar were creating the very danger they were supposed to suppress. European liberalism and constitutionalism should be supported within reason not only because they were the best means of preventing revolution but also to promote British influence abroad. "Those," said Palmerston in 1829, "who seek to check improvement, to cherish abuses, to crush opinions, and to prohibit the human race from thinking . . . will find their weapon snap short in their hand, when they most need its protection."

By the Treaty of Vienna, the Holy Alliance claimed the right to intervene in the internal affairs of any nation which threatened the sacred interests of legitimacy. They soon showed that they had every intention of exercising this right. In 1820 the restored Bourbon King of Spain, the cowardly and treacherous Ferdinand VII, was forced by an army revolt to grant a constitution. Thereupon the Holy Alliance authorised Charles X of France to invade Spain and restore the abominable Ferdinand to absolute power. In the same year revolts broke out in the kingdoms of Naples and Piedmont, and were promptly suppressed by Austrian troops sent with the blessing of the Holy Alliance.

In opposition to this interference by Austria, Russia and Prussia, which was upsetting the balance of power, the successive British foreign ministers, Castlereagh and Canning, proclaimed the policy of non-intervention in the internal affairs of other nations. What they meant was that there should be no intervention without British consent. "There were," said Canning, "*special* occasions when interference in the concerns of other states might be justified." His disciple and successor, Palmerston, also shared this unusual view of the meaning of non-intervention: "Intervention by all means short of

K

open war was perfectly compatible with the principle of non-intervention." "*Non-intervention*," wrote a French journalist during the Spanish Civil War a century later, "*est un mot métaphysique et politique qui signifie à peu près la même chose qu'intervention.*" ("Non-intervention is a metaphysical and political word which means more or less the same thing as intervention.")

Nor was Palmerston to stop short of open war.

3

Palmerston became the Secretary of State for Foreign Affairs in 1830 in the Whig Reform government of Earl Grey. He was already well into middle age. For twenty years, under five Tory prime ministers, he had toiled, an industrious nonentity, as Secretary at War, a junior office dealing only with army accounts. In the House of Commons, to which he was eligible as an Irish peer, he had made no mark save as an unattractive speaker, whose harsh voice had earned him the nickname of Lord Pumicestone. Although a colleague of Sidmouth and Castlereagh in the most tyrannical government in modern British history, he was sensitive to the winds of change, and at the appropriate moment broke with the diehard Wellington and followed Canning, who brought him into the Cabinet. In 1829, in an unexpected and remarkable speech, he attacked the Wellington government for not implementing Canning's policy of intervention in Greece and Portugal. Defeated in the election of 1830, he threw in his lot with the reforming Whigs, and became eligible for office in Grey's administration.

Before Canning's death in 1827, Palmerston had been angling for the office of Chancellor of the Exchequer for which he thought himself well qualified after balancing the army accounts for twenty years. Canning was agreeable, but then suddenly withdrew his offer. Palmerston publicly attributed this rebuff to the hostility of the King, George IV, who disliked him. It is true that Palmerston never acquired the knack of getting on well with royalty. He was detested not only by George but by his niece Victoria and her consort Albert, whom Palmerston thought to be a German spy. On the death of Albert, he visited the court, where everything was draped in black, dressed "in a brown overcoat, light grey trousers, green gloves and blue studs, with his whiskers freshly dyed".

But there was more to his rejection than royal disfavour. In 1826 Palmerston was in financial difficulties as a result of unlucky gambling and speculation. He was also accused of "carelessness" (the shareholders called it swindling) in the affairs of a company of which he was a director. The result was that he had a painful interview with Canning, whose offer of the Exchequer was "rudely withdrawn". Palmerston emerged from the interview "chastened and penitent". But this was not the end of the story.

Following the fashion of Regency aristocrats, Palmerston kept two mistresses, in a *menage à trois*. They were both married: Emily Lamb to Earl Cowper and the Princess Lieven to the Russian ambassador. Lord Cupid, as Palmerston was affectionately called, was the father of Emily's younger children, and became eventually her husband, thus establishing a rather irregular relationship with her two brothers, Lord Melbourne, who became Prime Minister twice, and the Hon. Frederick Lamb, who was ambassador at Vienna.

The Princess Lieven was in a different category. She was not merely the wife of the Russian ambassador but a Russian agent in her own right. According to the British diplomat and Turkophil, David Urquhart, in his articles in the *Free Press*, the Princess came to Palmerston's financial rescue by providing him with twenty thousand pounds of the Czar's money, through a Jew who ran a gambling den in London and was later made by Palmerston British consul in Leipzig. Admittedly, Urquhart was prejudiced, but it could explain why Palmerston fought Wellington's pro-Turkish and anti-Russian policy both in the cabinet and in the newspapers, on material undoubtedly supplied by the Lievens. The Princess rather tactlessly fell into the habit of referring to him as "our minister", and claimed that she persuaded Grey to appoint him Foreign Secretary. Her proprietary attitude eventually led to a breach between them, and she transferred her affections to Guizot, Louis-Philippe's chief minister, but her influence was lasting, and Urquhart's accusations at least offer an explanation of certain inconsistencies in Palmerston's career.

As Foreign Secretary, Palmerston wielded enormous power. Britain was the richest country and the greatest maritime power in the world. In the eighteenth century she had built

up an immense empire, which not only provided a market for
the products of machine-industry but was an endless source
of raw material and a bountiful field for capital investment.
She exceeded by far all her competitors in the output of coal,
iron, textiles, machinery and millwork; her railways covered
more than three times the mileage of the French; her mercantile tonnage was more than three times that of her nearest
rival, the United States; and the totals of her exports and imports
amounted to more than three times those of France. Always
alert for fresh fields for investment, British banks and financiers
spread their tentacles all over the world, in the Far East, the
Mediterranean, Latin America and the Pacific; and everywhere
the Navy was ready to protect those investments. British
power was therefore very great and not to be lightly challenged,
thus enabling Palmerston to become the most meddlesome
foreign minister in modern history.

4

Palmerston took office as Foreign Secretary at the tail end of
the Greek War of Independence and during the course of a
civil war in Portugal. He had already severely criticised Wellington and Aberdeen for their lukewarm and cautious policies to
these crises.

The Greek rebellion against the Turkish government was
fomented in Russia. In 1821 the first contingent of Greek
rebels assembled in Russia, and under the leadership of Ypsilanti,
one of the Czar's officers, crossed the Turkish border. Failing
to receive support from the Rumanians, the rebels were defeated
and massacred by the Turks. This was the signal for rebellions
throughout Greece, during which fearful atrocities were
committed by both sides.

Although it was plain that the Greek revolt was sponsored by
Russian imperialism, it aroused the utmost enthusiasm in
Western Europe. A whole people was rising up against the
Turkish oppressors and, nurtured on the traditions of classical
Greece, western intellectuals identified the Greek rebels with the
heroes of antiquity. The painter Delacroix, the poets Chateau-
briand and Byron, led the ecstatic chorus, and after the romantic
death of Byron at Missolonghi, the philhellenic fervour reached
its peak and had considerable political influence.

This enthusiasm was not shared by the very unromantic Duke of Wellington, who was deeply suspicious of Russia and anxious about British interests in the Near East. The Duke's policy was therefore to bolster up the Turkish Empire and to prevent its dismemberment. In 1827, however, he was replaced by Canning, who thought that he could restrain Russia by co-operating with her. This co-operation resulted in the entire destruction of the Egypto-Turkish fleet, bringing troops to the Morea, at Navarino, by the joint Russian, French and British fleets under the command of a British admiral. This, said Wellington on resuming office, was "an untoward event". He shook his head gloomily at the Russian declaration of war on Turkey, and refused to approve the despatch of a French army to drive the Egyptians out of the Morea. Forced by events to accept the principle of Greek independence, he tried to so whittle down the new state's frontiers that it would continue to be a Turkish dependency. He refused to accept the Poros agreement of 1828, by which the Greek frontier should be narrowly confined to a line from the Gulf of Arta to the Gulf of Volo, and wished to deprive the Greeks of the possession of the islands of Samos, Euboea and Crete. Greek troops were to evacuate Acarnania which they had occupied without the Duke's permission, and Aetolia was to remain Turkish. This attitude was hotly condemned by the Canningites, led by Palmerston, who argued that it was in British interests that Greece should be a viable state. Furnished with material from the Lievens, he attacked Wellington and Aberdeen in the Commons and in the newspapers. They were unable, he said, to pursue a straight course, for "inclination leading one way and necessity driving the other they were forced into the diagonal". A remarkable indictment by a future Foreign Secretary whose tortuous policies often mystified Europe.

In the meantime the Russian armies had brought Turkey to its knees, and had forced on the Sultan the Treaty of Adrianople, by which Russia occupied the Danubian provinces of Wallachia and Moravia, shortly to become Rumania, and secured the recognition of Greek independence which was proclaimed in 1830.

Palmerston was now in office. He ordered the British envoy in Greece to delay the Greek evacuation of Acarnania. He then issued a protocol stating that the Greek frontiers proposed at Poros and Adrianople had been drawn on the wrong map, and forced the harassed Sultan to cede to Greece Aetolia and Acarnania.

But it was the Czar Nicholas and not Palmerston who got the credit for the liberation of Greece, and who was to be regarded as the protector of Greece and the Balkan states against Turkish irredentism. The new state began as a republic under the presidency of Capo d'Istrias, a native of Corfu, who had been one of the Czar Alexander's ministers. On his assassination in 1831, the Powers decided to make Greece a kingdom, and appointed as king Otto of Bavaria, a youth of seventeen, who, according to Palmerston, was "devoid of all capacity for governing". His first act was to deny his new subjects a constitution.

5

Palmerston was confronted with other crises during his first year of office. One of the most important of these was the Polish rebellion of 1830.

In 1815, the Treaty of Viennna abolished the Grand Duchy of Warsaw, and re-partitioned Poland among Austria, Prussia and Russia, the last power taking the largest share which included Warsaw. The Czar Alexander, in the first flush of enthusiasm at having recovered what he thought to be his lost property, granted a constitution to the Poles. The two crowns were united, the Czar becoming King of Poland. A Diet and Council of State were established, freedom of press and person guaranteed, Polish was to be the official language, and there was to be a Polish army of forty thousand men. But it was a political contradiction that could not work: the autocrat of Russia could not be expected to act as the constitutional King of Poland. Nor did he. The Polish viceroy was superseded by a Russian, the Diet was seldom called, and at the first sign of dissatisfaction the freedom of press and person was abolished.

The Czar Nicholas was even more repressive, all the more so since he had discovered that some Poles had been involved in the Decembrist plot. In the first five years of his reign he succeeded in antagonising not only the Polish liberals and nationalists but also the gentry and the Catholic Church. Revolt was inevitable.

Inspired by the July Revolution in France, it broke out in 1830. On the night of November 28th, a group of Poles broke into the Viceroy's palace in the hope of assassinating the Grand Duke Constantine, the Czar's brother. In January 1831, the Polish Diet deposed the Czar, which amounted to a declaration of war.

The Polish rebels had many weaknesses. The rebellion was largely the work of junior officers, secret societies and the poorer gentry. Many of the greater landowners stood aloof from the rising, the middle class was small and largely alien, the lesser nobles refused to emancipate the serfs or to grant rights to the immigrant peasants from Hungary and Germany. Although the rebels fought bravely and had some initial success, they were doomed to defeat. The Czar's vengeance outraged liberal Europe. Hundreds were executed, all freedom destroyed, the censorship of books and newspapers clamped down, and all study of history and sociology forbidden. The Polish Constitution was replaced by what Nicholas called the Organic Statute.

The British Foreign Secretary was unmoved by the clamour of protests and by the calls for British intervention as a signatory of the Treaty of Vienna. It is true that he wrote to the Czar recommending clemency, but added, "We do not intrude our advice nor offer our mediation much as we have been pressed by several to do so." He told an astonished House of Commons that the Poles were to blame for "commencing the conflict" and for taking the unjustifiable step of dethroning the Czar, who in Palmerston's opinion, was a "man of high and generous feelings".

But in serving Russia, he went further. He rejected an offer by the French government for joint intervention, and prevented by threats a contemplated intervention by Sweden and Persia.

The Russian occupation of the free city of Cracow, which had remained free only because it was a bone of contention between Austria and Russia, brought no protest from Palmerston, although it was a flagrant breach of the Treaty of Vienna. The occupation, he said, was merely transitory. It was still transitory in 1836, when the Prussians and Austrians joined the Russians in abrogating the constitution of the free city. It was still transitory in 1846, when after the massacre of the Polish nobles in Galicia, the Czar graciously ceded the free city of Cracow to Austria.

Palmerston's inactivity on all questions involving the Czar

did not go unnoticed. Sir Robert Peel in the Commons demanded to know exactly whose representative Palmerston was.

Even when hard pressed by the opposition, Palmerston did not abandon the Czar. He exculpated him by blaming Metternich for the atrocities in Poland. He told the Austrian envoy in August 1932 that in his opinion it was "the settled design on the part of the Austrian government to put down constitutional freedom wherever it exists and to cherish bad government wherever it is to be found. . . . Austria as we *know*, counselled Russia to destroy the Polish constitution". While no doubt this assessment of the Austrian government was correct, the image of a guileless and highminded Nicholas was hard to swallow.

In striking contrast to Palmerston's passivity during the Greek and Polish crises was his energetic intervention in the affairs of Spain, Portugal and Holland.

6

The flight of the Portuguese royal family in British warships to Brazil, to escape the French, and the coronation of Joseph Bonaparte as King of Spain had led to the separation of Latin America from Portugal and Spain. The defeat of Napoleon had meant the restoration of all the discredited old rulers who had returned to their former realms "in the baggage of the allies". The Spaniards were rewarded for their resistance to Napoleon by having the wretched Ferdinand VII thrust upon them. Ferdinand, who was said to have had the heart of a tiger and the head of a mule, promptly abolished the constitution, re-established the Inquisition and filled his prisons with *afancescados*, a general term for collaborators with the French, but which the king applied to constitutionalists, whom he believed to be Jacobins. After Riego's rebellion he was restored to absolute power by a French army sent with the blessing of the Holy Alliance.

But the Spanish colonies in America refused to accept Ferdinand. They rose in revolt and were helped by Britain. An English army of six thousand "volunteers" helped Bolivar to secure the independence of equatorial America, and a brilliant British admiral, Lord Cochrane, in command of a small rebel fleet, cleared the Pacific of Spanish warships and helped to liberate Chile and Peru.

This was not altruism on the part of Britain. It was clear to the City of London that the new South American republics were offering it a new commercial empire, and it demanded that the British government should facilitate its expanding trade by recognising the rebel states. The demand became more pressing when Ferdinand asked France and the Holy Alliance to supply him with troops to reduce the rebels to obedience. Canning's reaction was prompt. In 1826 he recognised the independence of the republics of Mexico, Peru and Chile, and let it be known in Paris, Vienna and Moscow that the British fleet would if necessary prevent the transport of French, Austrian or Russian troops to Latin America.

British commercial interests were also vitally concerned with Portugal and her Brazilian empire. The exiled prince-regent of Portugal, afterwards John VI, had already shown his gratitude to his British protectors by concluding a commercial treaty in 1810 which gave British merchants extra-territorial rights in Brazil and limited the duties on British goods to 15 per cent as opposed to 24 per cent for foreigners and 16 per cent for Portuguese. But at the end of the Napoleonic War British influence in Portugal was supplanted by that of France, under the restored Bourbons, and the Holy Alliance. John VI had married a termagant sister of Ferdinand of Spain, Carlotta-Joaquina, who had twice conspired with the absolutists to have her husband declared insane. This ill-assorted couple had two sons, Pedro who lived with his father, and Miguel who was completely dominated by his absolutist mother. John himself was reluctant to leave Brazil, where he lived in idle luxury, and the ruling junta in Lisbon was disturbed by the infiltration of republicans and constitutionalists who were organised in Masonic lodges. In 1817 a premature rebellion led by the grand master of the Portuguese Masons, General Gomes Freire, was crushed by the Englishman, Beresford, who was then marshal of the Portuguese army, and Freire was shot. But to prevent further rebellion a *Cortes* was convened to draw up a constitution. In 1821 John was at last persuaded to return to Portugal, and his son, Dom Pedro, at once took advantage of his departure to proclaim himself independent Emperor of Brazil. In Portugal John was induced to accept the constitution, which was soon destroyed by the absolutists who had rallied round the Queen and Miguel. A military rising in Lisbon obliged John to take refuge in a British warship, and Miguel was proclaimed king. Fortunately for John, Canning, true to his peculiar view of non-intervention, had stationed a naval squadron and nearly a thousand marines at Lisbon, and with this assistance John was able to suppress the rising and banish Miguel.

John died in 1826, leaving the thrones of Portugal and Brazil to Dom Pedro who, comfortably ensconced in Brazil, benignly granted a constitutional charter to the Portuguese, which was brought to them by a British envoy. At the same time he announced his abdication of the throne of Portugal in favour of his infant daughter, Maria da Gloria, on condition that she was betrothed to his brother Miguel and that Miguel accepted the new constitution. Miguel was to become regent.

It was a crackpot scheme. Canning sent a British force under General Clinton to Lisbon to ensure the inauguration of the new constitution and to deter Spanish intervention. He also installed Miguel as lieutenant-governor of the realm. The Queen-Mother now descended on Lisbon with her absolutist cohorts, declared Pedro's charter invalid, and had Miguel crowned king. A constitutionalist rising at Oporto in favour of Maria was suppressed, and the refugees were brought to England and lodged in a Plymouth warehouse.

Canning lived just long enough to see the collapse of his whole policy. Portugal under Miguel was now in the camp of France, Spain and the Holy Alliance. Shortly before his death he wrote to Lord Liverpool, "Portugal appears to be the chosen ground on which the Continental Alliance have resolved to fight England hand to hand, and we must be prepared to meet and defeat them . . . or be driven from the field."

But the new Tory government did not share Canning's opinion. The Duke of Wellington, who had conceived a poor opinion of the Portuguese at the time of the Peninsular War, detested all forms of liberalism, thought Pedro a ruffian, and was disposed to recognise Miguel. This brought on his head the full wrath of the Canningites, notably Huskinson and Palmerston. The latter, in his famous speech on June 1st, 1829, roundly denounced both Wellington and Miguel: Canning's policy of non-intervention was both sound in principle and ought to be sacred and Britain should "non-intervene" in Portugal and secure the deposition of Miguel.

The following year Palmerston became Foreign Secretary in the Reform government. At the same time there took place the July Revolution in France and the succession of the "constitutionalist" king, Louis-Philippe. The French, anxious to assert their influence in the Peninsula, began with Palmerston's tacit consent to intervene in Portugal against Miguel. In 1833 Dom Pedro, expelled from Brazil by the Brazilian liberals, set sail for Europe to champion the Portuguese liberals and to recover the throne for his daughter. He established a government at Terceira in the Azores, and from there invaded and seized Oporto, and was at once besieged there by the Miguelists. The situation was further complicated by Metternich, who sent an Austrian force under General Bourmont to help Miguel. It was clear to Palmerston that the time had come for the most energetic non-intervention. An English naval officer, Charles Napier, under the name of Carlo Ponza, was sent with some new steam warships to take command of Pedro's fleet. He defeated and captured Miguel's fleet off Cape St. Vincent. Oporto was relieved and the Pedroist army took Lisbon. Early in the following year Miguel capitulated and was banished to Vienna.

Pedro survived his victory by less than three months. Maria da Gloria was declared of age. Her first husband having died on arrival, she married a German princeling of the Saxe-Coburg family who gave her eleven children and much bad advice. She soon became, in Marx's ungallant phrase, "a huge hill of flesh", and her government, under British protection, one of the most corrupt and oppressive in Europe.

Palmerston cared little about that. Portugal had been saved from the tyranny of France and Austria. It was a "constitutional state" and a "substantive power", by which Palmerston meant that it was a dependency of Britain. The Brazilian market was safe for British merchants and investors.

He also meddled in Spanish affairs. In 1833 Ferdinand VII died, and his queen Maria Cristina assumed the regency for Isabella II, then aged three. As the absolutists had gathered round Miguel in Portugal, so they now gathered round the infant queen's uncle, Don Carlos, in Spain. At the same time an ominous secret meeting between the rulers of the Holy Alliance at Münchengratz caused the deepest suspicion in

France and Britain. It seemed that in return for Austrian consent to Russian expansion in the East, Russia would support Austrian policy in Italy and Spain. Thus when Don Carlos launched his rebellion in 1834, he had the backing of Austria, while France and Britain competed with each other to support the "liberal" government of Isabella.

Isabella's "liberal" government took the form of a series of military dictatorships, some pro-British, like that of Espartero, some pro-French and some just anti-British. Palmerston was then out of office, but when he returned in 1846 he joined in the game with his usual gusto. He ordered Isabella to dismiss her ministers, to restrain her appetite for vengeance on the defeated Carlists, and to follow a pro-British policy. Spain retorted by expelling the British minister, Bulwer, who advised Palmerston to send the fleet to Cadiz.

The fleet was not sent. Palmerston and Bulwer faced a storm of criticism from Parliament and from the Palace, where Palmerston was no great favourite. The Queen wrote that she could not help "being struck how much such matters (i.e. Spain) must have been mismanaged".

The result of Palmerston's meddling in Spain was a triumph for French diplomacy. Already Palmerston and Louis-Philippe had quarrelled on the question of the Spanish marriages. Isabella had been offered the choice of two husbands, one pro-French and one pro-English, both equally repugnant. Not only did she choose the pro-French one but her sister, the Infanta, married Louis-Philippe's son, the Duc de Montpensier, in violation of the Treaty of Utrecht. Palmerston thought that he had been tricked, and heard of Louis-Philippe's fall the next year in the Revolution of 1848 with considerable satisfaction. But the fact remained that British influence in Spain was entirely eclipsed.

7

The victorious powers had in 1814–15 taken precautions against any renewal of French aggression that might disturb them in the enjoyment of their gains. France was encircled by a number of bulwarks: in the east Switzerland; in the south an enlarged Piedmont and the Austrian possessions of Lombardy and Venetia; in the north-east Prussia occupied Luxembourg and controlled the Rhine; and in the north not only were the barrier fortresses taken over by the troops of the Allies, but Belgium had been forcibly united to Holland under the House of Orange.

The creation of the United Kingdom of the Netherlands was a piece of monumental folly. The Belgians differed from the Dutch in language, race, culture and religion. They resented Dutch being the official language, which excluded the Walloons from all public life, and objected to the employment of Dutchmen in all important civil and military offices. Their resentment was encouraged by the French, who naturally wished to break the encirclement.

The matter came to a head after the July Revolution in France of 1830. In September a riot in Brussels changed into a rebellion and six hundred Belgians were killed in the streets by Dutch troops. The King of the Netherlands appealed for help to the Quadruple Alliance to maintain the Vienna settlement, and the representatives of the Great Powers met in London under the chairmanship of Palmerston. Britain was vitally concerned that the mouth of the Scheldt and Antwerp, "a pistol pointed at the heart of Britain", should not fall into the hands of a potentially hostile power. Palmerston therefore strenuously opposed the Austrian and Prussian proposal that Belgium should be partitioned between them, and won the support of the Czar by offering to continue paying the instalments of the notorious Dutch loan.

During the late wars Russia had borrowed from Messrs. Hope and Co. twenty-five million florins. By the Treaty of Vienna, the King of the United Netherlands undertook to pay off this loan on the express condition that there should be no separation of Belgium from Holland. At the same time Britain agreed to take over the main burden of paying these instalments to Russia as an act of compensation for seizing the Dutch colonies. Now Palmerston undertook to continue the payments to Russia after the separation of Belgium from Holland. It was British money, therefore, that the Czar used in suppressing the Polish rebellion. Payments were continued after the seizure of Cracow, a violation of the Vienna Treaty, and, astonishingly, throughout the Crimean War.

Having thus induced the powers to make Belgium an independent kingdom, Palmerston's next task was to secure a king who would be acceptable to Britain. France already had a candidate in Louis-Philippe's second son, the Duc de Nemours, who was unacceptable to everyone except the Belgians. When it appeared likely that the Belgians would accept Nemours, Palmerston staged a naval demonstration and threatened France with war. In this he was supported by the Czar who, disturbed by the July Revolution, was disposed to regard Louis-Philippe as a usurper and crypto-Jacobin.

Nemours withdrew, and Leopold of Coburg, Queen Victoria's meddlesome uncle, was elected king. The Dutch at once invaded Belgium, but were driven out by the French, with the consent of Palmerston. When the French stayed on and showed signs of seizing the barrier fortresses, Palmerston was again obliged to threaten war "within days". Nevertheless he again co-operated with the French in coercing the Dutch to accept the new situation by imposing a naval blockade and impounding Dutch ships. But it was not until 1839 that the Dutch were willing to recognise the *de jure* existence of Belgium. The Treaty of London of that year declared Belgium independent and perpetually neutral under a guarantee of the five great powers. This was the "scrap of paper" invoked by the British Government in its declaration of war in 1914.

8

Among those showing a vulturine interest in the rapid decomposition of the Turkish Empire was Mehemet Ali, the Pasha of Egypt. This former tobacco-seller from Albania ruled Egypt as an an independent monarch although nominally he was only the Sultan's viceroy. A man of ability and enterprise, he dreamed of revitalising and reconstituting the Turkish Empire, which would embrace all Arabic speaking states, with himself as ruler instead of the effete and discredited sultanate in Constantinople. Early in the century he conquered the Sudan and brought the ports and holy cities of Arabia under his control, and formed plans to dominate the Persian Gulf. His price for helping the Sultan in the Greek War of Independence was the cession of various naval and military bases in Greece and Anatolia, all pointed against Constantinople. Here he was foiled by the "untoward" destruction of his fleet at Navarino, but his agents continued to be busy throughout Turkey. Having such ambitions he had no love for the British, whom he had driven out in 1807, but, as an admirer of Napoleon, he had staffed his army with French officers and instructors. While he had private reservations about the French, especially after they had occupied Algiers, France looked on him as an agent through whom she could control the whole southern littoral of the Mediterranean.

In 1831 Mehemet openly rebelled. He sent his son Ibrahim to invade Syria. The Egyptian army under its French officers stormed the fortress of Acre, won the battle of Homs, destroyed the Turkish forces at Konieh and advanced on Constantinople. The distracted Sultan, his throne tottering, found comfort in the assurances of the British ambassador, Sir Stratford Canning, that the English fleet would protect him. But to the astonishment of Peel, Wellington and others, Palmerston, although British imperial interests were vitally involved, proved deaf to all appeals and did nothing at all. It would be a violation of the sacred principle of non-intervention, he explained to a dumbfounded Commons, to protect the Sultan against a rebellious subject. Marx's comment is more than adequate: "*Etiquette* prevented the noble lord from stopping Ibrahim's armies. *Etiquette* forbade his giving instructions to his consul at Alexandria to use his influence with Mehemet Ali. Like the Spanish grandee, the noble lord would rather let the Queen burn to ashes than infringe on *etiquette*, and interfere with her petticoats."

Thus abandoned by Britain, the wretched Sultan Mahmoud was forced to appeal to his dreaded northern neighbour. Russia was only too willing to help, but at a price. A Russian fleet sailed into the Bosphorus, and Russian troops on the Asiatic shore turned their batteries eastwards against Mehemet and seawards against French ships in the Dardanelles. No British fleet appeared to support the French, and the Sultan was obliged to accept the Russian terms, and sign the Treaty of Unkiar Skelessi, by which Turkey agreed to close the Dardanelles to all warships except Russian. Before signing it the Turks sent a copy of this humiliating treaty to the British Embassy with a final appeal for help. The Embassy informed the Russian envoy, who handed back to the Turks the copy of the Treaty with the advice to choose its confidants better. The Sultan was further obliged to recognise Mehemet's control of Syria and Adana.

In 1839 Mehemet struck again, this time with the full

support and encouragement of the French government of Louis-
Philippe. The Egyptians once again destroyed the Turkish
army at Nezib and advanced on Constantinople. The Turkish
fleet mutinied and joined Mehemet. The Sultan shattered by his
defeat died, and there were few who preferred his successor to the
virile Mehemet. Only direct foreign intervention could save the
whole of the Turkish Empire falling into the hands of Mehemet
and his French backers. Louis Philippe was prepared to fight-
Russia, which he considered not to be ready for a major war, and
he had some tacit understanding with Austria, which was
jealous of the Eastern encroachment of her Holy Ally. But this
time Palmerston, in striking contrast to his apathy in the earlier
crisis, sprang to the rescue of Turkey and Russia. He and the
Czar bullied Metternich into joining with Prussia a Quadruple
Alliance against France. The four powers decided to send a
joint naval expedition to the Dardanelles, and to allow a Prussian
army to assemble on the Rhine. Thiers, the French minister,
excitedly talked of war, and was reminded by Palmerston that
if France fought the four powers she would lose "her ships,
colonies and commerce . . . her army of Algiers will cease to
give her anxiety, and Mehemet Ali will just be chucked into the
Nile". English naval forces under Stopford and the dashing
Napier (Carlos da Ponza) captured Beirut and Acre from Mehemet. Louis-Philippe was forced to yield. Thiers was dismissed
and replaced by Guizot, and Mehemet Ali was compelled to
accept the terms offered by the powers. His position of Pasha of
Egypt was to be made hereditary, and he was to receive the
Pashalik of Acre, but he had to give up his claims to Syria and
Adana. The Czar agreed to a new Dardanelles convention by
which the Straits were to be closed to the warships of all the
powers, but open to all merchant ships.

Neither Russia nor France, to say nothing of Egypt and
Turkey, were satisfied by the outcome of the Mehemet Ali
rebellions. The conflict between them over the dismemberment
of Turkey was still to be resolved. The Czar Nicholas visited
London in the hope of getting "an upright and honest understanding" on the Eastern Question, by which he meant the
partition of Turkey between England and Russia. Palmerston
was out of office, and the Tory administration of Peel and
Aberdeen, torn between their distrust of France and suspicions

of Russia, did nothing, although Aberdeen for a while tinkered timidly with the idea of a Russian alliance. Palmerston was again out of office in 1854, when the rivalry in the Near East between France and Russia brought about the Crimean War. Aberdeen, "our own wretched pasha", as Palmerston called him, dithered as usual; the foreign secretary Clarendon mediated so ineptly that he antagonised everyone; Russell, anxious to return to office, identified himself with the popular war clamour; and Palmerston, invited to join the inner cabinet as an adviser, believed that the Czar, "a rational gentleman who could be trusted", would respond to a firm indication of how much of Turkey the Powers would allow him to take without objection. Palmerston was largely responsible for the Vienna Note which the Powers sent to Turkey demanding that the Sultan should accede to the Czar's claim to protect Christians in Moldavia and Wallachia. Nicholas declared himself satisfied with this, but the Sultan, encouraged by Louis-Napoleon, rejected the Note. It was obvious to Aberdeen that the French could not be allowed to "go it" alone in the Near East, and he and Clarendon, without consulting Palmerston, sent the British fleet to join the French in the Dardanelles, thus sliding into a war, which they did not want, which they conducted idiotically and which was concluded ineptly.

9

Palmerston's conduct of the Mehemet Ali crises reinforced the opinion of David Urquhart and other readers of the *Portfolio* that the British Foreign Minister was in fact a paid Russian agent.

Urquhart was an ardent Turkophil and therefore very anti-Russian. A number of damaging Russian documents, which had been seized in Warsaw by the insurgents during the Polish Rebellion had found their way to the Foreign Office. Through his friendship with the King's private secretary, he succeeded in interesting William IV, who hated Russia as much as he did the Duchess of Kent, in these documents. The King compelled a reluctant Palmerston to publish them in the *Portfolio*, with the official Foreign Office imprint. At about the same time Urquhart was appointed Secretary of the British Legation at Constantinople with the special mission of negotiating a

L

favourable commercial treaty with Turkey, which would help to restore Turkish finances and make that country less dependent on Russia. Then the King died. Immediately, Palmerston repudiated the documents published in the *Portfolio*, refused to pay the printer's bill and dismissed Urquhart from his Secretary-ship. This was bad enough, but on top of it came the scandalous affair of the *Vixen*.

By the Treaty of Adrianople in 1829, Russia had acquired from Turkey Circassia, the strategic region between the Black Sea, the Kuban River and the Greater Caucasus. The Circassians continued to resist the Russian occupation for another thirty years, but the Russians in violation of the Treaty, which allowed them only quarantine rights, proceeded to fortify the coast and claimed the right of searching and confiscating refractory foreign ships. The Wellington government had refused to recognise the Treaty of Adrianople, but it proved impossible to get any clear statement from Palmerston on his position, although he did declare that British merchants were within their rights in trading with the Black Sea ports.

Thus encouraged, in October 1836, a London merchant named George Bell sent a merchant ship, the *Vixen*, with a cargo of salt, on a direct voyage to Circassia. A month later the ship was seized at Soudjouk-Kale, off the Circassian coast, by a Russian warship, and the vessel, her cargo and crew were taken to Sevastopol. Here the *Vixen* was declared to be a lawful prize for smuggling salt which the Czar, without informing anybody, had privately decided was a prohibited import. The British flag was hauled down in a humiliating ceremony, the crew escorted to Turkey, the salt confiscated and the ship, re-named the *Soudjouk-Kale*, transferred to the Russian fleet as a transport.

In face of the resulting storm of protest, Palmerston's equivocation was equalled only by that of the Czar. The *Vixen*, it now appeared, had been guilty not of ordinary smuggling but of trying to run the blockade of Circassia proclaimed by the Czar. The real culprit, said Palmerston with characteristic irrelevance, was Austria for recognising the blockade. He denied having misled Bell and Urquhart, in spite of the evidence of the correspondence; on the contrary they had tried and failed to trap him into declaring war on Russia. Russia, he said, was an unaggressive power with no hostile intentions to anyone, and there was no danger of Londoners waking up to find the Czar's fleet in the Thames. Then, after months of dodging in the Commons, he suddenly sent a note to St. Petersburg recognising the Treaty of Adrianople, the Russian annexation of Circassia, and declaring that he saw "no sufficient reason to question the right of Russia to seize and confiscate the *Vixen*".

The Tories moved for a Select Committee to enquire into the allegations made by Bell against the Foreign Secretary. It was revealed during the debate that, on first coming to office in 1831, Palmerston had surreptitiously recognised both the Treaty of Adrianople and the Russian seizure of Circassia. He survived a vote of censure by only sixteen votes.

It is interesting to contrast Palmerston's attitude towards the protection of British subjects and property in the *Vixen* case with his attitude in the Don Pacifico crisis in 1850. Don Pacifico was a shady Portuguese who, having been born in Gibraltar, claimed to be a British subject. During one of the frequent riots in Athens his house had been pillaged, and he alleged that the mob had destroyed documents proving that the Portuguese government owed him £27,000, a sum which he now demanded in compensation from a sceptical Greek government. In support of this unlikely story, Palmerston ordered Admiral Parker to blockade Athens and to seize Greek ships and cargoes as security until the Greek government paid Pacifico the sum demanded.

In justification of this outrageous act, Palmerston made his famous *Civis Romanus Sum* speech: ". . . as the Roman in days of old held himself free from indignity when he could say '*Civis Romanus sum*', so also a British subject, in whatever land he may be, shall feel confident that the watchful eye and strong arm of England will protect him against injustice and wrong."

It would have been instructive to have heard the comments on that speech made by the unfortunate merchant Bell, who, by an act of what amounted to piracy, had lost for ever a valuable ship and cargo.

10

There has always been a tendency to judge politicians by their speeches rather than by their acts, despite Talleyrand's warning that language was invented so that we may conceal our thoughts.

Palmerston's speeches were often inconsistent with his acts and misled rulers and rebels alike. His pose as a constitutionalist and as an enemy of absolutism caused European liberals and nationalists to look upon him as an ally, only to find that at moments of crisis he appeared on the side of the absolutists. In the revolutions of 1848–49, when he was expected to support the Italians and the Hungarians, he made a lengthy speech in the Commons in favour of maintaining the complete integrity of the Austrian Empire, and concluded by saying, "Sir, to suppose that any Government of England can wish to excite revolutionary movements in any part of the world . . . shows a degree of ignorance and folly which I never supposed any public man could have been guilty of . . ." For once his speech was in accordance with his acts. He remained silent and unprotesting at the crushing of the Italians and Piedmontese by the Austrians, at the atrocities of King "Bomba" of Naples, at the invasion of Hungary by Russia, and at the appalling cruelties committed by the Austrians and Russians in Hungary and Croatia. He made no protest when the Russians occupied Transylvania, and at Russian request withdrew the British vice-consul from there because he had sided with the Hungarians; and when Russian troops invaded Rumania and drove out the revolutionaries, he defended their action as in accordance with treaty rights. It should also be noted that when Louis-Napoleon, in 1851, violently overthrew the Republic and proclaimed himself Emperor, the first to send him fulsome congratulations, without consulting the Queen or the Cabinet, was the champion of constitutionalism, Palmerston.

He was popular among the unthinking mass and he tried to live up to his image as "The Most English Minister" who was ready to give impertinent foreigners "a bloody nose"—his own expression, for he was a boxing enthusiast. This courting of popularity often made him unpredictable. When the Austrian general von Haynau, so notorious for his barbarities in Hungary and Italy that he was called by the English press General Hyena, foolishly visited England in 1850 and was thrown into a vat of beer by the draymen at Barclay's brewery, Palmerston offended the Queen, the Cabinet and the Austrian government, by saying that "he only got what he deserved". But this was merely playing up to public opinion, for he remained so pro-Austrian that the next year he refused to receive the Hungarian leader, Kossuth.

On occasion he made anti-Russian noises, but his acts were consistently in support of Russia. Urquhart's allegation that he received Russian money was evidently not given much credence by Marx, who makes no mention of it. Unlike Danton, who, according to Victor Hugo, was incorruptible because although he took bribes he did not deliver the goods, Palmerston delivered the goods without necessarily taking bribes. Marx denounced him for what he was: a brilliant aristocrat who while posing as the champion of liberty was the enemy of the people.

LESTER HUTCHINSON

THE STORY OF THE LIFE
OF LORD PALMERSTON

I

RUGGIERO[1] is again and again fascinated by the false charms of Alcine, which, as he knows, disguise an old witch,—

"Sans teeth, sans eyes, sans taste, sans everything,"

and the knight-errant cannot withstand falling in love anew with her whom he knows to have transmuted all her former adorers into asses and other beasts. The English public is another Ruggiero and Palmerston is another Alcine. Although a septuagenarian, and since 1807 occupying the public stage almost without interruption, he contrives to remain a novelty, and to evoke all the hopes that used to centre on an untried and promising youth. With one foot in the grave, he is supposed not yet to have begun his true career. If he were to die to-morrow, all England would be surprised to learn that he had been a Secretary of State half this century.

If not a good statesman of all work, he is at least a good actor of all work. He succeeds in the comic as in the heroic —in pathos as in familiarity—in tragedy as in farce; although the latter may be more congenial to his feelings. He is not a first-class orator, but an accomplished debater. Possessed of a wonderful memory, of great experience, of consummate tact, of never-failing presence of mind, of gentlemanlike versatility, of the most minute knowledge of Parliamentary tricks, intrigues, parties, and men, he handles difficult cases in an admirable manner and with a pleasant volatility, sticking to the prejudices and susceptibilities of his public, secured from any surprise by his cynical impudence, from any self-confession by his selfish dexterity, from running into a passion by his profound frivolity, his perfect indifference, and his aristocratic contempt. Being an exceedingly happy joker, he ingratiates himself with everybody. Never losing his temper, he imposes on an impassioned antagonist. When unable to master a subject, he knows how to play with it. If wanting in general views, he is always ready to weave a web of elegant generalities.

Endowed with a restless and indefatigable spirit, he abhors inactivity and pines for agitation, if not for action. A country like England allows him, of course, to busy himself in every corner of the earth. What he aims at is not the substance, but the mere appearance of success. If he can do nothing, he will devise anything. Where he dares not interfere, he intermeddles. When unable to vie with a strong enemy, he improvises a weak one. Being no man of deep designs, pondering on no combinations of long standing, pursuing no great object, he embarks on difficulties with a view to disentangle himself from them in a showy manner. He wants complications to feed his activity, and when he finds them not ready, he will create them. He exults in show conflicts, show battles, show enemies, diplomatical notes to be exchanged, ships to be ordered to sail, the whole ending in violent Parliamentary debates, which are sure to prepare him an ephemeral success, the constant and the only object of all his exertions. He manages international conflicts like an artist, driving matters to a certain point, retreating when they threaten to become serious, but having got, at all events, the dramatic excitement he wants. In his eyes, the movement of history itself is nothing but a pastime, expressly invented for the private satisfaction of the noble Viscount Palmerston of Palmerston.

Yielding to foreign influence in fact, he opposes it in words. Having inherited from Canning[2] England's mission to propagate Constitutionalism on the Continent, he is never in need of a theme to pique the national prejudices, to counteract revolution abroad, and, at the same time, to keep awake the suspicious jealousy of foreign powers. Having succeeded in this easy manner in becoming the *bête noire* of the continental courts, he could not fail to be set up as the truly English minister at home. Although a Tory by origin he has contrived to introduce into the management of foreign affairs all the shams and contradictions that form the essence of Whiggism. He knows how to conciliate a democratic phraseology with oligarchic views, how to cover the peace-mongering policy of the middle classes with the haughty language of England's aristocratic past—how to appear as the aggressor where he connives, and as the defender where he betrays—how to manage an apparent enemy, and how to exasperate a pretended ally—how to find himself, at the opportune moment of the dispute, on the side of the stronger against the weak, and how to utter brave words in the act of running away.

Accused by the one party of being in the pay of Russia, he is suspected by the other of Carbonarism.[3] If, in 1848, he had to defend himself against the motion of impeachment for having acted as the minister of Nicholas, he had, in 1850, the satisfaction of being persecuted by a conspiracy of foreign ambassadors, which was successful in the House of Lords, but baffled in the House of Commons. If he betrayed foreign peoples, he did it with great politeness—politeness being the small coin of the devil, which he gives in change for the life-blood of his dupes. If the oppressors were always sure of his active support, the oppressed never wanted a great ostentation of his rhetorical generosity. Poles, Italians, Hungarians, Germans, found him in office whenever they were crushed, but their despots always suspected him of secret conspiracy with the victims he had allowed them to make. Till now, in all instances, it was a probable chance of success to have him for one's adversary, and a sure chance of ruin to have him for one's friend. But, if his art of diplomacy does not shine in the actual results of his foreign negotiations, it shines the more brilliantly in the construction he has induced the English people to put upon them, by accepting phrases for facts, phantasies for realities, and high-sounding pretexts for shabby motives.

Henry John Temple, Viscount Palmerston, deriving his title from a peerage of Ireland, was nominated Lord of the Admiralty, in 1807, on the formation of the Duke of Portland's Administration. In 1809, he became Secretary for War, and continued to hold this office till May, 1828. In 1830, he went over, very skilfully too, to the Whigs, who made him their permanent Secretary for Foreign Affairs. Excepting the intervals of Tory administration, from November, 1834, to April, 1835, and from 1841 to 1846, he is responsible for the whole foreign policy England has pursued from the revolution of 1830 to December, 1851.

Is it not a very curious thing to find, at first view, this Quixote of "free institutions," and this Pindar of the "glories of the constitutional system," a permanent and an eminent member of the Tory administrations of Mr. Percival, the Earl of Liverpool, Mr. Canning, Lord Goderich, and the Duke of Wellington, during the long epoch when the Anti-Jacobin war was carried on, the monster debt contracted, the corn laws promulgated, foreign mercenaries stationed on the English soil, the people—to borrow an expression from his colleague, Lord Sidmouth—"bled" from time to time, the press gagged, meetings suppressed, the mass of the nation disarmed, individual liberty suspended together with regular jurisdiction, the whole country placed as it were under a state of siege—in one word, during the most infamous and most reactionary epoch of English history?

His *début* in Parliamentary life is a characteristic one. On February 3, 1808, he rose to defend—what?—secrecy in diplomatic negotiations, and the most disgraceful act ever committed by one nation against another nation, viz., the bombardment of Copenhagen, and the capture of the Danish fleet, at the time when England professed to be in profound peace with Denmark. As to the former point, he stated that, "in this particular case, his Majesty's ministers are pledged" by whom? "to secrecy"; but he went further: "I also object generally to making public the working of diplomacy, because it is the tendency of disclosures in that department to shut up future sources of information." Vidocq would have defended the identical cause in the identical terms. As to the act of piracy, while admitting that Denmark had evinced no hostility whatever towards Great Britain, he contended that they were right in bombarding its capital and stealing its fleet, because they had to prevent Danish neutrality from being, perhaps, converted into open hostility by the compulsion of France. This was the new law of nations, proclaimed by my Lord Palmerston.

When again speechifying, we find this English minister *par excellence* engaged in the defence of foreign troops, called over from the Continent to England, with the express mission of maintaining forcibly the oligarchic rule, to establish which William had, in 1688, come over from Holland with his Dutch troops. Palmerston answered to the well-founded "apprehensions for the liberties of the country," originating from the presence of the King's German Legion,[4] in a very flippant manner. Why should we not have 16,000 of those foreigners at home, while you know that we employ "a far larger proportion of foreigners abroad"?—(*House of Commons, March* 10, 1812.)

When similar apprehensions for the Constitution arose from the large standing army, maintained since 1815, he found "a sufficient protection of the Constitution in the very Constitution of our army", a large proportion of its officers being "men of property and connections."—(*House of Commons, March 8, 1816.*)

When a large standing army was attacked from a financial point of view, he made the curious discovery that "much of our financial embarrassments has been caused by our former low peace establishment."—(*House of Commons, March 8, 1816.*)

When the "burdens of the country" and the "misery of the people" were contrasted with the lavish military expenditure, he reminded Parliament that those burdens and that misery "were the price which we (viz., the English oligarchy) agreed to pay for our freedom and independence."—(*House of Commons, May 16, 1821.*)

In his eyes, military despotism was not to be apprehended except from the exertions of "those self-called, but misled reformers, who demand that sort of reform in the country, which, according to every first principle of government, must end, if it were acceded to, in a military despotism."—(*House of Commons, June 14, 1820.*)

While large standing armies were thus his panacea for maintaining the Constitution of the country, flogging was his panacea for maintaining the Constitution of the army. He defended flogging in the debates on the Mutiny Bill, on the 5th of March, 1824; he declared it to be "absolutely indispensable" on March 11, 1825; he recommended it again on March 10, 1828; he stood by it in the debates of April, 1833, and he has proved an amateur of flogging on every subsequent occasion.

There existed no abuse in the army he did not find plausible reasons for, if it happened to foster the interests of aristocratic parasites. Thus, for instance, in the debates on the Sale of Commissions.—(*House of Commons, March 12, 1828.*)

Lord Palmerston likes to parade his constant exertions for the establishment of religious liberty. Now, he voted against Lord John Russell's motion for the Repeal of the Test and Corporation Acts.[5] Why? Because he was "a warm and zealous friend to religious liberty," and could, therefore, not allow the

dissenters to be relieved from "imaginary grievances, while real
afflictions pressed upon the Catholics."—(*House of Commons,
February* 26, 1828.)

In proof of his zeal for religious liberty, he informs us of
his "regret to see the increasing numbers of the dissenters.
It is my wish that the established church should be the pre-
dominant church in this country," and from pure love and zeal
for religious liberty he wants "the established church to be fed
at the expense of the misbelievers." His jocose lordship accuses
the rich dissenters of satisfying the ecclesiastical wants of the
poorer ones, while, "with the Church of England, it is the poor
alone who feel the want of church accommodation. . . . It would
be preposterous to say that the poor ought to subscribe for
churches out of their small earnings."—(*House of Commons,
March* 11, 1825.)

It would be, of course, more preposterous yet to say, that the
rich members of the established church ought to subscribe for
the church out of their large earnings.

Let us now look at his exertions for Catholic Emancipation,
one of his great "claims" on the gratitude of the Irish people.
I shall not dwell upon the circumstances, that, having declared
himself for Catholic Emancipation[6] when a member of the
Canning Ministry, he entered, nevertheless, the Wellington
Ministry, avowedly hostile to that emancipation. Did Lord
Palmerston consider religious liberty as one of the rights of man,
not to be intermeddled with by legislature? He may answer for
himself:

"Although I wish the Catholic claims to be considered, I
never will admit these claims to stand upon the ground of
right. . . . If I thought the Catholics were asking for their
right, I, for one, would not go into the committee."—(*House
of Commons, March* 1, 1813.)

And why is he opposed to their demanding their right?

"Because the legislature of a country has the right to impose
such political disabilities upon any class of the community,
as it may deem necessary for the safety and the welfare of the
whole. . . . This belongs to the fundamental principles on
which civilised government is founded."—(*House of Commons,
March* 1, 1813.)

There you have the most cynical confession ever made, that the mass of the people have no rights at all, but that they may be allowed that amount of immunities the legislature—or, in other words, the ruling class—may deem fit to grant them. Accordingly Lord Palmerston declared, in plain words, "Catholic Emancipation to be a measure of grace and favour."—(*House of Commons, February* 10, 1829.)

It was then entirely upon the ground of expediency that he condescended to discontinue the Catholic disabilities. And what was lurking behind this expediency?

Being himself one of the great Irish landed proprietors, he wanted to entertain the delusion that "other remedies for Irish evils than Catholic Emancipation are impossible", that it would cure absenteeism, and prove a cheap substitute for Poor-laws.— (*House of Commons, March* 19, 1829.)

The great philanthropist, who afterwards cleared his Irish estates of their Irish natives, could not allow Irish misery to darken, even for a moment, with its inauspicious clouds, the bright sky of the landlords and moneylords.

> "It is true," he said, "that the peasantry of Ireland do not enjoy all the comforts which are enjoyed by all the peasantry of England [only think of all the comforts enjoyed by a family at the rate of 7s. a week]. Still," he continues, "still, however, the Irish peasant has his comforts. He is well supplied with fuel, and is seldom [only four days out of six] at a loss for food. [What a comfort!] But this is not all the comfort he has—he has a greater cheerfulness of mind than his English fellow-sufferer!"—(*House of Commons, May* 7, 1829.)

As to the extortions of Irish landlords, he deals with them in as pleasant a way as with the comforts of the Irish peasantry.

> "It is said that the Irish landlord insists on the highest possible rent that can be extorted. Why, sir, I believe that is not a singular circumstance; certainly in England the landlord does the same thing."—(*House of Commons, March* 7, 1829.)

Are we then to be surprised that this man, so deeply initiated into the mysteries of the "glories of the English Constitution," and the "comforts of her free institutions," should aspire to spread them all over the Continent?

2

When the Reform Movement had grown irresistible, Lord
Palmerston deserted the Tories, and slipped into the Whig-
gery camp. Although he had apprehended the danger of military
despotism springing up, not from the presence of the King's
German Legion on English soil, nor from keeping large standing
armies, but only from the "self-called reformers", he patronised,
nevertheless, already in 1828, the extension of the franchise to
such large industrial places as Birmingham, Leeds, and Manchester. But why? "Not because I am a friend to Reform, but
because I am its decided enemy."

He had persuaded himself that some timely concessions made
to the overgrown manufacturing interest might be the surest
means of escaping "the introduction of general Reform."—
(*House of Commons, June* 17, 1828.) Once allied with the Whigs,
he did not even pretend that their Reform Bill[7] aimed at breaking
through the narrow trammels of the Venetian Constitution,
but, on the contrary, at the increase of its strength and solidity,
by severing the middle classes from the people's Opposition.
"The feelings of the middle classes will be changed, and their
dissatisfaction will be converted into that attachment to the
Constitution which will give to it a vast increase of strength and
solidity." He consoled the peers by telling them that the Reform
Bill would neither weaken the "influence of the House of Lords",
nor put a stop to its "interfering in elections." He told the
aristocracy that the Constitution was not to lose its feudal
character, "the landed interest being the great foundation upon
which rests the fabric of society and the institutions of the
country." He allayed their fears by throwing out ironical hints
that "we have been charged with not being in earnest or sincere
in our desire to give the people a real representation," that "it
was said we only proposed to give a different kind of influence to
the aristocracy and the landed interest." He went even so far as

to own that, besides the inevitable concessions to be made to the middle classes, "disfranchisement," viz., the disfranchisement of the old Tory rotten boroughs for the benefit of new Whig boroughs, "was the chief and leading principle of the Reform Bill."—(*House of Commons, March* 24, 1831, and *March* 14, 1832.)

It is now time to return to the performances of the noble lord in the foreign branch of policy.

In 1823, when, in consequence of the resolutions of the Congress of Vienna, a French army was marched into Spain, in order to overturn the Constitution of that country, and to deliver it up to the merciless revenge of the Bourbon idiot and his suite of bigot monks, Lord Palmerston disclaimed any "Quixotic crusades for abstract principles," any intervention in favour of the people, whose heroic resistance had saved England from the sway of Napoleon. The words he addressed on that occasion to his Whig adversaries are a true and lively picture of his own foreign policy, after he had become their permanent Minister for Foreign Affairs. He said:

> "Some would have had us use threats in negotiation, without being prepared to go to war, if negotiation failed. To have talked of war, and to have meant neutrality; to have threatened an army, and to have retreated behind a state paper; to have brandished the sword of defiance in the hour of deliberation, and to have ended in a penful of protests on the day of battle, would have been the conduct of a cowardly bully, and would have made us the object of contempt, and the laughing stock of Europe."—(*House of Commons, April* 30, 1823.)

At last we arrive at the Greco-Turkish debates, which afforded Lord Palmerston the first opportunity of displaying publicly his unrivalled talents, as the unflinching and persevering advocate of Russian interests, in the Cabinet and in the House of Commons. One by one, he re-echoed all the watch-words given by Russia of Turkish monstrosities, Greek civilisation, religious liberty, Christianity, and so forth. At first we meet him repudiating, as the Minister for War, any intention of passing "a censure upon the meritorious conduct of Admiral Codrington," which has caused the destruction of the Turkish fleet at

Navarino, although he admits that "this battle took place against
a power with which we are not at war," and that it was "an
untoward event."—(*House of Commons, January* 31, 1828.)

Then, having retired from office, he opened the long series
of his attacks upon Lord Aberdeen,[8] by reproaching him with
having been too slow in executing the orders of Russia.

"Has there been much more energy and promptitude in
fulfilling our engagements to Greece? July, 1829, is coming
fast upon us, and the treaty of July, 1827, is still unexecuted.
. . . The Morea, indeed, has been cleared of the Turks. . . .
But why were the arms of France checked at the Isthmus of
Corinth? . . . The narrow policy of England stepped in, and
arrested her progress. . . . But why do not the allies deal with
the country north of the Isthmus, as they have done with that
to the south, and occupy at once all that which must be
assigned to Greece? I should have thought that the allies had
had enough of negotiating with Turkey about Greece."—
(*House of Commons, June* 1, 1829.)

Prince Metternich[9] was, as is generally known, at that time
opposing the encroachments of Russia, and accordingly her
diplomatic agents—I remind you of the despatches of Pozzo di
Borgo and Prince Lieven—had been advised to represent
Austria as the great enemy of Grecian emancipation and of
European civilisation, the furtherance of which was the exclusive object of Russian diplomacy. The noble lord follows, of
course, in the beaten track.

"By the narrowness of her views, the unfortunate prejudices
of her policy, Austria has almost reduced herself to the level of a
second-rate power"; and in consequence of the temporising
policy of Aberdeen, England is represented as "the keystone of
that arch of which Miguel and Spain, Austria and Mahmoud
are the component parts. . . . People see in the delay in executing
the treaty of July not so much fear of Turkish resistance, as
invincible repugnance to Grecian freedom."—(*House of
Commons, June* 11, 1829.)

For half a century one phrase has stood between Russia and
Constantinople—the phrase of the integrity of the Turkish
Empire being necessary to the balance of power. "I object,"
exclaims Palmerston on February 5, 1830, "to the policy of
making the integrity of the Turkish dominion in Europe an

object essentially necessary to the interests of Christian and civil-ised Europe."

Again he assails Aberdeen because of his anti-Russian diplomacy:

"I, for one, shall not be satisfied with a number of des-patches from the Government of England, which will no doubt read well and smooth enough, urging, in general terms, the propriety of conciliating Russia, but accompanied, perhaps, by strong expressions of the regard which England bears to Turkey, which, when read by an interested party, might easily appear to mean more than was really intended. . . . I should like to see, that whilst England adopted a firm resolution—almost the only course she could adopt—upon no consideration and in no event to take part with Turkey in that war—that that decision was fairly and frankly com-municated to Turkey. . . . There are three most merciless things,—time, fire, and the Sultan."—(*House of Commons, February* 16, 1830.)

Arrived at this point, I must recall to memory some few historical facts, in order to leave no doubt about the meaning of the noble lord's philo-Hellenic feelings.

Russia having seized upon Gokcha, a strip of land bordering on the Lake of Sevan (the indisputed possession of Persia), demanded as the price of its evacuation the abandonment of Persia's claims to another portion of her own territory, the lands of Kapan. Persia not yielding, was overrun, vanquished, and forced to subscribe to the treaty of Turcomanchai, in February, 1828. According to this treaty, Persia had to pay an indemnity of two millions sterling to Russia, to cede the provinces of Erivan and Nakhitchevan, including the fortresses of Erivan and Ab-bassabad, the exclusive purpose of this arrangement being, as Nicholas stated, to define the common frontier by the Araxes, the only means, he pretended, of preventing any future disputes between the two empires. But at the same time he refused to give back Talish and Mogan, which are situated on the Persian bank of the Araxes. Finally, Persia pledged herself to maintain no navy on the Caspian Sea. Such were the origin and the results of the Russo-Persian war.

As to the religion and the liberty of Greece, Russia cared at that epoch as much about them as the god of the Russians cares now about the keys of the Holy Sepulchre, and the famous Cupola. It was the traditional policy of Russia to excite the Greeks to revolt, and, then, to abandon them to the revenge of the Sultan. So deep was her sympathy for the regeneration of Hellas, that she treated them as rebels at the Congress of Verona, acknowledging the right of the Sultan to exclude all foreign intervention between himself and his Christian subjects. In fact, the Czar offered "to aid the Porte[10] in suppressing the rebellion"; a proposition which was, of course, rejected. Having failed in that attempt, he turned round upon the Great Powers with the opposite proposition, "To march an army into Turkey, for the purpose of dictating peace under the walls of the Seraglio." In order to hold his hands bound by a sort of common action, the other Great Powers concluded a treaty with him at London, July 6, 1827, by which they mutually engaged to enforce, if need be by arms, the adjustment of the differences between the Sultan and the Greeks. A few months after she had signed that treaty, Russia concluded another treaty with Turkey, the treaty of Akerman, by which she bound herself to renounce all inter-ference with Grecian affairs. This treaty was brought about after Russia had induced the Crown Prince of Persia to invade the Ottoman dominions, and after she had inflicted the injuries on the Porte in order to drive it to a rupture. After all this had taken place, the resolutions of the London treaty of July 6, 1827, were presented to the Porte by the English Ambassador, or in the name of Russia and the other powers. By virtue of the complications resulting from these frauds and lies Russia found at last the pretext for beginning the war of 1828 and 1829. That war terminated with the treaty of Adrianople, whose contents are summed up in the following quotations from O'Neill's celebrated pamphlet on the "Progress of Russia in the East";

"By the treaty of Adrianople the Czar acquired Anapa and Poti, with a considerable extent of coast on the Black Sea, a portion of the Pashalic of Akhilska, with the fortresses of Akhilska, and Akhalkaliki, the islands formed by the mouths of the Danube. The destruction of the Turkish fortress of Georgilvsk, and the abandonment by Turkey of the right bank of the Danube to the distance of several miles from the river, were stipulated. . . . Partly by force, and partly by the influence of the priesthood, many thousand families of the

M

Armenians were removed from the Turkish provinces in Asia to the Czar's territories. . . . He established for his own subjects in Turkey an exemption from all responsibility to the national authorities, and burdened the Porte with an immense debt, under the name of expenses for the war and for commercial losses—and, finally, retained Moldavia, Wallachia, and Silistria, in pledge for the payment. . . . Having by this treaty imposed upon Turkey the acceptance of the protocol of March 22, which secured to her the suzerainty of Greece, and a yearly tribute from the country, Russia used all her influence to procure the independence of Greece, which was erected into an independent state, of which Count Capo d'Istria, who had been a Russian Minister, was named President."

These are the facts. Now look at the picture drawn of them by the master hand of Lord Palmerston:

"It is perfectly true that the war between Russia and Turkey arose out of aggressions made by Turkey on the commerce and rights of Russia, and violations of treaties."— (*House of Commons, February* 16, 1830.)

When he became the Whig-incarnation of the Minister for Foreign Affairs, he improved upon this statement:

"The honourable and gallant member (Colonel Evans) has represented the conduct of Russia as one of unvarying aggression upon other States, from 1815 to the present time. He adverted more particularly to the wars of Russia with Persia and Turkey. Russia was the aggressor in neither of them, and although the result of the Persian war was an aggrandisement of her power, it was not the result of her own seeking. . . . Again, in the Turkish war, Russia was not the aggressor. It would be fatiguing to the House to detail all the provocations Turkey offered to Russia; but I believe there cannot be a doubt that she expelled Russian subjects from her territory, detained Russian ships, and violated all the provisions of the treaty of Akerman, and then, upon complaint being made, denied redress; so that, if there ever was a just ground for going to war, Russia had it for going to war with Turkey. She did not, however, on any occasion, acquire any increase of territory, at least in Europe. I know there was a continued occupation of certain points [Moldavia and Wallachia are only points, and the mouths of the Danube are mere zeros], and some additional acquisitions on the Euxine in Asia; but she had an agreement with the other European powers that success in that war should not lead to any aggrandisement in Europe."—(*House of Commons, August* 7, 1832.)

My readers will now understand Sir Robert Peel's telling the noble lord, in a public session of the House, that "he did not know whose representative he was."

3

At a recent meeting in London to protest against the action
of the British Embassy in the present controversy between
Russia and Turkey, a gentleman who presumed to find special
fault with Lord Palmerston was saluted and silenced by a storm
of indignant hisses. The meeting evidently thought that if
Russia had a friend in the ministry, it was not the noble viscount,
and would no doubt have rent the air with cheers had some one
been able to announce that his lordship had become prime
minister. This astonishing confidence in a man so false and hollow is another proof of the ease with which people are imposed
on by *brilliant abilities*, and a new evidence of the necessity of
taking off the mask from this wily enemy to the progress of
human freedom.

Accordingly, with the history of the last 25 years and the
debates of Parliament for guides, we proceed with the task of
exposing the real part which this accomplished actor has performed in the drama of modern Europe.

The noble viscount is generally known as the chivalrous
protector of the Poles, and never fails to give vent to his painful
feelings with regard to Poland, before the deputations which are
once every year presented to him by "dear, dull, deadly"
Dudley Stuart,[11] "a worthy who makes speeches, passes resolutions, votes addresses, goes up with deputations, has at all times
the necessary quantity of confidence in the necessary individual,
and can also, if necessary, give three cheers for the Queen."

The Poles had been in arms for about a month, when Lord
Palmerston came into office in November, 1830. As early as
August 8, 1831, Mr. Hunt presented to the House a petition
from the Westminster Union in favour of the Poles, and "for
the dismissal of Lord Palmerston from his Majesty's Councils."
Mr. Hume[12] stated on the same day he concluded from the
silence of the noble lord that the Government "intended to do

nothing for the Poles, but allow them to remain at the mercy of Russia." To this Lord Palmerston replied, "that whatever obligations existing treaties imposed, would at all times receive the attention of the Government." Now, what sort of obligations were, in his opinion, imposed on England by existing treaties? "The claims of Russia," he tells us himself, "to the possession of Poland bear the date of the treaty of Vienna"— (*House of Commons, July* 9, 1833), and that treaty makes this possession dependent upon the observance of the Polish Constitution by the Czar. But from a subsequent speech we learn that "the mere fact of this country being a party to the treaty of Vienna, was not synonymous with our England's guaranteeing that there would be no infraction of that treaty by Russia."— (*House of Commons, March* 26, 1834.)

That is to say, you may guarantee a treaty without guaranteeing that it should be observed. This is the principle on which the Milanese said to the Emperor Barbarossa: "You have had our oath, but remember we did not swear to keep it."

In one respect the treaty of Vienna was good enough. It gave to the British Government, as one of the contracting parties,

"a right to entertain and express an opinion on any act which tends to a violation of that treaty. . . . The contracting parties to the treaty of Vienna had a right to require that the Constitution of Poland should not be touched, and this was an opinion which I have not concealed from the Russian Government. I communicated it *by anticipation* to that Government previous to the taking of Warsaw, and before the result of hostilities was known. I communicated it again when Warsaw fell. The Russian Government, however, took a different view of the question."—(*House of Commons, July* 9, 1833.)

He had quietly anticipated the downfall of Poland, and had availed himself of this opportunity to entertain and express an opinion on certain articles of the treaty of Vienna, persuaded as he was that the magnanimous Czar was merely waiting till he had crushed the Polish people by armed force to do homage to a Constitution he had trampled upon when they were yet possessed of unbounded means of resistance. At the same time the noble lord charged the Poles with having "taken the uncalled for, and in his opinion, *unjustifiable*, step of the dethronement of the Emperor."—(*House of Commons, July* 9, 1832.)

"He could also say that the Poles were the aggressors, for they commenced the contest."—(*House of Commons, August 7, 1832.*)

When the apprehensions that Poland would be extinguished became universal and troublesome, he declared that "to exterminate Poland, either *morally or politically*, is so perfectly impracticable that I think there need be no apprehension of its being attempted."—(*House of Commons, June 28, 1832.*)

When reminded afterwards of the vague expectations thus held out, he averred that he had been misunderstood, that he had said so not in the political but the Pickwickian sense of the word, meaning that the Emperor of Russia was unable "to exterminate *nominally or physically* so many millions of men as the Polish kingdom in its divided state contained."—(*House of Commons, April 20, 1836.*)

When the House threatened to interfere during the struggle of the Poles, he appealed to his ministerial responsibility. When the thing was done, he coolly told them that "no vote of this House would have the slightest effect in reversing the decision of Russia."—(*House of Commons, July 9, 1833.*)

When the atrocities committed by the Russians, after the fall of Warsaw, were denounced, he recommended to the House great tenderness towards the Emperor of Russia, declaring that "no person could regret more than he did the expressions which had been uttered"—(*House of Commons, June 28, 1832*)—that "the present Emperor of Russia was a man of high and generous feelings"—that "where cases of undue severity on the part of the Russian Government to the Poles have occurred, we may set this down as a proof that the power of the Emperor of Russia is practically limited, and we may take it for granted that the Emperor has, in those instances, yielded to the influence of others, rather than followed the dictates of his spontaneous feelings."—(*House of Commons, July 9, 1833.*)

When the doom of Poland was sealed on the one hand, and on the other the dissolution of the Turkish Empire became imminent, from the rebellion of Mehemet Ali,[13] he assured the House that "affairs in general were proceeding in a satisfactory train."—(*House of Commons, January 26, 1832.*)

A motion for granting subsidies to the Polish refugees having been made, it was "exceedingly painful to him to oppose the grant of any money to those individuals, which the natural and spontaneous feelings of every generous man would lead him to acquiesce in; but it was not consistent with his duty to propose any grant of money to those unfortunate persons."—(*House of Commons, March* 25, 1834.)

This same tender-hearted man had secretly defrayed, as we shall see by and by, the cost of Poland's fall, to a great extent, out of the pockets of the British people.

The noble lord took good care to withhold all State papers about the Polish catastrophe from Parliament. But statements made in the House of Commons which he never so much as attempted to controvert, leave no doubt as to the game he played at that fatal epoch.

After the Polish revolution had broken out, the Consul of Austria did not quit Warsaw, and the Austrian Government went so far as to send a Polish agent, M. Walewski, to Paris, with the mission of negotiating with the Governments of France and England about the re-establishment of a Polish kingdom. The Court of the Tuileries declared "it was ready to join England in case of her consenting to the project." Lord Palmerston rejected the offer. In 1831, M. de Talleyrand,[14] the Ambassador of France at the Court of St. James, proposed a plan of combined action on the part of France and England, but met with a distinct refusal and with a note from the noble lord, stating that "an amicable intermediation on the Polish question would be declined by Russia; that the Powers had just declined a similar offer on the part of France; that the intervention of the two Courts of France and England could only be by force in case of a refusal on the part of Russia; and the amicable and satisfactory relations between the Cabinet of St. James and the Cabinet of St. Petersburg, would not allow his British Majesty to undertake such an interference. The time was NOT YET come to undertake such a plan with success against the will of a sovereign whose *rights were indisputable*."

This was not all. On February 23, 1848, Mr. Anstey[15] made the following declaration in the House of Commons:

"Sweden was arming her fleet for the purpose of making a diversion in favour of Poland, and of regaining to herself the provinces in the Baltic, which have been so unjustly wrested from her in the last war. The noble lord instructed our ambassador at the Court of Stockholm in a contrary sense, and Sweden discontinued her armaments. The Persian Court had, with a similar purpose, despatched an army three days on its march towards the Russian frontier, under the command of the Persian Crown Prince. The Secretary of Legation at the court of Teheran, Sir John M'Neill, followed the prince, at a distance of three days' march from his headquarters, overtook him, and there, under instructions from the noble lord, and in the name of England, threatened Persia with war if the prince advanced another step towards the Russian frontier. Similar inducements were used by the noble lord to prevent Turkey from renewing war on her side."

To Colonel Evans, asking for the production of papers with regard to Prussia's violation of her pretended neutrality in the Russo-Polish war, Lord Palmerston replied, "that the ministers of this country could not have witnessed that contest without the deepest regret, and it would be most satisfactory for them to see it terminated."—(*House of Commons, August* 16, 1831.)

Certainly he wished to see it terminated as soon as possible, and Prussia shared in his feelings.

On a subsequent occasion, Mr. H. Gally Knight thus summed up the whole proceedings of the noble lord with regard to the Polish revolution:

"There is something *curiously inconsistent* in the proceedings of the noble lord when Russia is concerned. . . . On the subject of Poland, the noble lord has disappointed us again and again; remember when the noble lord was pressed to exert himself in favour of Poland, then he admitted the justice of the cause —the justice of our complaints; but he said, 'Only restrain yourselves at present, there is an ambassador fast setting out, of known liberal sentiments; you will only embarrass his negotiation, if you incense the Power with whom he has to deal. So, take my advice, be quiet at present, and be assured that a great deal will be effected.' We trusted to those assurances; the liberal ambassador went; whether he ever approached the subject or not was never known, but all we got were the fine words of the noble lord, and no results."—(*House of Commons, July* 13, 1840.)

The so-called kingdom of Poland having disappeared from the map of Europe, there remained still, in the free town of Cracow, a fantastic remnant of Polish nationality. The Czar Alexander, during the general anarchy resulting from the fall of the French Empire, had not conquered the Duchy of Warsaw but simply seized it, and wished, of course, to keep it, together with Cracow, which had been incorporated with the Duchy by Bonaparte. Austria, once possessed of Cracow, wished to have it back. The Czar being unable to obtain it himself, and unwilling to cede it to Austria, proposed to constitute it a free town. Accordingly the Treaty of Vienna stipulated in Article VI, "the town of Cracow with its territory is to be for ever a free, independent and strictly neutral city, under the protection of Austria, Russia, and Prussia"; and in Article IX, "the courts of Russia, Austria, and Prussia, engage to respect, and to cause to be always respected, the neutrality of the free town of Cracow and its territory. *No armed force shall be introduced on any pretence whatever.*"

Immediately after the close of the Polish insurrection of 1830–31, the Russian troops suddenly entered Cracow, the occupation of which lasted two months. This, however, was considered as a transitory necessity of war, and in the turmoil of that time was soon forgotten.

In 1836, Cracow was again occupied by the troops of Austria, Russia, and Prussia, on the pretext of forcing the authorities of Cracow to deliver up the individuals concerned in the Polish revolution five years before.

On this occasion the noble lord refrained from all remonstrance, on the ground, as he stated in 1836 and 1840, "that it was difficult to give effect to our remonstrances." As soon, however, as Cracow was definitely confiscated by Austria, a simple remonstrance appeared to him to be "the only effectual means." When the three northern Powers occupied Cracow in 1836, its Constitution was abrogated, the three consular residences assumed the highest authority—the police was entrusted to Austrian spies—the senate overthrown—the tribunals suspended—the university put down by prohibiting the students of the neighbouring provinces from frequenting it—and the commerce of the free city, with the surrounding countries, destroyed.

In March, 1836, when interpellated on the occupation of Cracow, Lord Palmerston declared that occupation to be of a merely transitory character. Of so palliative and apologetic a kind was the construction he put on the doings of his three northern allies, that he felt himself obliged suddenly to stop and interrupt the even tenor of his speech by the solemn declaration, "I stand not up here to defend the measure, which on the contrary, I MUST censure and condemn. I have merely stated those circumstances which, though they do not excuse the forcible occupation of Cracow, might yet afford a justification, etc. . . ." He admitted that the Treaty of Vienna bound the three Powers to abstain from any step without the previous consent of England, but "they may be justly said to have paid an *involuntary* homage to the justice and plain dealing of this country, by supposing that we would never give our assent to such a proceeding".

Mr. Patrick Stewart having, however, found out that there existed better means for the preservation of Cracow than the "abstention from remonstrance," moved on April 20, 1836, "that the Government should be ordered to send a representative to the free town of Cracow as consul, there being three consuls there from the three other powers, Austria, Russia, and Prussia". The joint arrival of an English and French consul at Cracow would prove an event and must, in any case, have prevented the noble lord from afterwards declaring himself unaware of the intrigues pursued at Cracow by the Austrians, Russians, and Prussians. The noble viscount seeing that the majority of the House was favourable to the motion, induced Mr. Stewart to withdraw it, by solemnly promising that the Government "intended to send a consular agent to Cracow". On March 22, 1837, being interpellated by Lord Dudley Stuart with regard to his promise, the noble lord answered that "he had altered his intention, and had not sent a consular agent to Cracow, and it was not at present his intention to do so." Lord D. Stuart having given notice that he should move for papers to elucidate this singular transaction, the noble viscount succeeded in defeating the motion by the simple process of being absent, and causing the House to be counted out. He never stated why or wherefore he had not fulfilled his pledge, and withstood all attempts to squeeze out of him any papers on the subject.

In 1840, the "temporary" occupation still continued, and

the people of Cracow addressed a memorandum to the Governments of France and England, which says, amongst other things:

"The misfortunes which overwhelm the free city of
Cracow and its inhabitants are such that the undersigned see
no further hope for themselves and their fellow-citizens but
in the powerful and enlightened protection of the Governments of France and England. The situation in which they
find themselves placed gives them a right to invoke the intervention of every Power subscribed to the Treaty of Vienna."

Being interrogated on July 13, 1840, about this petition from
Cracow, Palmerston declared "that between Austria and the
British Government the question of the evacuation of Cracow
remained only a question of time". As to the violation of the
Treaty of Vienna "there were no means of enforcing the opin-
ions of England, supposing that this country was disposed to do
so by arms, because Cracow was evidently a place where no
English action could possibly take place."

Be it remarked, that two days after this declaration, July 15,
1840, the noble lord concluded a treaty with Russia, Austria,
and Prussia, for closing the Black Sea to the English navy,
probably in order that no English action could take place in those
quarters. It was at the very same time that the noble lord renewed the Holy Alliance with those Powers against France. As
to the commercial loss sustained by England, consequent upon
the occupation of Cracow, the noble lord demonstrated that
"the amount of general exports to *Germany* had not fallen off",
which, as Sir Robert Peel [16] justly remarked, had nothing to do
with Cracow, considerable quantities of English merchandise
being sent thither by the Black Sea, Moldavia, and Galicia—
and closely pressed to state his real intentions on the subject and
as to the consular agent to be sent to Cracow, "he thought
that his experience of the manner in which his unfortunate
assertion [made by the noble lord in 1836, in order to escape from
the censure of a hostile House] of an intention to appoint a
British consul at Cracow, had been taken up by honourable
gentlemen opposite, justified him in positively refusing to give
any answer to such a question, which might expose him to
similar unjustifiable attacks."

On August 16, 1846, he stated that "whether the treaty

of Vienna is or is not executed and fulfilled by the great Powers of Europe, depends not upon the presence of a consular agent at Cracow." On January, 28, 1847, Cracow was doomed, and when the noble lord was again asked for the production of papers relative to the *non-appointment* of a British consul at Cracow, he declared that "the subject had *no necessary* connection with the discussion on the incorporation of Cracow, and he saw no advantage in reviving an angry discussion on a subject which had *only a passing interest.*" He proved true to his opinion on the production of State papers, as expressed on March 7, 1837: "If the papers are upon the questions now under consideration, their production would be dangerous; if they refer to questions that are gone by, they can obviously be of no use."

The British Government was, however, very exactly informed of the importance of Cracow, not only from a political but also from a commercial point of view, their consul at Warsaw, Colonel Du Plat, having reported to them that

> "Cracow, since its elevation into an independent State, has always been the depôt of very considerable quantities of English merchandise sent thither by the Black Sea, Moldavia, and Galicia, and even *viâ* Trieste; and which afterwards find their way to the surrounding countries. In the course of years it came into railway communication with the great lines of Bohemia, Prussia, and Austria. . . . It is also the central point of the important line of railway communication between the Adriatic and the Baltic. It will come into direct communication of the same description with Warsaw. . . . Looking, therefore, to the almost certainty of every great point of the Levant, and even of India and China, finding its way up the Adriatic, it cannot be denied that it must be of the greatest commercial importance, even to England, to have such a station as Cracow, in the centre of the great net of railways connecting the Western and Eastern Continents."

Lord Palmerston himself was obliged to confess to the House that the Cracow insurrection of 1846 had been intentionally provoked by the three Powers. "I believe the original entrance of the Austrian troops into the territory of Cracow was in consequence of an application from the Government." But, then, those Austrian troops retired. Why they retired has never yet been explained. With them retired the Government and the authorities of Cracow; the immediate, at least the early, consequence of that retirement, was the establishment of a Provisional Government at Cracow.—(*House of Commons, August* 17, 1846.)

On the 22nd of February, 1846, the forces of Austria, and afterwards those of Russia and Prussia, took possession of Cracow. On the 26th of the same month, the Prefect of Tarnow issued his proclamation calling upon the peasants to murder their landlords, promising them "a sufficient recompense in money," which proclamation was followed by the Galician atrocities, and the massacre of about 2,000 landed proprietors. On the 12th appeared the Austrian proclamation to the "faithful Galicians who have aroused themselves for the maintenance of order and law, and destroyed the enemies of order." In the official *Gazette* of April 28th, Prince Frederick of Schwarzenberg stated officially that "the acts that had taken place had been *authorised* by the Austrian Government," which, of course, acted on a common plan with Russia and with Prussia, the lackey of the Czar. Now, after all these abominations had passed, Lord Palmerston thought fit to declare in the House:

"I have too high an opinion of the sense of justice and of right that must animate the Goverments of Austria, Russia, and Prussia, to believe that they can feel any disposition or intention to deal with Cracow otherwise than Cracow is entitled by treaty-engagements to be dealt with."—(*House of Commons, August* 17, 1846.)

For the noble lord the only business then in hand was to get rid of Parliament, whose session was drawing to a close. He assured the Commons that "on the part of the British Government everything shall be done to ensure a due respect being paid to the provisions of the treaty of Vienna." Mr. Hume giving vent to his doubts about Lord Palmerston's "*intention* to cause the Austro-Russian troops to retire from Cracow," the noble lord begged of the House not to give credence to the statements made by Mr. Hume, as he was in possession of better information, and was convinced that the occupation of Cracow was only a "TEMPORARY" one. The Parliament of 1846 having been got rid of, in the same manner as that of 1843, out came the Austrian proclamation of November 11, 1846, incorporating Cracow with the Austrian dominions. When Parliament re-assembled on January 19, 1847, it was informed by the Queen's speech that Cracow was gone, but that there remained in its place a protest on the part of the brave Lord Palmerston. In order to deprive this protest of even the appearance of a meaning the noble lord contrived, at that very epoch, to engage England in a quarrel with France on the occasion of the Spanish marriages,[17] very nearly setting the two countries by the ears; a performance which was sharply overhauled by Mr. Smith O'Brien in the House of Commons, on April 18, 1847.

The French Government having applied to Palmerston for his co-operation in a joint protest against the incorporation of Cracow, Lord Normanby,[18] under instructions from the noble viscount, answered that the outrage of which Austria had been guilty in annexing Cracow was not greater than that of France in effecting a marriage between the Duke of Montpensier and the Spanish Infanta—the one being a violation of the Treaty of Vienna, and the other of the Treaty of Utrecht. Now, the Treaty of Utrecht, renewed in 1782, was definitely abrogated by the Anti-Jacobin war; and had, therefore, ever since 1792, ceased to be operative. There was no man in the House better informed of this circumstance than the noble lord, as he had himself stated to the House on the occasion of the debates on the blockades of Mexico and Buenos Ayres, that

> "the provisions of the Treaty of Utrecht had long since lapsed in the variations of war, with the exception of the single clause relating to the boundaries of Brazil and French Guiana, because that clause had been expressly incorporated in the Treaty of Vienna."

We have not yet done with the exertions of the noble lord in resisting the encroachments of Russia upon Poland.

There once existed a curious convention between England, Holland, and Russia—the so-called Russian Dutch loan. During the Anti-Jacobin war the Czar, Alexander, contracted a loan with Messrs. Hope & Co., at Amsterdam; and after the fall of Bonaparte, the King of the Netherlands, "desirous to make a suitable return to the Allied Powers for having delivered his territory," and for having annexed to it Belgium, to which he had no claim whatever, engaged himself—the other Powers waiving their common claims in favour of Russia, then in great need of money—to execute a convention with Russia agreeing to pay her by successive instalments the twenty-five million florins she owed to Messrs. Hope & Co. England, in order to cover the robbery she had committed on Holland, of her colonies at the Cape of Good Hope, Demerara, Essequibo, and Berbice, became a party to this convention, and bound herself to pay a certain proportion of the subsidies granted to Russia. This stipulation became part of the Treaty of Vienna, but upon the *express condition* "that the payment should cease if the union between Holland and Belgium were broken prior to the liquidation of the debt." When Belgium separated herself from Holland by a revolution, the latter, of course, refused to pay her portion to Russia on the ground that the loan had been contracted to continue her in the undivided possession of the Belgian provinces, and that she no longer had the sovereignty of that country. On the other hand, there remained, as Mr. Herries stated in Parliament, "not the smallest iota of a claim on the part of Russia for the continuance of debt by England."—(*House of Commons, January* 26, 1832.)

Lord Palmerston, however, found it quite natural that "at one time Russia is paid for supporting the union of Belgium with Holland, and that at another time she is paid for supporting the separation of these countries."—(*House of Commons, July* 16, 1832.)

He appealed in a very tragic manner for the faithful observance of treaties—and above all, of the Treaty of Vienna; and he contrived to carry a new convention with Russia, dated November 16, 1831, the preamble of which expressly stated that it was contracted "in consideration of the general arrangements of the Congress of Vienna which remain in full force."

When the convention relating to the Russian Dutch loan had been inserted in the Treaty of Vienna, the Duke of Wellington exclaimed: "This is a master-stroke of diplomacy on the part of Lord Castlereagh;[19] for Russia has been tied down to the observance of the Vienna treaty by a pecuniary obligation."

When Russia, therefore, withdrew her observance of the Vienna treaty by the Cracow confiscation, Mr. Hume moved to stop any further annual payment to Russia from the British treasury. The noble viscount, however, thought that although

Russia had a right to violate the treaty of Vienna, with regard to Poland, England must remain bound by that very treaty with regard to Russia.

But this is not the most extraordinary incident in the noble lord's proceedings. After the Belgian revolution had broken out, and before Parliament had sanctioned the new loan to Russia, the noble lord defrayed the costs of the Russian war against Poland, under the false pretext of paying off the old debt contracted by England in 1815, although we can state, on the authority of the greatest English lawyer, Sir E. Sugden,[20] now Lord St. Leonards, that "there was not a single debatable point in that question and the Government had no power whatever to pay a shilling of the money"—(*House of Commons, June 26, 1832*); and, on the authority of Sir Robert Peel, "that Lord Palmerston was not warranted by law in advancing the money." —(*House of Commons, July 12, 1832.*)

Now we understand why the noble lord reiterates on every occasion that "nothing can be more painful to a man of proper feeling, than discussions upon the subject of Poland." We can also appreciate the degree of earnestness he is now likly to exhibit in resisting the encroachments of the Power he has so uniformly served.

4

The great and eternal themes of the noble viscount's self-glorification are the services he has rendered to the cause of constitutional liberty all over the Continent. The world owes him, indeed, the inventions of the "constitutional" kingdoms of Portugal, Spain, and Greece,—three political phantoms, only to be compared with the *homunculus* of Wagner in "Faust". Portugal, under the yoke of that huge hill of flesh, Donna Maria da Gloria,[21] backed by a Coburg, "must be looked upon as one of the *substantive* Powers of Europe."—(*House of Commons, March* 10, 1835.)

At the very time the noble viscount uttered these words, six British ships of the line anchored at Lisbon, in order to defend the "substantive" daughter of Don Pedro from the Portuguese people, and to help her to destroy the constitution she had sworn to defend. Spain, at the disposition of another Maria,[22] who, although a notorious sinner, has never founded a Magdalen, "holds out to us a fair, a flourishing, and even a formidable power among the European kingdoms."—(*Lord Palmerston, House of Commons, March* 10, 1837.)

Formidable, indeed, to the holders of Spanish bonds. The noble lord has even his reasons ready for having delivered the native country of Pericles and Sophocles to the nominal sway of an *idiot Bavarian boy*.[23] "King Otho belongs to a country where there exists a free constitution."—(*House of Commons, August* 8, 1832.)

A free constitution in Bavaria, the German Bastia! This passes the *licentia poetica* of rhetorical flourish, the "legitimate hopes" held out by Spain, and the "substantive" power of Portugal. As to Belgium, all Lord Palmerston did for her was burdening her with a part of the Dutch debt, reducing it by the Province of Luxemburg, and saddling her with a Coburg dynasty. [24] As to the *entente cordiale* with France, waning from

N

the moment he pretended to give it the finishing touch by the Quadruple alliance of 1834, we have already seen how well the noble lord understood how to manage it in the instance of Poland, and we shall hear, by and by, what became of it in his hands.

One of those facts, hardly adverted to by contemporaries, but broadly marking the boundaries of historical epochs, was the military occupation of Constantinople by the Russians, in 1833.

The eternal dream of Russia was at last realized. The barbarian from the icy banks of the Neva held in his grasp luxurious Byzantium, and the sunlit shores of the Bosphorus. The self-styled heir to the Greek Emperors occupied however temporarily the Rome of the East.

> "The occupation of Constantinople by Russian troops sealed the fate of Turkey as an independent power. The fact of Russia having occupied Constantinople even for the purpose (?) of saving it, was as decisive a blow to Turkish independence as if the flag of Russia now waved on the Seraglio."—(*Sir Robert Peel, House of Commons, March* 17, 1834.)

In consequence of the unfortunate war of 1828–29 and the Treaty of Adrianople,[25] the Porte had lost its prestige in the eyes of its own subjects. As usual with Oriental empires, when the paramount power is weakened, successful revolts of Pashas broke out. As early as October, 1831, commenced the conflict between the Sultan and Mehemet Ali, the Pasha of Egypt, who had supported the Porte during the Greek insurrection. In the spring of 1832, Ibrahim Pasha, his son, marched his army into Syria, conquered that province by the battle of Homs, crossed the Taurus, annihilated the Turkish army at the battle of Konieh, and moved on the way to Stamboul. The Sultan was forced to apply to St. Petersburg on February 2, 1833. On February 17, the French Admiral Roussin arrived at Constantinople, remonstrated with the Porte two days afterwards, and engaged for the retreat of the Pasha on certain terms, including the refusal of Russian assistance; but, unassisted, he was, of course, unable to cope with Russia. "You have asked for me, and you shall have me."

On February 20, a Russian squadron suddenly sailed from Sebastopol, disembarked a large force of Russian troops on the

shores of the Bosphorus, and laid siege to the capital. So eager
was Russia for the protection of Turkey, that a Russian officer
was simultaneously despatched to the Pashas of Erzerum and
Trebizond, to inform them that, in the event of Ibrahim's army
marching towards Erzerum, both that place and Trebizond
should be immediately protected by a Russian army. At the end
of May, 1833, Count Orloff*[26] arrived from St. Petersburg, and
intimated to the Sultan that he had brought with him a little
bit of paper, which the Sultan was to subscribe to, without the
concurrence of any minister, and without the knowledge of
any diplomatic agent at the Porte. In this manner the famous
treaty of Unkiar Skelessi[27] was brought about; it was concluded
for eight years to come. By virtue of it the Porte entered into an
alliance, offensive and defensive, with Russia; resigned the right
of entering into any new treaties with other powers, except with
the concurrence of Russia, and confirmed the former Russo-
Turkish treaties, especially that of Adrianople. By a secret
article, appended to the treaty, the Porte obliged itself "in favour
of the Imperial Court of Russia to close the Straits of the Dardanelles—viz., not to allow any foreign man-of-war to enter it
under any pretext whatever."

To whom was the Czar indebted for occupying Constan-
tinople by his troops and for transferring, by virtue of the treaty
of Unkiar Skelessi, the supreme seat of the Ottoman empire
from Constantinople to St. Petersburg? To nobody else but to the
Right Honourable Henry John Viscount Palmerston, Baron
Temple, a Peer of Ireland, a Member of His Majesty's Most
Honourable Privy Council, Knight of the Grand Cross of the
Most Honourable Order of the Bath, a Member of Parliament,
and His Majesty's Principal Secretary of State for Foreign
Affairs.

The treaty of Unkiar Skelessi was concluded on July 8,
1833. On July 11, 1833, Mr. H. L. Bulwer[28] moved for the
production of papers with respect to the Turco-Syrian affairs.
The noble lord opposed the motion

"because the *transactions* to which the papers called for
referred were *incomplete*, and the character of the whole
transaction would depend upon its termination. As the results

* The same Count Orloff was lately designated by *The Times* as the "head of the
Russian peace-party," and is now on a *pacific* errand to Vienna.

were not yet known, the motion was premature."—(*House of Commons, July* 11, 1833.)

Accused by Mr. Bulwer of not having interfered for the defence of the Sultan against Mehemet Ali, and thus prevented the advance of the Russian army, he began that curious system of defence and of confession, developed on later occasions, the *membra disjecta* of which I shall now gather together.

> "He was not *prepared* to deny that in the later part of last year an application was made on the part of the Sultan to this country for assistance."—(*House of Commons, July* 11, 1833.)
> "The Porte made formal application for assistance in the in the course of August."—(*House of Commons, August* 24, 1833.)

No, not in August. "The request of the Porte for naval assistance had been in the month of October, 1832."—(*House of Commons, August* 28, 1833.)

No, it was not in October. "Its assistance was asked by the Porte in November, 1832."—(*House of Commons, March* 17, 1834.)

The noble lord is as uncertain of the day when the Porte implored his aid, as Falstaff was of the number of rogues in buckram suits, who came at his back in Kendal green. He is not prepared, however, to deny that the armed assistance offered by Russia was rejected by the Porte, and that he, Lord Palmerston, was applied to. He refused to comply with its demands. The Porte again applied to the noble lord. First it sent M. Maurageni to London; then sent Namic Pasha, who entreated the assistance of a naval squadron on condition of the Sultan undertaking to defray all the expenses of that squadron, and promising in requital for such succour the grant of new *commercial* privileges and advantages to British subjects in Turkey. So sure was Russia of the noble lord's refusal, that she joined the Turkish envoy in praying his lordship to afford the succour demanded. He tells us himself:

> "It was but justice that he should state, that so far from Russia having expressed any jealousy as to this Government granting this assistance, the Russian ambassador officially communicated to him, while the request was still under consideration, that he had learned that such an application

had been made, and that, from the interest taken by Russia in the maintenance and preservation of the Turkish empire, it would afford satisfaction if ministers could find themselves able to comply with that request."—(*House of Commons, August* 28, 1833.)

The noble lord remained, however, inexorable to the demand of the Porte, although backed by disinterested Russia herself. Then, of course, the Porte knew what it was expected to do. It understood that it was doomed to make the wolf shepherd. Still it hesitated, and did not accept Russian assistance till three months later.

"Great Britain," says the noble lord, "never complained of Russia granting that assistance, but, on the contrary, was glad that Turkey had been able to obtain effectual relief from any quarter."—(*House of Commons, March* 17, 1834.)

At whatever epoch the Porte may have implored the aid of Lord Palmerston, he cannot but own that

"no doubt if England had thought fit to interfere, the progress of the invading army would have been stopped, and the Russian troops would not have been called in."—(*House of Commons, July* 11, 1833.)

Why then did he not "think fit" to interfere and to keep the Russians out?

First he pleads *want of time*. According to his own statement the conflict between the Porte and Mehemet Ali arose as early as October, 1831, while the decisive battle of Konieh was not fought till December 21, 1832. Could be find no time during all this period? A great battle was won by Ibrahim Pasha,[29] in July, 1832, and again he could find no time from July to December. But he was all that time waiting for a *formal* application on the part of the Porte which, according to his last version, was not made till the 3rd of November. "Was he then," asks Sir Robert Peel, "so ignorant of what was passing in the Levant, that he must wait for a formal application?"—(*House of Commons, March* 17, 1834.) And from November, when the formal application was made, to the latter part of February, there elapsed again four long months, and Russia did not arrive until February 20, 1833. Why did not he?

But he has better reasons in reserve.

The Pasha of Egypt was but a rebellious subject, and the Sultan was the Suzerain.

"As it was a war against the sovereign by a subject, and that sovereign was in alliance with the King of England, it would have been inconsistent with good faith to have had *any communication* with the Pasha."—(*House of Commons, August* 28, 1833.)

Etiquette prevented the noble lord from stopping Ibrahim's armies. *Etiquette* forbade his giving instructions to his consul at Alexandria to use his influence with Mehemet Ali. Like the Spanish grandee, the noble lord would rather let the Queen burn to ashes than infringe on *etiquette*, and interfere with her petticoats. As it happens the noble lord had already, in 1832, accredited consuls and diplomatic agents to the "subject" of the Sultan without the consent of the Sultan; he had entered into treaties with Mehemet, altering existing regulations and arrangements touching matters of trade and revenue, and establishing other ones in their stead; and he did so without having the consent of the Porte beforehand, or caring for its approbation afterwards—(*House of Commons, February* 23, 1848.)

Accordingly, we are told by Earl Grey, the then chief of the noble viscount, that "they had at the moment extensive commercial relations with Mehemet Ali which it would not have been their interest to disturb."—(*House of Commons, February* 4, 1834.)

What, commercial relations with the "rebellious subject"!

But the noble viscount's fleets were occupied in the Douro, and the Tagus, and blockading the Scheldt, and doing the services of midwife at the birth of the constitutional empires of Portugal, Spain, and Belgium, and he was, therefore, not in a position to spare one single ship—(*House of Commons, July* 11, 1833, and *March* 17, 1834).

But what the Sultan insisted on was precisely naval assistance. For argument's sake, we will grant the noble lord to have been unable to dispose of one single vessel. But there are great authorities assuring us that what was wanted was not a single *vessel*, but only a single *word* on the part of the noble lord. There is Lord Mahon, who had just been employed at the Foreign

Office under Sir Robert Peel, when he made this statement. There is Admiral Codrington,[30] the destroyer of the Turkish fleet at Navarino.

"Mehemet Ali," he states, "had of old felt the strength of our representations on the subject of the evacuation of the Morea. He had then received orders from the Porte to resist all applications to induce him to evacuate it, at the risk of his head, and he did resist accordingly, but at last prudently yielded, and evacuated the Morea."—(*House of Commons, April* 20, 1836.)

There is the Duke of Wellington.

"If, in the session of 1832 or 1833, they had plainly told Mehemet Ali that he should not carry on his contest in Syria and Asia Minor, they would have put an end to the war without the risk of allowing the Emperor of Russia to send a fleet and an army to Constantinople."—(*House of Lords, February* 4, 1834.)

But there are still better authorities. There is the noble lord himself.

"Although," he says, "his Majesty's Government did not comply with the demand of the Sultan for naval assistance, yet the moral assistance of England was afforded; and the communications made by the British Government to the Pasha of Egypt, and to Ibrahim Pasha commanding in Asia Minor, did materially contribute to bring about that arrangement (of Kiutayah) between the Sultan and the Pasha, by which that war was terminated."—(*House of Commons, March* 17, 1834.)

There is Lord Derby, then Mr. Stanley and a member of the Palmerston Cabinet, who

"boldly asserts that what stopped the progress of Mehemet Ali was the distinct declaration of France and England that they would not permit the occupation of Constantinople by his troops."—(*House of Commons, March* 17, 1834.)

Thus then, according to Lord Derby and to Lord Palmerston himself, it was not the Russian squadron and army at Constantinople, but it was a *distinct declaration* on the part of the British consular agent at Alexandria, that stopped Ibrahim's victorious march upon Constantinople, and brought about the arrangement of Kiutayah, by virtue of which Mehemet Ali obtained, besides Egypt, the Pashalic of Syria, of Adana and other places, added as an appendage. But the noble lord thought fit not to allow his consul at Alexandria to make this distinct declaration till after the Turkish army was annihilated, Constantinople overrun by the Cossack, the treaty of Unkiar Skelessi signed by the Sultan, and pocketed by the Czar.

If want of time and want of fleets forbade the noble lord to assist the Sultan, and a superfluity of *etiquette* to check the Pasha, did he at least employ his ambassador at Constantinople to guard against excessive influence on the part of Russia, and to keep her influence confined within narrow bounds? Quite the contrary. In order not to clog the movements of Russia, the lord took good care to have no ambassador at all at Constantinople during the most fatal period of the crisis.

> "If ever there was a country in which the weight and station of an ambassador were useful—or a period in which that weight and station might be advantageously exerted—that country was Turkey, during the six months before the 8th of July."—(*Lord Mahon, House of Commons, April* 20, 1836.)

Lord Palmerston tells us, that the British ambassador, Sir Stratford,[31] left Constantinople in September, 1832—that Lord Ponsonby, then at Naples, was appointed in his place in November, and that "difficulties experienced in making the necessary arrangements for his conveyance," although a man-of-war was in waiting for him, "and the unfavourable state of the weather prevented his getting to Constantinople until the end of May, 1833."—(*House of Commons, March* 17, 1834.)

The Russian was not yet in, and Lord Ponsonby was accordingly ordered to require seven months for sailing from Naples to Constantinople.

But why should the noble lord prevent the Russians from occupying Constantinople? "He, for his part, had great *doubts* that any intention to *partition* the Oottman empire at all entered into the policy of the Russian Government."—(*House of Commons, February* 14, 1839.)

Certainly not. Russia wants not to partition the empire,

but to keep the whole of it. Besides the security Lord Palmerston possessed in this *doubt*, he had another security

"in the *doubt* whether it enters into the policy of Russia *at present* to accomplish the object, and a third 'security' in his third '*doubt*' whether the Russian nation (just think of a Russian *nation*!) would be prepared for that transference of power, of residence, and authority to the southern provinces which would be the necessary consequence of the conquest by Russia of Constantinople."—(*House of Commons, July* 11, 1833.)

Besides these negative arguments, the noble lord had an affirmative one:

"If they had quietly beheld the temporary occupation of the Turkish capital by the forces of Russia, it was because they had full confidence in the honour and good faith of Russia. The Russian Government, in granting its aid to the Sultan, has pledged its honour, and in that pledge he reposed the most implicit confidence."—(*House of Commons, July* 11, 1853.)

So inaccessible, indestructible, integral, imperishable, inexpugnable, incalculable, incommensurable, and irremediable, so boundless, dauntless, and matchless was the noble lord's confidence, that still on March 17, 1834, when the Treaty of Unkiar Skelessi had become a *fait accompli*, he went on declaring that, "in their confidence ministers were not deceived." Not his is the fault if nature has developed his bump of confidence to altogether anomalous dimensions.

5

The contents of the Treaty of Unkiar Skelessi were published in the *Morning Herald* of August 21, 1833. On August 24, Sir Robert Inglis asked Lord Palmerston, in the House of Commons,

"whether there really had been concluded a treaty, offensive and defensive, between Russia and Turkey? He hoped that the noble lord would be prepared before the prorogation of Parliament, to lay before the House, not only the treaties that had been made, but all communications connected with the formation of those treaties between Turkey and Russia." Lord Palmerston answered that "when they were *sure* that such a treaty as that alluded to really did exist, and when they were in possession of that treaty, it would *then* be for them to determine what was the course of policy they ought to pursue. . . . It could be no blame to him if the newspapers were sometimes beforehand with the Government."—(*House of Commons, August* 24, 1833.)

Seven months afterwards, he assures the House that

"it was perfectly impossible that the treaty of Unkiar Skelessi, not to be ratified at Constantinople until the month of September, should have been officially known to him in August."—(*House of Commons, March* 17, 1834.)

He did know of the treaty, in August, but not *officially*.

"The British Government was surprised to find that when the Russian troops quitted the Bosphorus, they carried that treaty with them."—(*Lord Palmerston, House of Commons, March* 1, 1848.)

Yes, the noble lord was in possession of the treaty *before* it had been concluded.

"No sooner had the Porte received it (namely, the draft of the treaty of Unkiar Skelessi), than the treaty was communicated by them to the British Embassy at Constantinople, with the prayer for our protection against Ibrahim Pasha and against Nicholas. The application was rejected—but that was not all. With an atrocious perfidiousness, the fact was made known to the Russian Minister. Next day, the very copy of the treaty which the Porte had lodged with the British Embassy, was returned to the Porte by the Russian Ambassador, who ironically advised the Porte—'to choose better another time its confidants.' "—(*Mr. Anstey, House of Commons, February* 8, 1848.)

But the noble viscount had obtained all he cared for. He was interrogated with respect to the Treaty of Unkiar Skelessi, of whose existence he was not *sure*, on August 24, 1833. On August 29, Parliament was prorogued, receiving from the throne the consolatory assurance that "the hostilities which had disturbed the peace of Turkey had been terminated, and they might be assured that the King's attention would be carefully directed to any events which might affect the present state or the future independence of that Empire."

Here, then, we have the key to the famous Russian Treaties of July. In July they are concluded; in August something about them is transpiring through the public press. Lord Palmerston is interrogated in the Commons. He, of course, is aware of nothing. Parliament is prorogued,—and, when it reassembles, the treaty has grown old, or, as in 1841, has already been executed, in spite of public opinion.

Parliament was prorogued on August 29, 1833, and it reassembled on February 5, 1834. The interval between the prorogation and its reassembling was marked by two incidents intimately interwoven with each other. On the one hand, the united French and English fleets proceeded to the Dardanelles, displayed there the tricolour and the Union Jack, sailed on their way to Smyrna, and returned from thence to Malta. On the other hand, a new treaty was concluded between the Porte and Russia on January 29, 1834,—the Treaty of St. Petersburg. This treaty was hardly signed when the united fleet was withdrawn.

This combined manœuvre was intended to stultify the British people and Europe into the belief that the hostile demonstration on the Turkish seas and coasts, directed against the Porte, for having concluded the Treaty of Unkiar Skelessi, had enforced upon Russia the new Treaty of St. Petersburg. This treaty, by promising the evacuation of the Principalities, and reducing the Turkish payments to one-third of the stipulated amount, apparently relieved the Porte from some engagements enforced on it by the Treaty of Adrianople. In all other instances it was a simple ratification of the Treaty of Adrianople, not at all relating to the Treaty of Unkiar Skelessi, nor dropping a single word about the passage of the Dardanelles. On the contrary, the small alleviations it granted to Turkey were the purchase money for the exclusion of Europe, by the Treaty of Unkiar Skelessi, from the Dardanelles.

> "At the very time at which the demonstration (of the British fleet) was being made, an assurance was given by the noble lord to the Russian Ambassador at this court, that this combined movement of the squadrons was not intended in any sense hostile to Russia, nor to be taken as a hostile demonstration against her; but that, in fact, it meant nothing at all. I say this on the authority of Lord Ponsonby, the noble lord's own colleague, the Ambassador at Constantinople."—(*Mr. Anstey, House of Commons, February* 23, 1848.)

After the Treaty of St. Petersburg had been ratified, the noble lord expressed his satisfaction with the moderation of the terms imposed by Russia.

When Parliament had reassembled, there appeared in the *Globe*, the organ of the Foreign Office, a paragraph stating that

> "the Treaty of St. Petersburg was a proof either of the moderation or good sense of Russia, or of the influence which the union of England and France, and the firm and concerted language of those two powers, had acquired in the councils of St. Petersburg."—(*Globe, February* 24, 1835.)

Thus, on the one hand, the Treaty of Adrianople, protested against by Lord Aberdeen and the Duke of Wellington, was surreptitiously to be recognised on the part of England by Lord Palmerston officially expressing his satisfaction with the Treaty of St. Petersburg, which was but a ratification of that treaty; on the other hand, public attention was to be diverted from the Treaty of Unkiar Skelessi, and the animosity it had aroused in Europe against Russia was to be soothed down.

Artful as the dodging was, it would not do. On March 17,

1834, Mr. Sheil brought in a motion for "the copies of any treaties between Turkey and Russia, and of any correspondence between the English, Russian, and Turkish Governments, respecting those treaties, to be laid before the House."

The noble lord resisted this resolution to his utmost, and succeeded in baffling it by assuring the House that "peace could be preserved only by the House reposing confidence in the Government," and refusing to accede to the motion. So grossly contradictory were the reasons which he stated prevented him from producing the papers, that Sir Robert Peel called him, in his parliamentary language, "a very inconclusive reasoner", and his own Colonel Evans could not help exclaiming:—"The speech of the noble lord appeared to him the most unsatisfactory he had ever heard from him."

Lord Palmerston strove to convince the House that, according to the *assurances* of Russia, the Treaty of Unkiar Skelessi was to be looked upon "as one of reciprocity," that reciprocity being, that if the Dardanelles should be closed against England in the event of war, they should be closed against Russia also. The statement was altogether false, but if true, this certainly would have been Irish reciprocity, for it was all on one side. To cross the Dardanelles is for Russia not the means to get at the Black Sea, but, on the contrary, to leave it.

So far from refuting Mr. Sheil's statement that "the consequence [of the Treaty of Unkiar Skelessi] was precisely the same as if the Porte surrendered to Russia the possession of the Dardanelles," Lord Palmerston owned "that the treaty closed the Dardanelles to British men-of-war, . . . and that under its provision even *merchant vessels* might, . . . in effect, be practically excluded from the Black Sea," in the case of a war between England and Russia. But if the Government acted "with temper," if it "showed no unnecessary distrust," that is to say, if it quietly submitted to all further encroachments of Russia, he was "inclined to think that the case might not arise in which that treaty would be called into operation; and that, therefore, it would in practice remain a dead letter."—(*House of Commons, March* 17, 1834.)

Besides, "the assurances and explanations" which the British Government had received from the contracting parties to that treaty greatly tended to remove its objections to it. Thus, then.

it was not the articles of the Treaty of Unkiar Skelessi, but the assurances Russia gave with respect to them, not the acts of Russia, but her language, he had, in his opinion, to look upon. Yet, as on the same day his attention was called to the protest of the French *Chargé d'Affaires*, M. Le Grenée, against the Treaty of Unkiar Skelessi, and the offensive and contumelious language of Count Nesselrode, answering in the *St. Petersburg Gazette*, that "the Emperor of Russia would act as if the declaration contained in the note of Le Grenée had no existence"—the noble lord, eating his own words, propounded the opposite doctrine that "it was on all occasions the duty of the English Government to look to the acts of a foreign Power, rather than to the language which the Power might hold, on any particular subject or occasion."

One moment he appealed from the acts of Russia to her language, and the other from her language to her acts.

In 1837 he still assured the House that the "Treaty of Unkiar Skelessi was a treaty between two independent Powers." —(*House of Commons, December* 14, 1837.)

Ten years later, the treaty having long since lapsed, and the noble lord being just about to act the play of the truly English minister, and the "civis Romanus sum," he told the House plainly, *"the Treaty of Unkiar Skelessi was no doubt to a certain degree forced upon Turkey by Count Orloff, the Russian envoy, under circumstances* [created by the noble lord himself] which rendered it difficult for Turkey to refuse acceding to it. . . . It gave practically to the Russian Government a power of interference and dictation in Turkey, not consistent with the independence of that state."—(*House of Commons, March* 1, 1848.)

During the whole course of the debates about the Treaty of Unkiar Skelessi, the noble lord, like the clown in the comedy, had an answer of most monstrous size, that must fit all demands and serve all questions—the Anglo-French Alliance. When his connivance with Russia was pointed at in sneers, he gravely retorted:

"If the present relations established between this country and France were pointed at in these sneers, he would only say, that he should look with feelings of pride and satisfaction at the part he had acted in bringing about that good understanding."—(*House of Commons, July* 11, 1833.)

When the production of the papers relating to the Treaty of Unkiar Skelessi was demanded, he answered that "England and France had now cemented a friendship which had only grown stronger."—(*House of Commons, March* 17, 1834.)

"He could but remark," exclaimed Sir Robert Peel, "that whenever the noble lord was thrown into a difficulty as to any part of our European policy, he at once found a ready means of escape, by congratulating the House upon the close alliance between this country and France."

Simultaneously the noble lord took good care not to quench the suspicions of his Tory opponents, that he had "been compelled to connive at the aggression upon Turkey by Mehemet Ali," because France had directly encouraged it.

At that time, then, the ostensible *entente* with France was to cover the secret infeoffment to Russia, as in 1840 the clamorous rupture with France was to cover the official alliance with Russia.

While the noble lord fatigued the world with ponderous folios of printed negotiations on the affairs of the constitutional kingdom of Belgium and with ample explanations, verbal and documentary, with regard to the "substantive power" of Portugal, to this moment it has proved quite impossible to wrest out of him any document whatever relating to the first Syrio-Turkish War, and to the Treaty of Unkiar Skelessi. When the production of the papers was first demanded, on July 11, 1833, "the motion was premature, . . . the transactions incomplete, . . . and the results *not yet* known."

On August 24, 1833, "the treaty was not officially signed, and he was not in possession of it." On March 17, 1834, "communications were still carrying on . . . the discussions, if he might so call them, were not yet completed." Still in 1848, when Mr. Anstey told him that in asking for papers he did not ask for the proof of the noble lord's collusion with the Czar, the chivalrous minister preferred killing time by a five hours' speech, to killing suspicion by self-speaking documents. Notwithstanding all this, he had the cynical impudence to assure Mr. T. Attwood, on December 14, 1837, that "the papers connected with that treaty [viz., the Treaty of Unkiar Skelessi] were laid before the House three years ago," that is to say in 1834, when "peace could be preserved only" by withholding them from the House. In 1834, he enjoined the House not to press him, as "*peace* could be preserved only by the House reposing confidence in the Government," which, if left alone, would certainly protect the interests of England from encroachment. Now in 1837, in a thin House, composed almost entirely of his retainers, he told Mr. Attwood, that it had never been "the intention of the Government to have recourse to *hostile measures* to compel Russia and Turkey, two independent Powers, to cancel the treaty made between them."

On the same day, he told Mr. Attwood that "this treaty was a matter which had gone by, it was entered into for a limited period, . . . and that period having expired, its introduction by the honourable member . . . was wholly unnecessary and uncalled for."

According to the original stipulation, the Treaty of Unkiar Skelessi was to expire on July 8, 1841. Lord Palmerston tells Mr. Attwood that it had already expired on December 14, 1837.

"What trick, what device, what starting hole, canst thou now find to hide thee from this open and apparent shame? Come, let's hear, Jack—what trick hast thou now?"[32]

6

There is no such word in the Russian vocabulary as "honour."
As to the thing itself, it is considered to be a French delusion.

"*Schto takoi honneur? Ett Fransusski chimere*," is a Russian
proverb. For the invention of Russian honour the world is
exclusively indebted to my Lord Palmerston, who, during a
quarter of a century, used at every critical moment to pledge
himself in the most emphatic manner, for the "honour" of the
Czar. He did so at the close of the session of 1853, as at the close
of the session of 1833.

Now, it happens that the noble lord, while he expressed
"his most implicit confidence in the honour and good faith"
of the Czar, had just got into possession of documents, concealed from the rest of the world, and leaving no doubt, if
any existed, about the nature of Russian honour and good
faith. He had not even to scratch the Muscovite in order to
find the Tartar. He had found the Tartar in his naked hideous-
ness. He found himself possessed of the self-confessions of the
leading Russian ministers and diplomatists, throwing off their
cloaks, opening out their most secret thoughts, unfolding,
without constraint, their plans of conquest and subjugation,
scornfully railing at the imbecile credulity of European courts
and ministers, mocking the Villèles, the Metternichs, the
Aberdeens, the Cannings, and the Wellingtons; and devising
in common, with the savage cynicism of the barbarian, miti-
gated by the cruel irony of the courtier, how to sow distrust
against England at Paris, and against Austria at London, and
against London at Vienna, how to set them all by the ears, and
how to make all of them the mere tools of Russia.

At the time of the insurrection in Warsaw, the vice-royal
archives kept in the palace of Prince Constantine, and con-
taining the secret correspondence of Russian ministers and
ambassadors from the beginning of this century down to 1830,

o

fell into the hands of the victorious Poles. Polish refugees brought these papers over first to France, and, at a later period, Count Zamoyski, the nephew of Prince Czartoryski, placed them in the hands of Lord Palmerston, who buried them in Christian oblivion. With these papers in his pocket, the noble viscount was the more eager to proclaim in the British Senate and to the world, "his most implicit confidence in the honour and good faith of the Emperor of Russia."

It was not the fault of the noble viscount, that those startling papers were at length published at the end of 1835, through the famous *Portfolio*. King William IV, whatsoever he was in other respects, was a most decided enemy of Russia. His private secretary, Sir Herbert Taylor, was intimately connected with David Urquhart,[33] introducing this gentleman to the King himself, and from that moment Royalty was conspiring with these two friends against the policy of the "truly English" minister.

"William IV. ordered the above-mentioned papers to be given up by the noble lord. They were given up and examined at the time at Windsor Castle, and it was found desirable to print and publish them. In spite of the great opposition of the noble lord, the King compelled him to lend the authority of the Foreign Office to their publication, so that the editor who took the charge of revising them for the press, published not a single word which had not the signature or initials attached. I, myself, have seen the noble lord's initial attached to one of these documents, although the noble lord has denied these facts. Lord Palmerston was compelled to place the documents in the hands of Mr. Urquhart for publication. Mr. Urquhart was the real editor of the *Portfolio*."—(*Mr. Anstey, House of Commons, February* 23, 1848.)

After the death of the King, Lord Palmerston refused to pay the printer of the *Portfolio*, disclaimed publicly and solemnly all connection on the part of the Foreign Office with it, and induced, in what manner is not known, Mr. Backhouse, his under-secretary, to set his name to these denials. We read in *The Times* of January 30, 1839:

"It is not for us to understand how Lord Palmerston may feel, but we are sure there is no misapprehending how *any other person* in the station of a gentleman, and in the position of a minister, *would feel* after the notoriety given to the correspondence between Mr. Urquhart, whom Lord Palmerston dismissed from office, and Mr. Backhouse, whom the noble viscount has retained in office, by *The Times* of yesterday. There never was a fact apparently better established through this correspondece than that the series of official documents contained in the well-known publication called the *Portfolio*, were printed and circulated by Lord Palmerston's authority, and that his lordship is responsible for the publication of them, both as a statesman to the political world here and abroad, and as an employer of the printers and publishers, for the pecuniary charge accompanying it."

In consequence of her financial distress, resulting from the exhaustion of the treasury by the unfortunate war of 1828–29, and the debt to Russia stipulated by the Treaty of Adrianople, Turkey found herself compelled to extend that obnoxious system of monopolies, by which the sale of almost all articles was granted only to those who had paid Government licences. Thus a few usurers were enabled to seize upon the entire commerce of the country. Mr. Urquhart proposed to King William IV a commercial treaty to be concluded with the Sultan, which treaty, while guaranteeing great advantages to British commerce, intended at the same time to develop the productive resources of Turkey, to restore her exchequer to health, and thus to emancipate her from the Russian yoke. The curious history of this treaty cannot be better related than in the words of Mr. Anstey:

"The whole of the contest between Lord Palmerston on the one hand, and Mr. Urquhart on the other, was directed to this treaty of commerce. On the 3rd of October, 1835, Mr. Urquhart obtained his commission as Secretary of Legation at Constantinople, given him for the one purpose of securing the adoption there of the Turkish commercial treaty. He delayed his departure, however, till June or July, 1836. Lord Palmerston pressed him to go. The applications to him urging his departure were numerous, but his answer invariably was, 'I will not go until I have this commercial treaty settled with the Board of Trade and the Foreign Office: and then I will accompany it and procure its acceptance at the Porte. . . .' Finally, Lord Palmerston gave his approbation to the treaty, and it was forwarded to Lord Ponsonby, the Ambassador at Constantinople. [In the meantime the latter had been instructed by Lord Palmerston to take the negotiations entirely out of the hands of Mr. Urquhart into his own, contrary to the engagement entered into with Mr. Urquhart.] As soon as the removal of Mr. Urquhart from Constantinople had been effected through the intrigues of the noble lord, the treaty was immediately thrown overboard. Two years later the noble lord resumed it, giving Mr. Urquhart, before Parliament, the compliment of being the author of it, and disclaiming for himself all merits in it. But the noble lord had destroyed the treaty, falsified it in every part, and converted it to the ruin of commerce. The original treaty of Mr. Urquhart placed the subjects of Great Britain in Turkey upon the footing of the most favoured nation, viz. the Russians. As altered by Lord Palmerston, it placed the subjects of Great Britain upon the footing of the taxed and oppressed subjects of the Porte. Mr. Urquhart's treaty stipulated for the removal of all transit duties, monopolies, taxes, and duties of whatever character, other than those stipulated by the treaty itself. As falsified by Lord Palmerston, it contained a clause, declaring the perfect right of the Sublime Porte to impose whatever regulations and restrictions it pleased, with regard to commerce. Mr Urquhart's treaty left exportation subject only to the old duty of three shillings; that of the noble lord raised the duty from three shillings to five shillings. Mr. Urquhart's treaty stipulated for an *ad valorem* duty in this manner, that if any article of commerce was so exclusively the production of Turkey as to insure it a ready sale at the prices usually received under the monopoly in foreign ports, then the export duty, to be assessed by two commissioners appointed on the part of England and Turkey, might be a high one, so as to be remunerative and productive of revenue, but that, in the case of commodities produced elsewhere than in Turkey, and not being of sufficient value in foreign ports to bear a high duty, a lower duty should be assessed. Lord Palmerston's treaty stipulated a fixed duty of twelve shillings *ad valorem* upon every article, whether it would bear the duty or not. The original treaty extended the benefit of free trade to Turkish ships and produce; the substituted treaty contained no stipulation whatever on the subject. . . . I charge these falsifications, I charge also the concealment of them, upon the noble lord, and further—I charge the noble lord with having falsely stated to the House that his treaty was that which had been arranged by Mr. Urquhart."—(*Mr. Anstey, House of Commons, February* 23, 1848.)

So favourable to Russia, and so obnoxious to Great Britain, was the treaty as altered by the noble lord, that some English merchants in the Levant resolved to trade henceforth under the protection of Russian firms, and others, as Mr. Urquhart states, were only prevented from doing so by a sort of national pride.

With regard to the secret relations between the noble lord and William IV, Mr. Anstey stated to the House:

"The King forced the question of the process of Russian encroachment in Turkey upon the attention of the noble lord. . . . I can prove that the noble lord was obliged to take the direction in this matter from the late King's private secretary, and that his existence in office depended upon his compliance with the wishes of the monarch. . . . The noble lord did, on one or two occasions, as far as he dared, resist, but his resistance was invariably followed by *abject* expressions of *contrition* and *compliance*. I will not take upon myself to assert that on one occasion the noble lord was actually out of office for a day or two, but I am able to say that the noble lord was in danger of a most unceremonious expulsion from office on that occasion. I refer to the discovery which the late King had made, that the noble lord consulted the feelings of the Russian Government as to the choice of an English Ambassador at the Court of St. Petersburg, and that Sir Stratford Canning, originally destined for the embassy, was set aside to make room for the late Earl of Durham, an ambassador more agreeable to the Czar."—(*House of Commons, February* 23, 1853.)

It is one of the most astonishing facts that, while the King was vainly struggling against the Russian policy of the noble lord, the noble lord and his Whig allies succeeded in keeping alive the public suspicion that the King—who was known as a Tory—was paralysing the anti-Russian efforts of the "truly English" Minister. The pretended Tory predilection of the monarch for the despotic principles of the Russian Court, was, of course, made to explain the otherwise inexplicable policy of Lord Palmerston. The Whig oligarchs smiled mysteriously when Mr. H. L. Bulwer informed the House, that "no longer ago than last Christmas Count Apponyi, the Austrian Ambassador at Paris, stated, in speaking of the affairs of the East, that this Court had a greater apprehension of French principles than of Russian ambition."—(*House of Commons, July* 11, 1833.)

They smiled again, when Mr. T. Attwood interrogated the noble lord: "what reception Count Orloff, having been sent over to England, after the treaty of Unkiar Skelessi, had met with at his Majesty's Court?"—(*House of Commons, August* 28, 1833.)

The papers entrusted by the dying King and his secretary, the late Sir Herbert Taylor, to Mr. Urquhart, "for the purpose of vindicating, upon the fitting opportunity, the memory of William IV," will, when published, throw a new light upon the past career of the noble lord and the Whig oligarchy, of which the public generally know little more than the history of their pretensions, their phrases, and their so-called principles—in a word, the theatrical and fictitious part—the mask.

This is a fitting occasion to give his due to Mr. David Urquhart, the indefatigable antagonist for twenty years of Lord Palmerston, to whom he proved a real adversary—one not to be intimidated into silence, bribed into connivance, charmed into suitorship, while, what with cajoleries, what with seductions, Alcine Palmerston contrived to change all other foes into fools. We have just heard the fierce denunciation of his lordship by Mr. Anstey:

"A circumstance most significant is that the accused minister sought the member, viz. Mr. Anstey, and was content to accept his co-operation and private friendship without the forms of recantation or apology. Mr. Anstey's recent legal appointment by the present Government speaks for itself."— (*D. Urquhart's Progress of Russia.*)

On February 23, 1848, the same Mr. Anstey had compared the noble viscount to "the *infamous* Marquis of Carmarthen, Secretary of State to William III, whom, during his visit to his Court, the Czar, Peter I, found means to corrupt to his interests with the gold of British merchants."—(*House of Commons, February* 23, 1848.)

Who defended Lord Palmerston on that occasion against the accusations of Mr. Anstey? Mr. Sheil; the same Mr. Sheil who had, on the conclusion of the Treaty of Unkiar Skelessi, in 1833, acted the same part of accuser against his lordship as Mr. Anstey in 1848. Mr. Roebuck, once his strong anatagonist, procured him the vote of confidence in 1850. Sir Stratford

Canning, having denounced during a decennium, the noble lord's connivance with the Czar, was content to be got rid of as ambassador to Constantinople. The noble lord's own dear Dudley Stuart was intrigued out of Parliament for some years, for having opposed the noble lord. When returned back to it, he had become the *âme damnée* of the "truly English" Minister. Kossuth,[34] who might have known from the Blue Books that Hungary had been betrayed by the noble viscount, called him "the dear friend of his bosom," when landing at Southampton.

7

One glance at the map of Europe will show you on the western littoral of the Black Sea the outlets of the Danube, the only river which, springing up in the very heart of Europe, may be said to form a natural highway to Asia. Exactly opposite on the eastern side, to the south of the river Kuban, begins the mountain-range of the Caucasus, stretching from the Black Sea to the Caspian in a south-easterly direction for some seven hundred miles, and separating Europe from Asia.

If you hold the outlets of the Danube, you hold the Danube, and with it the highway to Asia, and a great part of the commerce of Switzerland, Germany, Hungary, Turkey, and above all, of Moldo-Wallachia. If you hold the Caucasus too, the Black Sea becomes your property, and to shut up its door, you only want Constantinople and the Dardanelles. The possession of the Caucasus mountains makes you at once master of Trebizond, and through their domination of the Caspian Sea, of the northern seaboard of Persia.

The greedy eyes of Russia embraced at once the outlets of the Danube and the mountain-range of the Caucasus. There, the business in hand was to conquer supremacy, here to maintain it. The chain of the Caucasus separates southern Russia from the luxurious provinces of Georgia, Mingrelia, Imertia, and Giuriel, wrested by the Muscovite from the Mussulman. Thus the foot of the monster empire is cut off from its main body. The only military road, deserving to be called such, winds from Mozdok to Tiflis, through the eyry-pass of Dariel, fortified by a continuous line of entrenched places, but exposed on both sides to the never-ceasing attacks from the Caucasian tribes. The union of these tribes under one military chief might even endanger the bordering country of the Cossacks. "The thought of the dreadful consequences which a union of the hostile Circassians[35] under one head would produce in the south of Russia, fills one with terror," exclaims Mr. Kapffer, a German who presided over the scientific commission which, in 1829, accompanied the expedition of General Etronnel to Elbruz.

At this very moment our attention is directed with equal anxiety to the banks of the Danube, where Russia has seized the two corn magazines of Europe, and to the Caucasus, where she is menaced in the possession of Georgia. It was the Treaty of Adrianople that prepared Russia's usurpation of Moldo-Wallachia, and recognised her claims to the Caucasus.

Article IV of that treaty stipulates:

"All the countries situated north and east of the line of demarcation between the two Empires (Russia and Turkey), towards Georgia, Imertia, and the Giureil, as well as all the littoral of the Black Sea, from the mouth of the Kuban, as far as the port of St. Nicholas exclusively, shall remain under the domination of Russia."

With regard to the Danube the same treaty stipulates:

"The frontier line will follow the course of the Danube to the mouth of St. George, leaving all the islands formed by the different branches in the possession of Russia. The right bank will remain, as formerly, in the possession of the Ottoman Porte. It is, however, agreed that the right bank, from the point where the arm of St. George departs from that of Sulina, shall remain uninhabited to a distance of two hours (six miles) from the river, and that no kind of structure shall be raised there, and, in like manner, on the islands which still remain in the possession of the Court of Russia. With the exception of quarantines, which will be there established, it will not be permitted to make any other establishment or fortification."

Both these paragraphs, inasmuch as they secure to Russia an "extension of territory and exclusive commercial advantages," openly infringed on the protocol of April 4, 1846, drawn up by the Duke of Wellington at St. Petersburg, and on the treaty of July 6, 1827, concluded between Russia and the other great Powers at London. The English Government, therefore, refused to recognise the Treaty of Adrianople. The Duke of Wellington protested against it.—(*Lord Dudley Stuart, House of Commons, March* 17, 1837.)

Lord Aberdeen protested:

"In a despatch to Lord Heytesbury, dated October 21, 1829, he commented with no small dissatisfaction on many parts of the Treaty of Adrianople, and especially notices the stipulations respecting the islands of the Danube. He denies that peace (the Treaty of Adrianople) has respected the territorial rights of the sovereignty of the Porte, and the condition and the interests of all maritime states in the Mediterranean."—(*Lord Mahon, House of Commons, April* 20, 1836.)

Earl Grey declared that "the independence of the Porte would be sacrificed, and the peace of Europe endangered, by this treaty being agreed to."—(*Earl Grey, House of Lords, February* 4, 1834.)

Lord Palmerston himself informs us:

"As far as the extension of the Russian frontier is concerned in the south of the Caucasus, and the shores of the Black Sea, it is certainly not consistent with the solemn declaration made by Russia in the face of Europe, previous to the commencement of the Turkish war."—(*House of Commons, March* 17, 1837.)

The eastern littoral of the Black Sea, by blockading which and cutting off supplies of arms and gunpowder to the north-western districts of the Caucasus, Russia could alone hope to realise her nominal claim to these countries—this littoral of the Black Sea and the outlets of the Danube are certainly no places "where an English action could possibly take place," as was lamented by the noble lord in the case of Cracow. By what mysterious contrivance, then, has the Muscovite succeeded in blockading the Danube, in blocking up the littoral of the Euxine, and in forcing Great Britain to submit not only to the Treaty of Adrianople, but at the same time to the violation by Russia herself of that identical treaty?

These questions were put to the noble viscount in the House of Commons on April 20, 1836, numerous petitions having poured in from the merchants of London, of Glasgow, and other commercial towns, against the fiscal regulations of Russia in the Black Sea, and her enactments and restrictions tending to intercept English commerce on the Danube. There had appeared on

February 7, 1836, a Russian ukase, which, by virtue of the
Treaty of Adrianople, established a quarantine on one of the
islands formed by the mouths of the Danube. In order to execute
that quarantine, Russia claimed a right of boarding and search,
of levying fees and seizing and marching off to Odessa refractory
ships proceeding on their voyage up the Danube. Before the
quarantine was established, or rather before a custom-house and
fort were erected, under the false pretence of a quarantine, the
Russian authorities threw out their feelers, to ascertain the risk
they might run with the British Government. Lord Durham[36]
acting upon instructions received from England, remonstrated
with the Russian Cabinet for the hindrance which had been
given to British trade.

"He was referred to Count Nesselrode,[37] Count Nesselrode
referred him to the Governor of South Russia, and the
Governor of South Russia again referred him to the Consul
at Galatz, who communicated with the British Consul at
Ibraila, who was instructed to send down the captains from
whom toll had been exacted, to the Danube, the scene of their
injuries, in order that inquiry might be made on the subject,
it being well known that the captains thus referred to were
then in England."—(House of Commons, April 20, 1936.)

The formal ukase of February 7, 1836, aroused, however,
the general attention of British commerce.

"Many ships had sailed, and others were going out, to
whose captains strict orders had been given not to submit to
the right of boarding and search which Russia claimed. The
fate of these ships must be inevitable, unless some expression
of opinion was made on the part of that House. Unless that
were done, British shipping, to the amount of not less than
5,000 tons, would be seized and marched off to Odessa, until
the insolent commands of Russia were complied with."—
(Mr. Patrick Stewart, House of Commons, April 20, 1836.)

Russia required the marshy islands of the Danube, by virtue
of the clause of the Treaty of Adrianople, which clause itself
was a violation of the treaty she had previously contracted with
England and the other Powers, in 1827. The bristling the gates
of the Danube with fortifications, and these fortifications with
guns, was a violation of the Treaty of Adrianople itself, which

expressly prohibits any fortifications being erected within six miles of the river. The exaction of tolls, and the obstruction of the navigation, were a violation of the Treaty of Vienna, declaring that "the navigation of rivers along their whole course, from the point where each of them becomes navigable to its mouth, shall be entirely free," that "the amount of the duties shall in no case exceed those now (1815) paid" and that "no increase shall take place, except with the common consent of the states bordering on the river." Thus, then, all the argument on which Russia could plead not guilty was the Treaty of 1827, violated by the Treaty of Adrianople, the Treaty of Adrianople violated by herself, the whole backed up by a violation of the Treaty of Vienna.

It proved quite impossible to wring out of the noble lord any declaration whether he did or did not recognise the Treaty of Adrianople. As to the violation of the Treaty of Vienna, he had

> "received no official information that anything had occurred which is not warranted by the treaty. When such a statement is made by the parties concerned, it shall be dealt with in such manner as the law advisers of the Crown shall deem consistent with the rights of the subjects of this country."— (*Lord Palmerston, House of Commons, April* 20, 1836.)

By the Treaty of Adrianople, Art. V, Russia guarantees the "prosperity" of the Danubian Principalities, and full "liberty of trade" for them. Now, Mr. Stewart proved that the Principalities of Moldavia and Wallachia were objects of deadly jealousy to Russia, as their trade had taken a sudden development since 1834 as they vied with Russia's own staple production, as Galatz was becoming the great depôt of all the grain of the Danube, and driving Odessa out of the market. If, answered the noble lord,

> "my honourable friend had been able to show that whereas some years ago we had had a large and important commerce with Turkey, and that that commerce had, by the aggression of other countries, or by the neglect of the Government of this, dwindled down to an inconsiderable trade, then there might have been ground to call upon Parliament."

In lieu of such an occurrence,

"my honourable friend has shown that during the last few years the trade with Turkey has risen from next to nothing to a very considerable amount."

Russia obstructs the Danube navigation, because the trade of the Principalities is growing important, says Mr. Stewart. But she did not do so when the trade was next to nothing, retorts Lord Palmerston. You neglect to oppose the recent encroachments of Russia on the Danube, says Mr. Stewart. We did not do so at the epoch these encroachments were not yet ventured upon, replies the noble lord. What "circumstances" have *therefore* "occurred against which the Government are not likely to guard unless driven thereto by the direct interference of this House?" He prevented the Commons from passing a resolution by assuring them that "there is no disposition of His Majesty's Government to submit to aggression on the part of any Power, be that Power what it may, and be it more or less strong," and by warning them that "we should also cautiously abstain from anything which might be construed by other Powers, and *reasonably* so, as being a provocation on our part." A week after these debates had taken place in the House of Commons, a British merchant addressed a letter to the Foreign Office with regard to the Russian ukase. "I am directed by Viscount Palmerston," answered the Under Secretary at the Foreign Office, to

"acquaint you that his lordship has called upon the law adviser for the Crown for his opinions as to the regulations promulgated by the Russian ukase of February 7, 1836; but in the meantime Lord Palmerston directs me to acquaint you, with respect to the latter part of your letter, that it is the opinion of His Majesty's Government that no toll is justly demanded by the Russian authorities, at the mouth of the Danube, and that you have acted properly in directing your agents to *refuse* to pay it."

The merchant acted according to this letter. He is abandoned to Russia by the noble lord; a Russian toll is, as Mr. Urquhart states, now exacted in London and Liverpool by Russian Consuls, on every English ship sailing for the Turkish ports of the Danube; and "the quarantine still stands on the island of Leti". Russia did not limit her invasion of the Danube to a quarantine established, to fortifications erected, and to tolls exacted. The only mouth of the Danube remaining still navigable, the Sulina mouth, was acquired by her through the Treaty of Adrianople. As long as it was possessed by the Turks, there was kept a depth of water in the channel of from fourteen to sixteen feet. Since in the possession of Russia, the water became reduced to eight feet, a depth wholly inadequate to the conveyance of the vessels employed in the corn trade. Now Russia is a party to the Treaty of Vienna, and that treaty stipulates, in Article CXIII, that "each State shall be at the expense of keeping in good repair the towing paths, and shall maintain the necessary work in order that no obstructions shall be experienced by the navigation". For keeping the channel in a navigable state, Russia found no better means than gradually reducing the depth of the water, paving it with wrecks, and choking up its bar with an accumulation of sand and mud. To this systematic and protracted infraction of the Treaty of Vienna, she added another violation of the Treaty of Adrianople, which forbids any establishment at the mouth of the Sulina, except for quarantine and light-house purposes, while at her dictation, a small Russian fort has there sprung up, living by extortions upon the vessels, the occasion for which is afforded by the delays and expenses for lighterage, consequent upon the obstruction of the channel.

"*Cum principia negante non est disputandum*—of what use is it to dwell upon abstract principles with despotic Governments, who are accused of measuring might by power, and of ruling their conduct by expediency, and not by justice?"— (*Lord Palmerston, April* 30, 1823.)

According to his own maxim, the noble viscount was contented to dwell upon abstract principles with the despotic Government of Russia; but he went further. While he assured the House on July 6, 1840, that the freedom of the Danube navigation was "guaranteed by the Treaty of Vienna," while he lamented on July 13, 1840, that the occupation of Cracow being a violation of the Treaty of Vienna, "there were no means of enforcing the opinions of England, because Cracow was evidently a place where no English action could possibly take place"; two days later he concluded a Russian treaty, closing the Dardanelles to England "during times of peace with Turkey," and thus

depriving England of the only means of "enforcing" the
Treaty of Vienna, and transforming the Euxine into a place
where no English action could possibly take place

This point once obtained, he contrived to give a sham
satisfaction to public opinion by firing off a whole battery of
papers, reminding the "despotic Government, which measures
right by power, and rules its conduct by expediency and not
by justice," in a sententious and sentimental manner, that
"Russia, when she compelled Turkey to cede to her the outlet
of a great European river, which forms the commercial highway
for the mutual intercourse of many nations, undertook duties
and responsibilities to other States which she should take a pride
in making good." To this dwelling upon abstract principles,
Count Nesselrode kept giving the inevitable answer that "the
subject should be carefully examined," and expressing from time
to time, "a feeling of soreness on the part of the Imperial
Government at the mistrust manifested as to their intentions."

Thus, through the management of the noble lord, in 1853,
things arrived at the point where the navigation of the Danube
was declared impossible, and corn was rotting at the mouth of
the Sulina, while famine threatened to invade England, France,
and the south of Europe. Thus, Russia was not only adding, as
The Times says, "to her other important possessions that of an
iron gate between the Danube and the Euxine," she possessed
herself of the key to the Danube, of a bread-screw which she
can put on whenever the policy of Western Europe becomes
obnoxious to punishment.

8

The petitions presented to the House of Commons on April 26, 1836, and the resolution moved by Mr. Patrick Stewart in reference to them, referred not only to the Danube, but to Circassia too, the rumour having spread through the commercial world that the Russian Government, on the plea of blockading the coast of Circassia, claimed to exclude English ships from landing goods and merchandise in certain ports of the eastern littoral of the Black Sea. On that occasion Lord Palmerston solemnly declared:

> "If Parliament will place their confidence in us—if they will leave it to us to manage the foreign relations of the country —we shall be able to protect the interests and to uphold the honour of the country without being obliged to have recourse to war."—(*House of Commons April* 26, 1836.)

Some months afterwards, on October 29, 1836, the *Vixen* a trading vessel belonging to Mr. George Bell and laden with a cargo of salt, set out from London on a direct voyage for Circassia. On November 25, she was seized in the Circassian Bay of Soudjouk-Kale by a Russian man-of-war, for "having been employed on a blockaded coast."—(*Letter of the Russian Admiral Lazareff to the English Consul, Mr. Childs, December* 24, 1836.) The vessel, her cargo, and her crew were sent to the port of Sebastopol, where the condemnatory decision of the Russians was received on January 27, 1837. This time, however, no mention was made of a "blockade," but the *Vixen* was simply declared a lawful prize, because "it was guilty of smuggling," the importation of salt being prohibited, and the Bay of Soudjouk-Kale, a Russian port, not provided with a customhouse. The condemnation was executed in an exquisitely ignominious and insulting manner. The Russians who effected the seizure were publicly rewarded with decorations. The British flag was hoisted, then hauled down, and the Russian flag hoisted in its stead. The master and crew, put as captives on board the *Ajax*—the captor—were despatched from Sebastopol to Odessa, and from Odessa to Constantinople, whence they were allowed to return to England. As to the vessel itself, a German traveller, who visited Sebastopol a few years after this event, wrote in a letter addressed to the *Augsburg Gazette*: "After all the Russian ships of the line which I visited, no vessel excited my curiosity more than the *Soudjouk-Kale*, formerly the *Vixen*, under the Russian colours. She has now changed her appearance. This little vessel is now the best sailer in the Russian fleet, and is generally employed in transports between Sebastopol and the coast of Circassia."

The capture of the *Vixen* certainly afforded Lord Palmerston a great occasion for fulfilling his promise "to protect the interests and to uphold the honour of the country." Besides the honour of the British flag, and the interests of British commerce, there was another question at stake—*the independence of Circassia*. At first, Russia justified the seizure of the *Vixen* on the plea of an infraction of the blockade proclaimed by her, but the ship was condemned on the opposite plea of a contravention against her custom-house regulations. By proclaiming a blockade, Russia declared Circassia a hostile foreign country, and the question was whether the British Government had ever recognised that blockade? By the establishment of custom-house regulations, Circassia was, on the contrary, treated as a Russian dependency, and the question was whether the British Government had ever recognised the Russian claims to Circassia?

Before proceeding, let it be remembered that Russia was at that epoch far from having completed her fortification of Sebastopol.

Any Russian claim to the possession of Circassia could only be derived from the Treaty of Adrianople, as explained in a previous article. But the treaty of July 6, 1827, bound Russia to not attempting any territorial aggrandisement, nor securing any exclusive commercial advantage from her war with Turkey. Any extension, therefore, of the Russian frontier, attendant on the Treaty of Adrianople, openly infringed the treaty of 1827, and was, as shown by the protest of Wellington and Aberdeen, not to be recognised on the part of Great Britain. Russia, then, had no right to receive Circassia from Turkey. On the other

P

hand, Turkey could not cede to Russia what she never possessed, and Circassia had always remained so independent of the Porte, that, at the time when a Turkish Pasha yet resided at Anapa, Russia herself had concluded several conventions with the Circassian chieftains as to the coast trade, the Turkish trade being exclusively and legally restricted to the port of Anapa. Circassia being an independent country, the municipal, sanitary or customs' regulations with which the Muscovite might think fit to provide her were as binding as his regulations for the port of Tampico.

On the other hand, if Circassia was a foreign country, hostile to Russia, the latter had only a right to blockade, if that blockade was no paper blockade—if Russia had the naval squadron present to enforce it, and really dominated the coast. Now, on a coast extending 200 miles, Russia possessed but three isolated forts, all the rest of Circassia remaining in the hands of the Circassian tribes. There existed no Russian fort in the Bay of Soudjouk-Kale. There was, in fact, no blockade, because no maritime force was employed. There was the offer of the distinct testimony of the crews of two British vessels who had visited the bay—the one in September, 1834, the other, that of the *Vixen*—confirmed subsequently by the public statements of two British travellers who visited the harbour in the years 1837 and 1838, that there was no Russian occupation whatever of the coast.—(*Portfolio, VIII, March* 1, 1844.)

When the *Vixen* entered the harbour of Soudjouk-Kale

"there were no Russian ships of war in sight nor in the offing. . . . A Russian vessel of war came into the harbour thirty-six hours after the *Vixen* had cast anchor, and at the moment when the owner and some of the officers were on shore fixing the dues demanded by the Circassian authorities, and payable on the value of the goods. . . . The man-of-war came not coast-wise, but from the open sea."—(*Mr. Anstey, House of Commons, February* 23, 1848.)

But need we give further proofs of the St. Petersburg Cabinet itself seizing the *Vixen* under pretext of blockade and confiscating it under pretext of custom-house regulations?

The Circassians thus appeared the more favoured by accident, as the question of their independence coincided with the question of the free navigation of the Black Sea, the protection of British commerce, and an insolent act of piracy committed by Russia on a British merchant ship. Their chance of obtaining protection from the mistress of the seas seemed less doubtful, as

> "the Cirassian declaration of independence had a short time ago been published after mature deliberation and several weeks' correspondence with different branches of the Government, in a periodical (the *Portfolio*) connected with the foreign department, and as Circassia was marked out as an independent country in a map revised by Lord Palmerston himself."—(*Mr. Robinson, House of Commons, January* 21, 1838.)

Will it then be believed that the noble and chivalrous viscount knew how to handle the case in so masterly a way, that the very act of piracy committed by Russia against British property afforded him the long-sought-for occasion of formally recognising the Treaty of Adrianople, and the extinction of Circassian independence?

On March 17, 1837, Mr. Roebuck moved, with reference to the confiscation of the *Vixen*, for "a copy of all correspondence between the Government of this country and the Governments of Russia and Turkey, relating to the Treaty of Adrianople, as well as all transactions or negotiations connected with the port and territories on the shores of the Black Sea by Russia since the Treaty of Adrianople."

Mr. Roebuck, from fear of being suspected of humanitarian tendencies and of defending Circassia, on the ground of abstract principles, plainly declared: "Russia may endeavour to obtain possession of all the world, and I regard her efforts with indifference; but the moment she interferes with our commerce, I call upon the Government of this country [which country exists in appearance somewhat beyond the limits of all the world] to punish the aggression." Accordingly, he wanted to know "if the British Government had acknowledged the Treaty of Adrianople?"

The noble lord, although pressed very hard, had ingenuity enough to make a long speech, and

> "to sit down without telling the House who was in actual possession of the Circassian coast at the present moment—

whether it really belonged to Russia, and whether it was by right of a violation of fiscal regulations, or in consequence of an existing blockade, that the *Vixen* had been seized, and whether or not he recognised the Treaty of Adrianople."— (*Mr. Hume, House of Commons, March* 17, 1837.)

Mr. Roebuck states that, before allowing the *Vixen* to proceed to Circassia, Mr. Bell had applied to the noble lord, in order to ascertain whether there was any impropriety or danger to be apprehended in a vessel landing goods in any part of Circassia, and that the Foreign Office answered in the negative. Thus, Lord Palmerston found himself obliged to read to the House the correspondence exchanged between himself and Mr. Bell. Reading these letters one would fancy he was reading a Spanish comedy of the cloak and sword rather than an official correspondence between a minister and a merchant. When he heard the noble lord had read the letters respecting the seizure of the *Vixen*, Daniel O'Connell exclaimed, "He could not keep calling to his mind the expression of Talleyrand, that language had been invented to conceal thoughts."

For instance, Mr Bell asks "whether there were any restrictions on trade recognised by His Majesty's Government? as, if not, he intended to send thither a vessel with a cargo of salt." "You ask me," answers Lord Palmerston, "whether it would be for your advantage to engage in a speculation in salt?" and inform him "that it is for commercial firms to judge for themselves whether they shall enter or decline a speculation." "By no means," replies Mr. Bell; "all I want to know is, whether or not His Majesty's Government recognises the Russian blockade on the Black Sea to the south of the river Kuban?" "You must look at the *London Gazette*," retorts the noble lord, "in which all the notifications, such as those alluded to by you, are made." The *London Gazette* was indeed the quarter to which a British merchant had to refer for such information, instead of the ukases of the Emperor of Russia. Mr. Bell, finding no indication whatever in the *Gazette* of the acknowledgement of the blockade, or of other restrictions, despatched his vessel. The result was, that some time after he was himself placed in the *Gazette*.

"I referred Mr. Bell," says Lord Palmerston, "to the *Gazette*, where he would find no blockade had been communicated or declared to this country by the Russian Government—consequently, none was acknowledged." By referring Mr. Bell to the *Gazette*, Lord Palmerston did not only deny the acknowledgment on the part of Great Britain of the Russian blockade, but simultaneously affirmed that, in his opinion, the coast of Circassia formed *no part* of the Russian territory, because blockades of their own territories by foreign States—as, for instance, against revolted subjects—are *not* to be notified in the *Gazette*. Circassia, forming no part of the Russian territory, could not, of course, be included in Russian custom-house regulations. Thus, according to his own statement, Lord Palmerston denied, in his letters to Mr. Bell, Russia's right to blockade the Circassian coast, or to subject it to commercial restrictions. It is true that, throughout his speech, he showed a desire to induce the House to infer that Russia had possession of Circassia. But, on the other hand, he stated plainly, "As far as the extension of the Russian frontier is concerned, on the south of the Caucasus and the shores of the Black Sea, it is certainly not consistent with the solemn declaration made by Russia in the face of Europe, previous to the commencement of the Turkish war." When he sat down, pledging himself ever "to protect the interests and uphold the honour of the country," he seemed to labour beneath the accumulated miseries of his past policy, rather than to be hatching treacherous designs for the future. On that day he met with the following cruel apostrophe:

"The want of vigorous alacrity to defend the honour of the country which the noble lord had displayed was most culpable; the conduct of no former minister had ever been so vacillating, so hesitating, so uncertain, so cowardly, when insult had been offered to British subjects. How much longer did the noble lord propose to allow Russia thus to insult Great Britain, and thus to injure British commerce? The noble lord was degrading England by holding her out in the character of a bully—haughty and tyrannical to the weak, humble and abject to the strong."

Who was it that thus mercilessly branded the truly English Minister? Nobody else than Lord Dudley Stuart.

On November 25, 1836, the *Vixen* was confiscated. The stormy debates of the House of Commons, just quoted, took place on March 17, 1837. It was not till April 19, 1837, that the noble lord requested the Russian Government "to state the reason on account of which it had thought itself warranted to seize in time of peace a merchant vessel belonging to British subjects." On May 17, 1837, the noble lord received the following despatch from the Earl of Durham, the British Ambassador at St. Petersburg:

> "MY LORD,
> "With respect to the military *de facto* occupation of Soudjouk-Kale, I have to state to your lordship that there is a fortress in the bay which bears the name of the Empress (Alexandrovsky), and that it has always been occupied by a a Russian garrison.
> > "I have, etc.,
> > "DURHAM."

It need hardly be remarked that the fort Alexandrovsky had not even the reality of the pasteboard towns, exhibited by Potemkin before the Empress Catherine II on her visit to the Crimea. Five days after the receipt of this despatch, Lord Palmerston returns the following answer to St. Petersburg:

> "His Majesty's Government, considering in the first place that Soudjouk-Kale, which was acknowledged by Russia in the Treaty of 1783 as a Turkish possession, now belongs to Russia, as stated by Count Nesselrode, by virtue of the Treaty of Adrianople, see no sufficient reason to question the right of Russia to seize and confiscate the *Vixen*."

There are some very curious circumstances connected with the negotiation. Lord Palmerston requires six months of premeditation for opening, and hardly one to close it. His last despatch of May 23, 1837, suddenly and abruptly cuts off any further transactions. It quotes the date before the Treaty of Kutchuk-Kainardji,[38] not after the Gregorian but after the Greek chronology. Besides, "between April 19 and May 23," as Sir Robert Peel said, "a remarkable change from official declaration to satisfaction occurred—apparently induced by the *assurance* received from Count Nesselrode that Turkey had ceded the coast in question to Russia by the Treaty of Adrianople. Why did he not protest against this ukase?"—(*House of Commons, June 21, 1838*.)

Why all this? The reason is very simple. King William IV had secretly instigated Mr. Bell to despatch the *Vixen* to the coast of Circassia. When the noble lord delayed negotiations, the king was still in full health. When he suddenly closed the negotiations, William IV was in the agonies of death, and Lord Palmerston disposed as absolutely of the Foreign Office, as if he was himself the autocrat of Great Britain. Was it not a master-stroke on the part of his jocose lordship to formally acknowledge by one dash of the pen the Treaty of Adrianople, Russia's possession of Circassia, and the confiscation of the *Vixen*, in the name of the dying king, who had despatched that saucy *Vixen* with the express view to mortify the Czar, to disregard the Treaty of Adrianople, and to affirm the independence of Circassia?

Mr. Bell, as we stated, went into the *Gazette*, and Mr. Urquhart, then the first secretary of the Embassy at Constantinople, was recalled, for "having persuaded Mr. Bell to carry his *Vixen* expedition into execution."

As long as King William IV was alive, Lord Palmerston dared not openly countermand the *Vixen* expedition, as is proved by the Circassian Declaration of Independence, published in the *Portfolio*; by the Circassian map revised by his lordship; by his uncertain correspondence with Mr. Bell; by his vague declarations in the House; by the supercargo of the *Vixen*; Mr. Bell's brother receiving, when setting out, despatches from the Foreign Office, for the Embassy at Constantinople, and direct encouragement from Lord Ponsonby, the British Ambassador to the Sublime Porte.

In the earlier times of Queen Victoria the Whig ascendency seemed to be safer than ever, and accordingly the language of the chivalrous viscount suddenly changed. From defence and cajolery, it became at once haughty and contemptuous. Interrogated by Mr. T. H. Attwood, on December 14, 1837, with regard to the *Vixen* and Circassia: "As to the *Vixen* Russia had given such explanations of her conduct as ought to satisfy the Government of this country. That ship was not taken during a blockade. It was captured because those who had the management of it contravened the municipal and customs' regulations of Russia." As to Mr. Attwood's apprehension of Russia's encroachment—"I say that Russia gives to the world quite as much security for the preservation of peace as England."— (*Lord Palmerston, House of Commons, December* 14, 1837.)

At the close of the session the noble lord laid before the House the correspondence with the Russian Government, the two most important parts of which we have already quoted.

In 1838 party aspects had again changed, and the Tories recovered an influence. On June 21 they gave Lord Palmerston a round charge. Sir Stratford Canning, the present Ambassador at Constantinople, moved for a Select Committee to inquire into the allegations made by Mr. George Bell against the noble lord, and in his claims of indemnification. At first his lordship was highly astonished that Sir Stratford's motion should be of "so trifling a character." "You," exclaimed Sir Robert Peel, "are the first English minister who dares to call trifles the protection of the British property and commerce." "No individual merchant," said Lord Palmerston, "was entitled to ask Her Majesty's Government to give an opinion on questions of such sort as the right of Russia to the sovereignty of Circassia, or to establish those customs and sanitary regulations she was enforcing by the power of her arms." "If that be not your duty, what is the use of the Foreign Office at all?" asked Mr. Hume. "It is said," resumed the noble lord, "that Mr. Bell, this innocent Mr. Bell, was led into a trap by me, by the answers I gave him. The trap, if there was one, was laid, not for Mr. Bell, but by Mr. Bell," namely, by the questions he put to innocent Lord Palmerston.

In the course of these debates (June 21, 1838), out came at length the great secret. Had he been willing to resist in 1836 the claims of Russia, the noble lord had been unable to do so for the very simple reason that already, in 1831, his first act on coming into office was to acknowledge the Russian usurpation of the Caucasus, and thus, in a surreptitious way, the Treaty of Adrianople. Lord Stanley (now Lord Derby) stated that, on August 8, 1831, the Russian Cabinet informed its representative at Constantinople of its intention "to subject to sanitary regulations the communications which freely exist between the inhabitants of the Caucasus and the neighbouring Turkish provinces," and that he was "to communicate the above-mentioned regulations to the foreign missions at Constantinople, as well as to the Ottoman Government." By allowing Russia the establishment of so-called sanitary and custom-house regulations on the coast of Circassia, although existing nowhere except in the above letter, Russian claims to the Caucasus were acknowledged and consequently the Treaty of Adrianople, on which they were grounded. "Those instructions," said Lord Stanley, "had been communicated in the most formal manner to Mr. Mandeville (Secretary to the Embassy) at Constantinople, expressly for the information of the British merchants, and transmitted to the noble Lord Palmerston." Neither did he, nor dared he, "according to the practice of former Governments, communicate to the committee at Lloyd's the fact of such a notification having been received." The noble lord made himself guilty of "a six years concealment," exclaimed Sir Robert Peel.

On that day his jocose lordship escaped from condemnation by a majority of sixteen: 184 votes being against, and 200 for him. Those sixteen votes will neither out-voice history nor silence the mountaineers, the clashing of whose arms proves to the world that the Caucasus does not "now belong to Russia, as stated by Count Nesselrode," and as echoed by Lord Palmerston.

SUPPLEMENTARY NOTES

1. Ruggiero, a character in *Orlando Furioso* by Ludovico Ariosto, 1474–1533. Tempted by the witch Alcine.

2. Canning, George, 1770–1827. Foreign Secretary 1807–9 and 1822–27. Prime Minister 1827. (See introduction.)

3. Carbonarism. The *Carbonari*, the charcoal-burners, a middle-class secret insurrectionary society in the early nineteenth century. Active in revolts in Spain, Piedmont, Naples and France. Played an important part in the Italian *Risorgimento*.

4. The German Legion. Hessian and Hanoverian troops maintained in Britain by the Hanoverian kings. They were often used for garrison duties abroad.

5. The Test Act, 1673, was intended to keep Roman Catholics and other non-conformists out of public office. All crown officers had to accept the Anglican creed. Repealed 1828. The Corporation Act, 1661, was intended to weaken the power of non-conformists in towns. All members of a corporation had to be Anglicans. Repealed 1828.

6. Catholic Emancipation Act passed in 1829 after a long and bitter struggle. Former penal legislation was repealed and Catholics permitted to hold office under the crown and to sit in Parliament.

7. The Reform Bill finally passed in 1832 in spite of strong Tory opposition. Rotten and pocket boroughs abolished and the franchise given to the new industrial towns. The right to vote restricted by property qualifications.

8. Aberdeen, George Hamilton Gordon, 4th Earl of, 1784–1860, Tory and Peelite minister. Foreign secretary 1828–30, 1841–46. Prime Minister 1852–55.

9. Metternich, Clemens Wenzel Lothar, Prince, 1773–1859. Austrian Foreign Minister and Chancellor, 1809–48. Extreme conservative, relying on censorship, espionage and armed force to repress nationalist and liberal movements.

10. The Porte, more properly the Sublime Porte, was the name given to the Government of the Ottoman Empire in

Constantinople. The name arose from a high gateway in the central government building.

11. Stuart, Lord Dudley Coutts, 1803–54. M.P. for Arundel 1830–37, for Marylebone 1847–54.

12. Hume, Joseph, 1777–1855, M.P. 1818–41, and 1842–55.

13. Mehemet Ali, 1769–1849, Pasha of Egypt. Former Albanian tobacco-seller, destroyed power of Mamelukes in 1811. Supported the Sultan in Greek War of Independence, when his fleet was destroyed by Admiral Codrington at Navarino. Rebelled twice (1833 and 1839) against Sultan. His pashalik made hereditary. Egyptian royal family descended from him. (See introduction.)

14. Talleyrand, Charles Maurice de, 1754–1838. Bishop of Autun, 1788. Excommunicated by pope, 1791. Foreign Minister under the Directory and under Napoleon. As Foreign Minister of Louis XVIII wielded great influence at the Congress of Vienna. Ambassador to London, 1830–34.

15. Anstey, Thomas Chisholm, 1816–73. Lawyer and politician. M.P. for Youghal. Severe critic of Palmerston's foreign policy which he declared encouraged the despots and destroyed the liberties of Europe.

16. Peel, Sir Robert, 1788–1850. Leader of Tory Opposition in Commons, 1830–34. Prime Minister, 1834–35, 1841–46.

17. The Spanish Marriages. King Louis-Philippe wished to marry his son, the Duc de Montpensier, to the young Queen of Spain, Isabella II. Foiled in this by British protests, he arranged for Isabella to marry her cousin, Don Francisco, believed to be impotent, while the Duc de Montpensier married her sister, the heir to the throne. In this way, Louis-Philippe hoped eventually to unite the crowns of France and Spain in violation of the Treaty of Utrecht. (See introduction.)

18. Normanby, Constantine Henry Phipps, 2nd Earl of Mulgrave, 1797–1863. British ambassador in Paris, 1846–52.

19. Castlereagh, Robert Stewart, 2nd Viscount, 1769–1822. Foreign Secretary, 1812–22. Committed suicide.

20. Sugden, Edward Burtenshaw, Sir, afterwards 1st Baron St. Leonards, 1781–1875. Lord Chancellor.

21. Donna Maria II da Gloria, 1819–53, Queen of Portugal.

Daughter of Dom Pedro, 1798–1832. King of Portugal and Emperor of Brazil. (See introduction.)

22. Maria Cristina, 1806–78, Queen-Regent of Spain.

23. Otho of Bavaria, 1815–67, first King of Greece. Deposed 1862. (See introduction.)

24. Saxe-Coburg, duchy of. The ducal dynasty produced Leopold I, King of the Belgians, and Prince Albert, consort of Queen Victoria. Duchy abolished in 1918.

25. Treaty of Adrianople, 1829, ended Russo-Turkish War of 1828–29. Turkey ceded to Russia territory on the Black Sea, allowed Russian occupation of Moldavia and Wallachia, recognised the Czar as protector of all the Sultan's Christian subjects. Dardanelles opened to all merchant shipping. Autonomy given to Serbia and promised to Greece. (See introduction.)

26. Orloff (Orlov), Alexis Feodorovitch, Count, 1787–1862. Russian diplomat.

27. Treaty of Unkiar-Skelessi, 1833. Russia undertook to protect the Sultan against Mehemet Ali of Egypt in return for the closing of the Dardanelles to all warships except Russian. (See introduction.)

28. Bulwer, Sir Henry Lytton Earle, 1801–72. British envoy successively to Madrid, Washington, Florence, the Porte. Created 1st Baron Dalling and Bulwer.

29. Ibrahim Pasha, 1789–1848, son and heir of Mehemet Ali and commander of Egyptian forces in Syria and Asia Minor.

30. Codrington, Sir Edward, admiral, 1770–1851. In command of the combined fleets of France, Russia and Britain at the battle of Navarino, 1827.

31. Canning, Sir Stratford, Viscount Stratford de Redcliffe, 1786–1880. British diplomat. Nephew of George Canning.

32. Shakespeare, *Henry IV*, Part I, Act II, Scene IV.

33. Urquhart, David, 1805–77. British diplomat. Secretary at the British Embassy at Constantinople, 1836. Dismissed by Palmerston while negotiating commercial treaty with Turkey. Founded in 1835 the diplomatic journal *Portfolio*. Attacked Palmerston as a Russian agent. M.P. for Stafford, 1847. Moved for the impeachment of Palmerston. (See introduction.)

34. Kossuth, Louis, 1802–94. Hungarian patriot. President of Hungarian Republic, 1849. After destruction of Republic by the Russians spent the rest of his life in exile.

35. Circassia, region between Black Sea, the Kuban River and Greater Caucasus, now in Krasnadar and Stavropol Territories. Ceded by Turkey to Russia by the Treaty of Adrianople, 1829, Circassia resisted Russian conquest until 1864. The Circassians now enjoy autonomy within the Soviet Union.

36. Durham, John George Lambton, Earl of, 1792–1840. British ambassador to St. Petersburg.

37. Nesselrode, Karl Robert, Count, 1780–1862. Russian minister. Controlled Russian foreign policy from 1816 to 1856.

38. Treaty of Kutchuk-Kainardji, 1774. Crimea declared independent of Turkey, thus preparing annexation by Russia in 1783.